daughter,
and in recognition
of a
common heritage.

 FriesenPress

Suite 300 - 990 Fort St
Victoria, BC, Canada, V8V 3K2
www.friesenpress.com

Cover photo
The Appian Way (Copyright Sonia Halliday Photo Library, photograph by F.H.C. Birch)

Front cover and interior design
Robert Barclay

**ISBN**
978-1-4602-7749-2 (Paperback)
978-1-4602-7750-8 (eBook)

*1. Political Science, Commentary & Opinion*

Distributed to the trade by The Ingram Book Company

*For Anne*

# Cobblestones

A Personal and
Political Journey

**Dirk de Vos**

"I learn by going where I have to go."

Theodore Roethke
*The Waking*

# PREFACE

This is the story of a journey of discovery that began in 1934, the year I was born. In the land of apartheid—South Africa.

The journey brought many lessons but the strange thing was that the lessons seemed to come to me. I had not sought them out. That's why I was so struck by something found in Joseph Cardinal Ratzinger's book, *Truth and Tolerance*. The Christian faith, the future Pope Benedict said, was "not the product of our own experiences; rather it is an event that comes to us from the outside." Elsewhere he had written that "mere *praxis* gives no light."

Could it therefore be that like faith, the insights we develop—the meaningful ones—may come to us in the same way? Is it just a matter of being in the right place at the right time? But would that not require that we should not be sitting still?

That's precisely what Benedict meant, because he also said that we have to break out of the confines of our own circles into "the wide open spaces of truth that is common to all." He did not mean that truth was a Christian prerogative. It might belong to people of many faiths and even to people of no particular faith, and the same can be said of this book.

Speaking of truth, something else I admired in Pope Benedict was his open-mindedness, notwithstanding the firmness of his convictions. Without being open-minded, how could we ever learn the truth? And therefore I would have to add that when we encounter the new and the unfamiliar we should be willing to recognize them for what they are. For example, my father taught me that I should be alert to events that could well be important turning points in history. Thus he drew my attention to the Bandung Conference of the so-called non-aligned nations as soon as it took place in Indonesia in 1955. Now, looking back, we know that it was a harbinger of a resurgent East.

I could add another qualification about encounters with the new and the unfamiliar. Leaving events and people to speak for themselves was the secret behind the American writer Allen Drury's remarkably perceptive portrayal of life in the land of apartheid, *A Very Strange Society.* Which is what I, too, have tried to do in this book.[1]

After my experiences in the land of apartheid, little did I know that I would eventually end up in yet another very strange society in the far north: a society that held itself up as a microcosm of—and indeed a model for—the world. I believe that no country other than Canada could have yielded the lessons—*insights of general application*—I would garner in a land whose leaderships not only treated their polity as a cultural laboratory, an experimental farm (as Chairman Mao had so famously done), but were bold enough to acknowledge it.

Looking back, I began to see that this was not that much different from experiments conducted by another leadership in the land of my birth, except that in South Africa the change agents did not purport to preach to the rest of the world, as a certain Barack Obama would do many years later in front of the Brandenburg Gate in Berlin, when—believe it or not—he would urge people everywhere to join him in a project to fundamentally change not only the United States of America, but the world itself.

Only belatedly would I discover that the political philosopher Eric Voegelin had seen it all. What I saw in practice, and what he described in his *New Science of Politics,* was an age-old mind set, generally known as Gnosticism. The Gnostic spirit is not easily defined because, like Proteus, the old god of the sea, it has constantly changed its shape. Gnosticism

---

1     The reader will soon notice the virtual absence of footnotes or endnotes in this work, as well as the absence of a bibliography. This is mainly because this is not an academic treatise, but even so, every quote and assertion in the text is supported by an extensive and cross-indexed database.

also happens to be the oldest of the Christian heresies and may even have pre-dated the birth of Christianity. An early Church Father, Irenaeus, inveighed against it in his famous treatise *Adversus Haereses*. Even the apostle Paul had problems with it. *Except that in those days, and for many years after, it was not political.*

As we ourselves shall see, the Gnostic spirit has continued to mutate, but it is alive and well, rearing its head in surprising places. And so, when Europeans and Americans alike struggle with the mounting challenges of the interplay between the politics of human rights, multiculturalism, and groupism, they may well be interested in lessons one person has learned on his journey of discovery.

Not every reader will want to grapple with the complexities of some of the concluding chapters in the book—important, relevant, and topical as I believe they are. But it is my hope that they will be useful to readers who are interested in the world of politics, and especially to teachers and students in schools of government and international affairs and departments of political science, and thus help a younger generation to recognize and better understand the nature and the origins of many a problematical development in the public life of the nation.

From time to time certain kinds of political and cultural change agents may suddenly appear on the scene. As Eric Voegelin had done, at first I was merely puzzled before gradually coming to realize that the most troublesome transformationists (admittedly rare birds) conformed to a recognizable *type*. Moreover, and because it is Gnostic, a type that has recurred and will continue to recur in human affairs. But unlike Voegelin, who was an academic, I was also interested in the *methods* those kinds of people employed—or were trying to employ—in their peculiar urge to fundamentally transform both 'man and his world.' Whether, and to what extent, those change agents have succeeded, or are succeeding, in their quest, is a separate question; and naturally debatable. Many do not, but some do.

Hence the intermediate sections of the book focus on the means and the methods to be found among the socio-cultural and political trans-formationist's most favoured devices. So let us not prevaricate, because such people seem to relish not only the *process* but the mere thought of manipulating others. In their hands we are but as clay. Astonishingly, they are often not even interested in actually achieving the goals they purport to pursue. Thus they will often trot out goals that are impossible of achievement not only by any reasonable standard, but sometimes on their own admission! Voegelin attributed it to a psychological inability or even a refusal to distinguish reality from the dream.

But equally often the pursuit and enjoyment of the transformational processes go hand in hand with a belief that there is nothing but process and that meaning resides in—and is confined to—the means and the methods themselves, *and nothing else.* An interest in the mindsets behind such a 'belief' system leads us directly to the concluding sections of the book. What are those belief systems rooted in, ultimately? What do they represent? That is the really important question.

# ACKNOWLEDGEMENTS

Along with my indebtedness to Eric Voegelin, I'm indebted to Harry Antonides of the Christian Work Research Foundation for his timely gift of Cornelio Fabro's monumental study of the phenomenon of immanence. I have to thank Philip Bom for having first whetted my interest with his early monograph on *Trudeau's Canada*, and Kenneth Hamilton, without whose constant prodding and counsel this story would not have been told. Without the professional help, technical competence, and patience of Robert Barclay, the physical production of a publishable text would have been unimaginable.

Dirk de Vos
Ottawa, 2015

# LIST OF ILLUSTRATIONS

# TABLE OF CONTENTS

# PROLOGUE

My father is down on the ground. They're about to kill him and there's nothing I can do.

They've dragged him outside to the front of the hall, the city hall of a South African town called Vereeniging. He had come here to talk about the iniquities of the *Broederbond*, a secret brotherhood who have worked for years in pursuit of apartheid and white domination. A member of the Bond, the minister of the local Dutch Reformed church, had stood at the back of the hall, waiting to give the signal. Before the thugs surged forward, some armed with broken bottles, my father had taunted them. He had stepped to the very edge of the platform holding out a sheet of paper by a corner, between the tips of two fingers, to show them that he did not even tremble.

He had been forewarned that he would not be allowed to speak. As I shall again discover far into the future, in another land—and as Karl Popper has written of a Marx and a Lenin—where certain ideologies rule, the very Question is *verboten*.

A national newspaper, the *Rand Daily Mail*, will complain that one of its reporters was "flung off the stage, and was struck three or four blows in the face... 'now put your face in the paper,' his assailant jeered;" that, "chairs were smashed and windows broken;" and that when the speaker, "took up the Bible and began to read from the Book of Jeremiah, there were shouts of 'put down the Bible,' and three men jumped onto the platform and warned him that they would not let him continue until he closed his Bible." It was then that "he was pulled off the platform by a mob, the members of which assaulted him, and hustled him through the doors."

## Cobblestones

All of a sudden a *bakkie*—a small pickup truck, as appositely named as the Russian *bobik* in Lionel Davidson's *Kolymsky Heights*—comes charging through the crowd. The newspaper will report that "the mob had carried him outside for 100 yards..." Two burly men jump out. They pull my father from under his attackers, drag him to the truck, and toss him in the back. Along with other pictures and press reports, which will rest among the special collections in an American archive, one of the pictures will show apprehension as my father pulls back from his rescuers, who have him by the arms. He does not know who these people are. Afterwards, Jan Serfontein, a theology student, will say that he had never been so afraid in his life. Still in my 'teens, I'm frightened too. I had sat behind my father on the platform, at a small desk, his secretary.

The *bakkie* takes off, scattering gravel in its wake. I start to run after it, in the dark. It seems a long way. But at night it feels faster. In the far distance brake lights flicker outside a house; a safe house, it turns out. I find my father sitting in a front room, shades drawn, cool as the proverbial cucumber, sipping water from a glass. His coat is torn and every button missing from his vest.

# PART ONE

# CHAPTER ONE
# BEGINNINGS

"Just as the initial conditions in an equation determine the solution, so it was with my life. It's been an interesting one, for sure."

Michal Heller, 2008 Templeton Prize winner

Old Mrs Saltzman, a widow, had brought the toys from Hitler's Germany back to her farm. Spread out on the floor of the farmhouse, they were the most exquisite toys I could have imagined or hoped for. A finely crafted train set. A working model of a real steam ship, actually a river boat, its boiler heated with a wick burning methylated spirits. A set of bowling pins. I was only two or three years old but I can still smell those toys, a smell intermingled with that of a South African homestead and the scent of bluegum trees and old oil on rusting farm machinery. In the background the constant *koer-koer* of the *tortelduifie*; the 'little blue pigeon with the mournful eyes.'

Mrs Saltzman was one of those Afrikaners, the Boers, who lived in the hope of a German victory in the coming war. She had returned, my parents told me later, with wondrous tales of *autobahnen*, prosperity, and joy. I too was an Afrikaner, a true African. In those days blacks were not Africans. They were *kaffirs*; as pejorative a label as its American equivalent. Truth to tell, in the mouth of an Englishman, *Boer* was pejorative as well. In the mouth of a kaffir, *Boer* conveyed resentment, even hatred.

The district of Reddersburg, where we lived, was the hometown of the most famous of the Boer generals, a guerilla fighter named Christiaan de Wet. The British forces never managed to pin him down. During the

Anglo-Boer War, at the turn of the century, envelopes were sold on the streets of London supposedly containing a picture of the general, except that the envelopes were empty, but for a card, reading, *He has escaped again!* There was to come the day when I narrowly lost a speaking contest at school, where you were given a card with the topic printed on it, and then had to turn around at once to make your speech. Flushed with excitement I blurted out a story my father had told me, and which was bound to evoke the most hostile response from the audience, with my telling of how that great war hero, albeit a Christian, never made a move on the battlefield without first consulting a black witch doctor, who scattered bones on the ground before giving tactical advice.

I could not have known that one day, far into the future, I would be defending in court the chief witch doctor (or 'medicine man' in current parlance) of Southern Africa—the head of the African Dingaka Association—who was often harassed and even persecuted by the white regime on account of the legitimate fear that religious or quasi-religious activities and ceremonies among the blacks might be used to cloak black nationalistic and even subversive political purposes. So much so that the government banned publication of a master's thesis on the subject, a thesis written by the same Jan Serfontein who was so frightened one night, in a town called Vereeniging.

---

I'm already a prospective partner in the second largest law firm in the province—with a partnership contract in my pocket, though still a young articled clerk—in a legal practice built on a most respectable clientèle, including hospitals, banks, and building societies. So that there are 'reservations' in the firm about some of the clients I've been taking on. Things do not improve when the senior partner comes into my office to find me standing by respectfully, watching my witch doctor client kneel on the carpet, scatter his bones, and peer at them intently, to make sure that the expected legal advice has the blessing of his ancestors. When bones are not at hand client asks for a handful of coins; never returned! Occasionally, in court, we're in deep trouble with the magistrate when client arrives half naked, decked out in a lion skin, with ornate rings around his ankles, feathers on his head, and countless little multicoloured medicine bottles suspended on a string hanging from his neck.

When that most courageous missionary priest from the Community of the Resurrection in England, Father Trevor Huddleston, wrote *Naught For Your Comfort*—a devastating account of the ravages of apartheid—he was repudiated by a functionary of the regime in a commissioned book titled *You Are Wrong, Father Huddleston*. One of the few pictures in the book shows my client dressed in his official garb and standing with an entourage of women and children. The picture is meant to contrast the reprehensible and primitive activities of 'the medicine man' with civilized medical practice. Behind the group, on the wall of a house, is a painting of an ant-eating *aardvark,* with its characteristically long snout. No wonder the authorities are distrustful. Depicted in the rock art of that most ancient of Southern African tribes, the San people—also known as the Bushmen—the aardvark lives underground. It only comes out under cover of night, a 'power animal' whose claws and strong limbs enable it to "quite literally disappear into the ground in front of one's eyes." Nothing like an aardvark for subversion!

The slaughtering of bulls and calves and goats and chickens is a vital component of my client's practice, not to mention other African 'spiritualities.' The worst part of the witch doctor's craft is that he drinks blood directly from a stab wound in the neck of the live animal. Sometimes I think I can smell the blood on my client's breath. Years later, on January 7, 2012, an American newspaper will report that:

> A bull bellowed in sacrifice Saturday as South Africa's ruling ANC paid tribute to its ancestors and founding leaders, who 100 years ago paved the way for Nelson Mandela's rainbow nation.

> President Jacob Zuma led the slaughter of a black bull in a ceremony on the second day of the African National

Congress centenary festivities to celebrate its rich anti-apartheid legacy now tarnished by scandals and challenges.

"Today our leaders, traditional leaders and traditional healers, had to perform certain rituals before we get into serious business of celebration," said Zuma after the sacrifice at the church site where the ANC was founded in 1912.

"In other words, to remember our ancestors, to remember our own gods in a traditional way."

Overlooked by giant portraits of former leaders such as Mandela, healers and cultural groups dressed in beads, porcupine head-dresses and animal skins sang, danced and prepared food as politics gave way to African drums and tradition.

Two goats and two chickens were slaughtered ahead of the bull, which was a gift from neighbouring Lesotho King Letsie III, in traditional rituals to communicate with the ancestors.

"Everything has been done. We have spoken to the ancestors," Zuma said before the sacrifice.

Yet another esteemed client in the spiritual domain is a black bishop, albeit entirely self-elected and self-ordained. A slight man, Bishop Wellington Pitse's badge of honour, and perhaps even badge of office, is a most impressive gold Rolex watch; fake, naturally. In the course of a consultation he casually rests his forearm on my desk, with his shirt cuff surreptitiously pulled up from his wrist, so that I can not possibly overlook the symbol of his authority.

At the other end of the spectrum, so to speak, is Mrs. Betty Moretlo. A widow, a teacher, Mrs Moretlo lives in the local *lokasie*, a sprawling black township outside the city. Mrs Moretlo too has lots of problems when she's trying to lead a respectable life in the midst of much crime and poverty and, worse, almost daily humiliation at the hands of the authorities. She comes in, neatly dressed, sits down, ankles crossed, handbag on her lap, hands folded. Always it takes her a while to compose herself before the consultation begins. I remember her address: 2950 Bochabela. For several years after my wife and I left South Africa for the first time—we emigrated twice—we exchanged Christmas cards.

---

These things happened in Bloemfontein, the capital city of the Orange Free State, one of the four South African provinces. The same Bloemfontein where I was born and where both a Rudyard Kipling and a J.J.R. Tolkien left their traces; and where my great-grandfather, Tobias Jan Ferdinand de Villiers, who was a member for twenty years (and the chairman for twelve of them) of the *Volksraad*, the legislative assembly of the old Republic of the Orange Free State. That was before the British forces came and took it all away. His son, my grandfather, landed in a prisoner of war camp at Ahmednagar, in India, not far from the legendary Poona, where he learned that three of his daughters had died in the course of a single week in a British concentration camp back home, while farms were devastated and homesteads burned to ashes. In those camps 26,000 women and children were destined to perish. The British were conducting a scorched earth campaign and created the camps to prevent the women from staying on their farms and feeding their husbands and sons who were fighting in the Boer commandos.[2]

Not only Africans, but white Afrikaners too had to regain, and eventually assert, their dignity and self-respect. They had gone through the defeat and devastation of the Anglo-Boer War, only to be demoralized once more by the immense poverty and deprivation inflicted by the Great Depression and the accompanying drought. It, in turn, gave rise to what

---

2    My grandfather's diaries and letters are now preserved in the archives of the Pitts Theology Library at Emory University in the American state of Georgia. They reveal the piety and the unbreakable faith of a man of God, the same spirit that imbued so many of the old pioneers whose main, and often only, literature was a big old family Bible written in High Dutch.

became known as the Poor White Problem. In the Depression, my father told me, for a penny he could buy a whole sheep, which he would bring home in a wheelbarrow. In 1938 the Afrikaners saw an opportunity to express and bolster their national pride by re-enacting and commemorating the Great Trek of the 1830s, when the Voortrekkers (as they were called) moved *en masse* into the interior, and out of the Cape Province, to escape the reach of the British Crown. The *Ossewatrek* of 1938—a celebration of the diaspora of a hundred years before—had overtones of the Exodus and the arduous journey of the people of Israel to the Promised Land. Several ox wagon teams (exact replicas of those carrying the pioneers) had started out from different points in the south, triggering highly emotional celebrations in every town along the way, marked by speeches, songs, hymns, and prayers. On December 16, 1938 the wagons converged on the laying of the cornerstone of a massive granite monument—the Voortrekker Monu-ment—that was to arise outside the capital city of Pretoria, exactly one hundred years from the day the Boers had defeated the forces of the Zulu king, Dingaan, in the Battle of Blood River.

My parents took a leading role in the festivities in the mining town of Roodepoort, in the Transvaal, where we had settled a short while before. Roodepoort was destined to be linked to the victims of some of the most notorious tortures and killings in the history of apartheid—including the murder of an African resistance leader by the name of Steven Biko—but it was also the birthplace of a courageous and internationally renowned church leader who was to follow in my father's footsteps, a man named Beyers Naudé.

The 1938 celebration—on what became known as the Day of the Covenant—became the effective impetus behind a new spirit of nationalism that was to culminate in the election, ten years later, of a government infused with the ideology of apartheid.

---

My wife and I are sitting in the audience in a down town church in the Canadian capital, Ottawa. The guest speaker has come from South Africa, to speak of his ongoing fight against the injustices of apartheid, and the role in the Dutch Reformed Church of a secret society known as the *Broederbond*: Beyers Naudé. Afterwards I walk forward to shake his hand and give him my name. "*My God*," he blurts out, "*maar jou vader was mos ons voorloper.*" He's saying that my father had been their forerunner. And he also mentions my father's fight with the *Broederbond*.

——————

A picture in the official publication commemorating the event shows the local organizing committee, the women decked out in traditional Voortrekker dress, with my father half sitting and half lying on one elbow in the front row, and with me in front of him, striking the exact same pose, now at the age of four. My father also commissioned a special painting of the nearby scene on the hills where the Boers of the Transvaal stymied an attempt by an agent of the imperialist Cecil John Rhodes (best remembered as the founder of the Rhodes Scholarships) to invade their republic and gain control of the newly developing gold mining industry.

My only enduring memory of the time sees me sitting, on my own, under the canvas top of a shaking and creaking wagon drawn by weary, sweating and complaining oxen. They've come a thousand miles on their way to the culminating ceremonies, and are now labouring up the side of a hillock henceforth to be known as *Monumentkoppie*. My father has placed me, facing towards the rear, on a dark brown, coarse and roughly folded blanket, and I'm reassured because, wearing his broad-brimmed hat, he stands in front of me on a swaying platform attached to the back. I'm the only passenger, other than the two drivers up front. (Now, so many years later, I can still hear the sharp crack of the whip and the clatter of the hooves on the hard surface of the road.) I shall return to the scene once again on the day when the completed monument will be inaugurated, with a marble sarcophagus at the very heart of the structure. A ray of sunlight will strike it through a hole in the ceiling, at noon, on the sixteenth day of December, year after year.

Thus was the spirit of Afrikanerdom first nurtured in my breast, because December 16, 1938 was as much a religious as a nationalistic experience, with fervent and moving anthems and hymns rolling out across the *veld*. Not unlike the euphoria of the liberated people of Poland when they were assembled to listen to their supreme spiritual leader, Karol Wojtyla. On the eve of December 16, 1838 the Boers had entered into a covenant with their God, pledging that if they were delivered from the black *impis* of Dingaan they would forever remain faithful in the service of the Almighty. Their leader, Jan Celliers, made that promise on their behalf, standing with one foot on the carriage of their one and only piece of artillery and holding the Bible aloft. Here were the makings of the destiny of not only the Afrikaner nation, but, by extension, of the white race.

And indeed, the Battle of Blood River had been a miracle, when a small band of 470 men routed a force of more than 12,000 Zulu warriors, of whom at least 3,000 were left dead on the battlefield, at the cost of only three Voortrekkers wounded, and no lives lost. What a pity that in the event my people were to fail to carry out their side of their bargain with God. Remarkable similarities among the 'covenant' peoples of South Africa, Ireland, and Israel—even to the extent of the design of their (defensive) homesteads—have been noted by a Canadian historian.

Harking back to 1938, imagine my emotions when, in faraway Canada, and years later, we watched on television the swearing-in of Nelson Mandela as the president of a rejuvenating country. In front of the presidential podium a black 'praise singer', clad in an animal skin and waving a weapon, was stamping his feet and uttering blood curdling cries. Looming on the far distant horizon, over the shoulder of the new president, I could see the granite hulk of Afrikanerdom's shrine. On that day I went outside to cry my heart out, because it was the end of an era, of a history of my family—and a people—going back more than 300 years.

Covenants matter. They matter not only because my word is supposed to be my bond, but above all, because covenants, as distinct from mere contracts, embrace the Godhead as well. In an age when people are so ready to assert and enforce their rights; when nations have seen such a proliferation of human rights codes and tribunals (even to the extent of overriding national sovereignties); and when I came to live in a country, Canada, which was so transformed by a new and constitutionally entrenched Charter of Rights and Freedoms, the very idea of a solemn covenant no longer had traction. And no country, to the best of my knowledge, has a charter of duties and responsibilities, because that's what covenants entail.

---

The next year, 1939, we moved to the city of Durban in the province of Natal, where my father was to take up a position as the associate minister in the main Dutch Reformed Church. I caught my first sight of the sea as we were coming over the top of a hill in Zululand, seeing and sensing the mysterious stillness of that pastel blue expanse stretching beyond miles of green fields of sugar cane. When they breasted those same hills, would someone in the retinue of the Trek leader, the legendary Piet Retief, have known of that ageless cry uttered by the remnants of Xenophon's Ten Thousand when—at the end of their arduous trek to the safety of the Black Sea—they would have seen a similar sight when they cried out: *Thalassa! Thalassa!* [3]

There was a famous Afrikaner with whom my father's path would soon cross. General Jan Christiaan Smuts (a future prime minister and world statesman) would have known about those Greeks. He even carried a Greek New Testament in his saddlebags throughout the Anglo-Boer War. And most likely General James Barrie Hertzog, another future prime minister (who had a doctorate in law from the University of Leiden) would have known too, except that he may have carried a digest of the *Institutes*

---

3     Tim Rood, a son of my oldest living friend, and a Fellow and Tutor in Classics at an Oxford college, has told the fascinating story of an army of Greek mercenaries who survived a war against the Persians in 400 BC. See Tim Rood, *The Sea! The Sea! The Shout of the Ten Thousand in the Modern Imagination* (London, 2004).

*of Justinian*, where Justinian spelled out the three elements of justice. Both men were fighting in a war against rank injustice at the end of a whole century of wrong (*Een Eeuw van Onrecht;* the title of a book written by Jan Smuts). Those Trekkers at least carried their old Dutch Bibles with them, so that when at last they saw the sea, having manhandled their wagons over the mighty Drakensberg and thought they had reached the end of their vicissitudes, might they not have experienced the feeling of a new birth in a land called Natalia?

I could not have been aware that an idyllic childhood in the subtropical lushness of life in wartime Durban would come to an abrupt end just five years later, when my family was overtaken by political forces that had been unleashed, not only on December 16, 1938 but by previous events in which my father had also been involved.

The fecundity of Africa has to be experienced to be appreciated. To a young child, subtropical Durban was a cornucopia of sights, sounds, and smells, especially when we went to the Indian market, replete with stalls laden with a profusion of fruits and vegetables, brightly coloured and pungent spices, and endless displays of all kinds of brassware from India, all in the midst of a noisy throng of humanity, the women decked out in their dazzling saris. Thousands of Indians had been brought to the province as indentured labour on the sugar estates. This was where a young lawyer by the name of Mahatma Gandhi first honed his political skills. For many years Asians were forbidden to settle in my native Province of the Orange Free State and could not even travel across the province without running into trouble if their stay exceeded the prescribed time limit of twenty-four hours. Long afterwards, as we were looking at a film of the life of Gandhi, I realized that a famous sermon featured in the story (with Gandhi in the congregation) must have been filmed in the very Presbyterian church on Richmond Common, outside London, where our daughter was baptized. And the day would come when I would take along with me only one book, Gandhi's autobiography, on a voyage up the east coast of Africa, en route to Venice, only to put it aside, thoroughly put off by the man's extraordinary preoccupation with his own bodily functions.

It was in Durban that I first learned of clashing cultures. Domestic help was the prerogative of black men (not women) despite the warrior tradition of the Zulu nation. Their servant garb consisted of a white cotton shirt and shorts, with the edges piped in either blue or red. They were mostly barefoot. The blacks resented and distrusted the Indians, and it was reciprocal. Eventually deadly riots would break out with black and Indian factions pitted against one another. My own tribe, the Afrikaners, were a white minority; greatly outnumbered by English-speaking people. They had to struggle to preserve their language and support their own schools. My father stocked our school library out of his own pocket when a new school was carved out of the bush, where monkeys sat on the window sills looking in on our classes. My parents showered me with books. The new ones I can still smell. I read so much that my eyesight suffered and I had to learn eye relaxation exercises, lying in the dark imagining black objects. At night I most dangerously put a candle under my bed, having pulled the blankets down to the floor to hide the light, reading into the small hours, no matter the subject. I devoured everything in sight: stories of explorers in the Far East; several volumes of a history of war; and the many volumes of the collected works of one of the greatest and most prolific of early Afrikaans writers, C.J. Langenhoven. Inside a compendium of great detective stories I discovered that my father had hollowed out a space to hide his revolver; highly illegal because all private firearms had been confiscated for fear of a new Boer uprising under the spell of Adolf Hitler. There had already been a rebellion at the time of the First World War, when General Smuts, now the Prime Minister, paid a heavy political price for the execution of one of the ringleaders. Should I then have already suspected that my father was in some kind of jeopardy, perhaps connected with the war?

Understandably, for a young child the most exciting thing about life in Durban had to be the war. Everything was blacked out at night, car head-lights having been left with only a tiny slit. Searchlights criss-crossed the night sky. My mother was deadly afraid of drunken sailors on the streets. We practised bomb scare exercises at school, having to crouch below our desks on knees and elbows, clenching a pencil between our teeth. Our home was high up on a hill overlooking the harbour where, every day, big Sunderland and Catalina flying boats came down and took off leaving streaks of foamy water in their wake. Most impressive was the sight of a mighty aircraft carrier limping toward dry dock, missing half of its bow. She had been either torpedoed or bombed off the island of Malta. How a ship in that condition could still float defied the imagination. On occasion my father took me down to the docks to witness the departure of passenger liners laden with troops, while the famous 'lady in white' sang for them from the quay, as she did for every one of those visiting vessels. One of them was the *Ile de France,* which was to carry 626,000 fighting men in the course of the war. Huge convoys anchored off the coast. My father was an honorary chaplain to the armed forces and came home with tales of how the sinkings by enemy submarines caused so many bodies to wash ashore that the cold storage facilities in the city had to be converted into morgues. At another time hundreds of mules destined for the war in the highlands of Abyssinia were left swimming in the ocean after their trans-port had been torpedoed. A memorable morning for me was when we were on holiday on the south coast and woke up to find the beach covered, for as far as the eye could see, in eggs and oranges, most of the former miraculously unbroken. We lined up eggs as targets for shooting practice. Air guns had not been confiscated.

It was also the war—as wars do in the lives of so many people—that precipitated a moment of truth in the life of my family. I wondered why a young uniformed soldier who used to visit us at home wore red tabs on his shoulders. It turned out that many Afrikaners looked upon the *rooi lussie* as the mark of a traitor to the *volk* because the wearer had volunteered to fight the Italians and the Germans in North Africa; sending regular soldiers abroad was forbidden by law. It became known that my father was the only Dutch Reformed minister in Durban, and most likely in the province, who was willing to marry, and administer the sacraments to, those volunteers. Also, my father was in touch with, and apparently at loggerheads with, the leadership of a nation-wide band of ruffians known as the *Ossewabrandwag,* literally, the Oxwagon Watch. Their closest approximation would have been Hitler's storm troopers under Ernst Roehm. One of my uncles, by marriage, was a member, and it was not unknown for him to make the rounds to discipline errant fellow-members with a heavy whip called the *sjambok,* carved out of thick hide, preferably from a hippopotamus. On the coast of South West Africa a German submarine landed one of the leading lights of the *Ossewabrandwag,* a boxer whose main claim to fame was that he had represented South Africa at the 1936 Olympic Games in Berlin.

When I was at university in the early 1950s the former leader of the *Ossewabrandwag,* the man with whom my father wrangled in Durban, came to deliver a public lecture, though not on university premises. A picture of his burial, not long after, showed the grave surrounded by men giving the Nazi salute. I've been told by a former fellow student, having forgotten all about it, that I got up "with eyes ablaze" to lambast the speaker with hostile questions. A future minister of justice and eventual prime minister, my father told me, had been in hiding from General Smuts's intelligence apparatus. Disguised as a car mechanic, he was pulled out by his feet from under a car at a service station in a Free State town, to be interned for the rest of the war. At times my father's sense of humour was positively sardonic as when, after the war, he bought up at an auction the entire contents of John Vorster's internment cell; the man after whom the most notorious interrogation center in the country, John Vorster Square, was named. When Vorster became Prime Minister after the assassination of South Africa's ideological father of apartheid, Dr Hendrik French Verwoerd, my father went down to the Houses of Parliament in Cape Town to present to Vorster in person, in his office, the tin bowl (or *blikskottel*) he had used during his internment to wash and shave. By that time my father had established a theological seminary, where he deployed, as his blackboard, a large wooden board Vorster had suitably painted for his lectures to fellow internees.

There were other problems as well. My father was a powerful public speaker and preacher, whose style—down to balancing an open Bible on his right hand—was the closest I have ever seen to the American evangelist Billy Graham. My father could hold audiences of thousands spellbound, so much so that much jealousy ensued among the ministers of other parishes whose congregations were depleted on Sundays on account of the people flocking to my father's services, where loudspeakers had to be erected outside to accommodate the throng. A particular problem developed between him and his associate minister that arose from the hostility of the minister's wife. It came to the point that he was summoned to appear before a special session of the Dutch Reformed regional synod in a town close to the place where the Zulu king, Dingaan, so treacherously murdered the Voortrekker leader Piet Retief and his entourage of sixty-nine men, who thought that they were going up to Dingaan's kraal to sign a treaty of friendship. The synod placed my father under suspension.

What had really happened, and precipitated the trouble, I believe, was that he had set off one of those rare religious revivals that have broken out at different times in different parts of the western world. He saw himself as following in the footsteps of a 19th century revivalist by the name of Dr Andrew Murray, whose spiritual books are still reprinted and read in the United States. When my father established a theological seminary a couple of years later, he initially named it the Andrew Murray Bible School. Murray's Huguenot Seminary (for young Christian ladies) in the town of Wellington at the Cape—as well as other similar seminaries established in other parts of South Africa—had been modelled on Mount Holyoke College in Massachusetts, from where a succession of missionary teachers ventured forth to lend the Reverend Murray a hand. My paternal grandmother was one of Murray's first students at Wellington. In the collection of our family documents archived at Emory University is an original letter of advice, in Murray's handwriting, apparently addressed to one of his children.

But the most serious problem involved the *Broederbond*, a secret band of brothers—at one stage estimated at 12,000 in number—who had been working indefatigably, ever since around the year 1918, to liberate Afrikanerdom from the remnants of the British yoke, and eventually in pursuit of the dream of apartheid. When I think of the *Broederbond* I could even see a certain historical, political, and theological analogue in the Egyptian Muslim Brotherhood. Members of the *Broederbond* were steadily infiltrating key positions across a range of institutions, such as school boards, the civil service, and other organs of the state, but above all, the Afrikaans church hierarchies, and especially in the echelons of the biggest of them all, the Dutch Reformed Church. Hence my lifelong antipathy to political priests and ministers of religion—not to mention the contemporary scourge of political correctness that has even tainted modern translations of the Christian Bible, thereby not only defying commonsense and the rules of grammar—but often destroying the dignity and poetic quality of the language. It may well be that, given his talents, there would have been efforts to recruit my father into the ranks of the *Broederbond*. He seemed to know a lot about them. At the time some of his utterances appear to have been highly ambivalent, which meant that he may have been misunderstood. Government agents regularly monitored the broadcasts of his sermons on the radio. They complained because he so unpredictably changed the volume and pitch of his delivery that it upset their equipment. One could imagine them busily twirling their knobs to prevent fuses from blowing out.

The Prime Minister of the day, Jan Smuts, now a Field Marshal, was alarmed by the political infiltration of the churches but he had to tread most carefully. He refrained from taking drastic measures not only against the *Broederbond* but also, surprisingly, against the *Ossewabrandwag*. The son of Smuts's wartime Director of Military Intelligence told me that his father was exasperated by Smuts's failure to harness the full power of the state against subversives, and there was even reason to believe that some kind of mutual understanding of permissible limits had been reached with the leader of the *Brandwag*. What precisely initiated my father's association with Jan Smuts is not known, and although it was not discussed in our home until much later, I gradually became aware that such an association had developed. History may show that my father's suspension as a minister of the church had as much to do with politics as with religion. He, evidently, earned the suspicion that he had become a traitor to his people, as also happened with Smuts himself.

Shortly before Smuts died, in 1950—just a couple of years after his defeat in the General Election of 1948—my father saw him for the last time in his parliamentary office in Cape Town, then as Leader of the Opposition. Smuts had sat back behind his desk, tenting his fingers—as he would do when in deep thought—and saying (addressing my father by his nickname) "Jannie, I've achieved so much in my life, but never have I been able to cope with the things that crawl in the night." And this from a Renaissance man of the highest calibre. He had conquered so many heights: as a mountaineer, literally; as a jurist; as a philosopher (the father of the philosophy of Holism); as a botanist; as a linguist (Latin and Greek included); as a military leader; as a statesman of international renown; and, yes, as the Chancellor of the University of Cambridge. And a very brave man, who stood upright in the back of an open car, had himself driven without a bodyguard or an escort, into the heart of a bloodthirsty mob of striking miners, and gave them just half an hour to disperse. I have a vision of a Charles de Gaulle standing upright in the Basilica of Notre Dame in Paris with a German sniper firing from the shadows above, and everybody else cowering on the floor.

In Durban, as a nine-year old boy, I had no inkling of the forces gathering around us. We had had a most enjoyable interlude when we moved back to the Cape for a year to be near the University of Stellenbosch, where my father completed the requirements for his doctorate in psychology. In the early 1930s he had made a fruitless attempt to garner the support of Prof Hendrik French Verwoerd for the award of a study bursary. I have before me a letter Dr Verwoerd addressed to my father, under his own hand, to convey the bad news.

It was around midnight, on April 21, 1944, that a turning point was reached in the life of my family. My parents had returned late at night and must have woken me up, saying they had something to tell. We sat around our oval family dining table, of sturdy oak (now, fully restored, it's where I'm writing at this moment) as we faced the old fashioned short wave radio with its circular dial, from which, at times, would thunder forth—amidst much crackling in the ether and fading in and out—the rantings of Adolf Hitler, courtesy of Radio Zeesen. I can still hear that voice. Earlier in the evening, my parents said, they had gathered under the ancient tree outside their church that, according to legend, had sheltered the Trekker leader Piet Retief and his men shortly before they set out on their fateful journey to the kraal of the king of the Zulus. With my parents, under the tree, had been virtually the entire *kerkraad* (the ruling council of elders and deacons). They had walked out of the Dutch

Reformed Church to start a new Reformed denomination, the first major split of its kind in Afrikanerdom since the 19th century.

The die was cast. Within a matter of weeks we found ourselves sitting on the sidewalk outside our home with our furniture and belongings, having been summarily evicted from the manse. Soon my parents, accompanied by my younger siblings, took off for the interior of the country to build and expand an entirely new church organization, effectively to become the fourth of the main Afrikaans church groups whose collective history went back to the arrival of the first permanent Dutch settlers at the Cape of Good Hope on April 6, 1652. I was left behind in the care of English people, a family of Plymouth Brethren. My only cause for misery in their home was that they often served boiled pork.

1944 was a turning point in another, increasingly important, sense because it was also the year when the Nationalist leader of the Opposition was the first person in parliament to use the word *apartheid*. A word that was to colour the history of South Africa for many decades to come.

# CHAPTER TWO
# STILL EARLY DAYS

Farming and a love of wide open spaces ran in our blood, so that when my parents bought a semi-rural property outside the city of my birth, Bloemfontein, and I was able to rejoin them, I was in my element. The house nestled in a valley at the foot of a *koppie* (a small hill). From the front *stoep* we were able to see for miles and miles, as far as the blue mountain of Thaba Nchu, where the local tribe found refuge from the marauding *impis* of Shaka, the Zulu king.

Many years later, when I—along with my family—emigrated to Canada and settled in Ottawa, one of the attractions, to me at least, was the mere thought that if one was to travel north in a straight line for thousands of miles, the chances of encountering any people, let alone human settlements, all the way to the North Pole, were negligible. In the Canadian winters the cold northern light, with that almost eerie quality of silver-blue steel; the stillness; and the purity of the air, grew into something I would not want to miss. The snowy landscape was the very embodiment of pristine beauty. As remarkable to us was that we had come to live near a majestic river whose source was one of the hundreds of thousands of lakes dotting the vast Canadian shield, and virtually untainted by industrial pollution. Because water was scarce on the South African plateau, where we seemed to live from drought to drought. One Marq de Villiers—a fellow descendant from the same Huguenot family as mine, and Bloemfonteiner to boot, and who had also moved to Canada— would become known as the author of a bestseller titled *Water*. With him we shared the genes of freedom-loving *Voortrekkers*: men and women who could not be hedged in, in any sense.

But what I did miss in Canada were the glittering stars of the Milky Way; the same night sky that so inspired my father when, as a young boy, and barefoot to boot, he herded sheep in the high mountains of the district of Sutherland and the place where eventually South Africa's best observatories would be located. And perhaps, for us, had it been a harbinger of sorts that in the winter the mountains of the *Koue Bokkeveld* were not only the coldest but also the snowiest region in a country where snow was virtually unknown. There, at times, my father was so snowed in on the mountains that his life was only saved by the closely huddled sheep around him.

Was there a more profound meaning to a love of wide open spaces and a sense of wonder under the expanse of the night sky? Was this an element in the psyches of my own Voortrekker forefathers who abandoned the comforts of home and hearth at the southern tip of the continent, when they trekked into the unknown, courting hardship and danger? Was it an element in the travel writer Bruce Chatwin's love for the life of the nomad and his saying that "all our activities are linked to the idea of journeys?" Was that why Chatwin quoted W.H. Hudson's insight in *Idle Days in Patagonia* that "desert wanderers discover in themselves a primæval calmness... which is perhaps the same as the Peace of God?" I could not help noticing when a future Pope Benedict wrote most evocatively of how, for the people of Israel, wanderers in the desert, "it (was) always a matter of tearing Israel out of its cultural identity," and how "this leaving behind of ones own"—starting with the wanderings of Father Abraham—became a "continual transcending of the limits of (their) own culture into the wideopen spaces of truth that is common to all."

Yes, the love of freedom was in our blood, because we were the children of Huguenots who were driven out of France after the revocation of the Edict of Nantes (1685). Wine farmers they were, from the district of La Rochelle, the three brothers de Villiers who eventually set sail from the port of Texel in Holland on January 8, 1689. The governors of the Dutch East India Company had armed them with a letter of introduction, commending the expertise that would give such a boost to viticulture at the Cape of Good Hope. The brothers settled in a verdant and breathtakingly beautiful valley they promptly named *La Petite Rochelle,* which became known as *Le Coin Français* (the French Corner), and eventually by its Dutch equivalent, Fransch Hoek. There they hewed vineyards out of the bush and built stately homes with their elegant 17th century Dutch gables. At first they possessed only one horse. Each Sunday the women and children took turns on its back on a fourteen-mile trip to the nearest church. Later on, across the mountain, sprang up the town of Villiersdorp, from where my mother's forebears moved to the interior.

---

On a rainy morning in the spring of 2014, I find myself in a quaint and obviously very old multi-storey building on the central square of the ancient Dutch port of Hoorn, not too far north from Amsterdam. It has been an effort to locate a small museum dedicated to the history of the Dutch East India Company. The curator seems to have taken a liking to his visitor. On the wall over there, he says, is the only known extant painting of a board meeting of the *Here Zeve*, who must have been the gentlemen who sent your forefathers to the Cape of Good Hope, because their point of departure, Texel, is not far from here. Arranged on a side table are small jute bags with samples of the spices those old seafarers had brought back from the Far East. He shows me two ship models, one of which had a very narrow deck, with pronouncedly bulging sides. Why was that? The reason: in those days taxes were levied on ships in proportion to their deck surfaces! As I am leaving, I dislodge a number of coat hangers. They clatter on the floor. The curator comes around the corner, asking me (in Dutch) "Have your teeth fallen out?"

---

Traces of the achievements of freedom-loving Huguenots can be found in the most surprising places. A Canadian historian told me that he was unable to find a Canadian publisher (eventually having to turn to the *Salisbury Review* in Britain) for his story that Samuel de Champlain, one of the earliest and most celebrated explorers, and a founder of Catholic Canada, was a hireling and acted as an emissary of a Huguenot entrepreneur and financier based back in France, a man by the name of Pierre Dugua de Mons. And when I was living with my family in the university town of Cambridge, in England (from where I commuted every day to my job in the City of London) I did not realize then that Cambridge too had such a strong association with French Huguenots. Those Huguenots were mainly thread- and lace-makers. Some of them also settled in the marshy fenlands, where the houses sat at weird angles in the soft peaty soil, and where Charles Kingsley's legendary Hereward the Wake plied the waterways. The Huguenots were said to have "brought different and beneficial skills to fenland and integrated well into the area. Their descendants are around today although the spellings of their names have changed due to the difficulty in the pronunciation of 'foreign' names by the local fen men." I was reminded of my Dutch ancestry and of the times when those nifty *Watergeuse* were able to resist the Spanish occupiers as they too plied their little boats along the waterways and among the reeds of the Low Country. So too would the people of the southern marshes of Iraq resist the regime of a 21$^{st}$ century tyrant until he took the extreme step of driving them out by completely draining their habitat.

On the subject of Calvinists (and Huguenots) I was intrigued by Joel Kotkin's contention, in *Tribes: How Race, Religion, and Identity Determine Success in the New Global Economy*, that Calvinists were one of the 'tribes' whose beliefs, skills and accomplishments had such a wide international reach. He cited Max Weber and the historian R.H. Tawney to the effect that the British ascendancy in the world "was propelled by the powerful moral and cultural influence of Calvinism." Calvinism "fostered attitudes conducive both to trade and to an interest in the acquisition of technical knowledge." The Calvinist diaspora, he said, consisted of people who rejected the magical, were utterly pragmatic, and embraced "a gospel of discipline and constant self-improvement." And he specifically mentioned the Dutch financiers and the French Huguenot bankers who advanced large sums of money to the British government and the private sector, effectively underwriting the imperial expansion. Though working in the financial heartland of London, I did not realize that the Cazenove banking family had been one of those powerful Huguenot financial props of empire. My South African Huguenot forebears who fought against the British in the Anglo-Boer War would have turned in their graves if they had known about this. Indeed, to this day (at least at the time this writing) the Cazenove business is still going strong, "providing capital management and equities and international market investment services to the country's elite." "The company," we are told, "counts the Queen of England among its clients, as well as nearly half of the country's largest 100 companies."

––––––––––

And covenants once again! The very name Huguenot had a covenantal or 'confederate' origin, believed to have derived from the German dialectical *Eidgenosse*, derived in turn from the Middle High German *eitgenoz*, meaning *eit* or oath plus *genoz*, a companion. *Eidgenossen* were companions bound by a solemn oath. An imaginative writer has contrasted *eidgenossen* with the word *neidgenossen*. In my mother tongue, Afrikaans, the word *nyd* connotes a particular form of hatred intermingled with envy. These days *neidgenossen* might be an apposite description of radical Islamists, who might well be regarded as a brotherhood. Think of the Egyptian Muslim Brotherhood, many of whom are steeped in hatred and, some would argue, associated with a deeply held envy.

––––––––––

The same de Villiers family was also destined to serve the cause of justice in the land, as barristers and judges, practising the Roman-Dutch system of common law, of which the last remnants could still be found in the jurisprudence of just three countries: South Africa, Sri Lanka, and— before that country succumbed to barbarism—Zimbabwe. Back in Holland, Roman-Dutch law was cut off at the roots, so to speak, when it was summarily replaced by the Code Napoléon. But strong traces have also survived in Scottish law, so full of commonsense, and so different from the artificial constructs of English law and its procedures. Which was one reason why, at one stage, I found myself working in a law office on the banks of the River Tay in the old Scottish borough of Perth. Quaintness was not the word! An old farmer would come in to effect a property transfer armed with a smelly stack of old transfer deeds written on sheepskin, with little tufts of wool still sticking out of the sides. Among the books on my shelf I found an ancient tome titled *The Law of Horses*, written by an author by the name of Oliphant.

Avoiding Oxford and Cambridge, the best Scottish legal scholars flocked to universities on the continent—to Leiden, Paris, Pisa and Bologna—to be immersed in the philosophies of a Justinian, of a Johannes Voet and of the father of international law, Hugo de Groot (best known by his Latin name Grotius). In 1983 I was on a Dutch train when I noticed a fellow traveller reading a newspaper and looking at an odd headline *Man in de kist.* ("Man in the chest.") It turned out that 1983 was the 400th anniversary of the birth of Grotius, and that, on March 22, 1621, his wife Maria had smuggled him out of prison in a chest used to transport library books, whereupon he fled to Paris. Before graduating from law school I had to study extracts from the *Institutes of Justinian* in the original Latin. Justinian's definition of the three elements of justice I shall not forget.[4]

From that most excellent example of English expository prose, Sir Henry Main's *Ancient Law,* I learned that "Politics, Moral Philosophy, and even Theology, found in Roman law not only a vehicle of expression, but a *nidus* in which some of their profoundest inquiries were nourished into maturity." And as for the equality of all persons (at least before the law), Henry Main recounts that "the Roman jurisconsults of the Antonine era laid down that *'omnes homines natura aequales sunt...'*" What a pity that in modern law schools the teaching of Jurisprudence, the philosophy of law, has largely fallen by the wayside.

Without a doubt the remarkable record of the South African courts in standing up to the cruelties and illegalities wreaked by the apartheid regime could be ascribed to the inherent sense of justice inculcated in them by their common law traditions. And so it was Sir Henry de Villiers, a judge, who was selected to preside over the Convention that gave rise

---

4    *Alterum non laedere, honeste vivere, suum cuique tribuere* (to not harm another, to live honestly, to render to each his own).

to the formation of the Union of South Africa in 1910. Afterwards he became the first Chief Justice of the land.

––––––––––

We—a sprightly old gentleman and I—are sitting around a campfire in a small and quite primitive village on the Pacific coast of Mexico. Only a single public telephone serves the 5,000 inhabitants of the village. At night, wandering local pigs root and grunt below the window of our hotel room, to my wife's utter consternation. The other animals in the village maintain a distinct nightly noise hierarchy. Whenever there's a disturbance, the dogs begin to bark. Soon they're followed by the roosters and the hens. Only then do the donkeys join in the chorus. The hotel too is quite basic, owned and managed by an American woman and her Mexican husband. Everything is spotlessly clean. One also marvels at the spotless clothing of the people who emerge from their modest huts (thatched with palm leaves) every morning, poor as they are. At times, along the seashore, we find offerings of tiny clay pots and small but very sharp little arrows (not unlike the arrows of the Bushmen) left there, we are told, by primitive Indians who came down from the high Sierra Madre to petition the gods. The harbour at San Blas, now silted up, had seen Chinese vessels come to trade, hundreds of years ago. The remains of a very old structure on a hill behind us attest to those days. Every year old General Maurice Pope, with his wife, the *Comtesse* de Bergendal, would drive down all the way from Canada in his ancient Rover car. He had met her in the First World War. In Flanders he had commandeered a chateau and promptly fell in love with the daughter of the house. Now he's introducing me, a newcomer, to Canadian history. Already in his eighties, General Pope is descended from a Father of Confederation, whose son, Sir Joseph Pope, Maurice's father, founded and then served as the first head of the Canadian Department of Foreign Affairs. Maurice himself had been Canada's first ambassador to Spain, where he developed his love of the Spanish language and culture. Before that, during the war, he served as Prime Minister Mackenzie King's liaison with the Canadian armed forces. After the war he commanded the Canadian sector in occupied Berlin. He accompanied Mackenzie King to San Francisco at the founding of the United Nations. There, one night, a South African, Field Marshal Jan Christiaan Smuts, drafted in his own hand, in his hotel room, the Preamble to the Charter of the United Nations.

I think you will be interested to learn, says General Pope, that my father told me that his father, William Henry Pope, had told him that one day, around the year 1908, a South African judge by the name of Henry de Villiers turned up in his office on Prince Edward Island, saying that he had been chosen to chair the convention that would be drafting a constitution for a new South Africa, and that he wished to know, from the mouth of a Father of Confederation, what mistakes the Canadians had made that the South Africans should avoid. Many years after that conversation with Maurice Pope I learned that before the very first meeting of Canada's Fathers of Confederation—the historic Charlottetown Conference of September 1864—William Henry Pope hosted the delegates. "The elaborate luncheon given by him in his own spacious house and grounds on the outskirts of Charlottetown set the congenial tone of the gathering."

According to my father, says Mr Pope, de Villiers was strongly advised by my grandfather that instead of forming a confederation, the South Africans should strive to form a union. After much research (even digging through old ship manifests) I have been able to verify that yes, Sir Henry de Villiers did visit Canada in July of 1908, but only for a week. Part of the time he spent in Quebec as the representative of the South African colonies at the Quebec tercentenary celebrations. According to the only reference I could find on the subject "he returned a 'convinced and ardent unificationist' and informed the press that the Canadian Constitution had erred in giving wide powers to the provincial legislatures, *because it had prevented the merging of the French and British Canadians into a single nation.*" (Emphasis added.)

How persuasive William Henry Pope must have been, can be gathered from the fact that in vain did the French Canadian prime minister, Sir Wilfrid Laurier, write to General Smuts:

My opinion is very strong that with the duality of races, such as they have it in South Africa and such as we have it in Canada, the form of union should be federative. Even if there were homogeneity of races I would still favour the federative system... To me the point does not admit of discussion... I may add... that our Constitution has worked remarkably well.

One could only say that the proof was not in the pudding. Well into the 21st century French and English Canadians were no more united than they were in 1908. Quebec had not even accepted the new Canadian Constitution enacted in 1982. A wholly artificial country-wide official bilingualism had been imposed on Canadians, but with little effect, other than to greatly increase costs for both the public and the private sectors, and thereby exacerbating the already low productivity of the economy. The legislature of the Province of Quebec dubbed itself the National Assembly. The same exclusiveness applied to the diplomatic scene. From an official website one learned that a "*délégation générale* (general delegation) is Québec's most important government office abroad. Led by a delegate general appointed by the government, it provides services in the areas of economy, education, culture, and immigration..." (the latter because the province enjoyed exclusive jurisdiction over immigration policies and practices). Canada, one had to conclude, was even more divided than that other example of failed nationhood, Belgium. It brought back a memory of a visit I had made to the offices of the Belgian Prime Minister, where an interview with an official was to take place. I could not understand the delay in starting the meeting until a second official hurried in and sat down, but never spoke a word. I learned afterwards that no such meeting with a foreigner could be conducted without the presence of at least one representative from each of the two solitudes, Flemish and Walloon.

*This Union* is the title of a book presented to my wife as a parting gift by its author, a South African senator in whose law office she worked. The foreword was by Field Marshal Smuts, the man who, as the Attorney General of the Republic of the Transvaal, played such a pivotal role in the negotiation of the Peace Treaty which marked the end of the Anglo-Boer

War. That treaty was concluded in the town of Vereeniging (meaning uni-fication). Before his government was defeated and he was ousted as prime minister by the torchbearers of apartheid in the general election of 1948, it had been Jan Smuts, through his secret service, who took an interest in my father's physical security. That was during the years when my father was in the thick of his fight with clerical *Broederbonders*. Though Smuts had died in 1950 there may have been a lingering connection with the two mysterious men who, one night, would rescue my father from a mob in a town called Vereeniging.

Yes indeed, by this time—in the year 1945—my father is in the thick of his fight with the Dutch Reformed Church (virtually South Africa's establishment church); its influence in the affairs of the *Broederbond*; and the way the church, in a series of articles in its official journal *Die Kerkbode*, has been laying a theological foundation for the doctrine of apartheid. He writes, and we distribute, sometimes under the cover of darkness, pamphlets of various kinds, some of them quite scurrilous. (One of them a photograph of a Dutch Reformed cleric wearing nothing more than a long shirt, with a pair of suspenders holding up black socks on hairy legs.) We also publish a regular church journal. To such ends I learn to operate an ancient printing press, laboriously setting the letters cast in type metal, one by one, line after line (and of course the type has to be set backwards). Sometimes I work right through the night to see the sun rise on hands and arms smeared with black printer's ink. The smell of printer's ink is unforgettable.

Not surprisingly, my father is often involved in litigation. When it comes to hearings in the Supreme Court of the Orange Free State, I sit behind him with our law books spread out on a table, having care-fully assembled, ordered and indexed the supporting documents he may need because he's appearing without benefit of legal counsel. By my early 'teens I'm already the proud possessor of the multi-volume *Digest of South African Law*, known in the profession as *Bissett and Smith*. Am I one of those Huguenot descendants who had chosen the world of jurisprudence, because the law seems to be my destiny? And in this case out of necessity.

I have been studying the violin for several years, sometimes practising for two or three hours a day and something I shall pursue throughout my later school years and into my second year at university. Victor Pohl, my first teacher, a graduate of the Brussels Conservatoire of Music, is also a writer of stories of the South African *veld*. He shares with the writer Laurence van der Post—who will have such an influence in the life of a future heir to the throne, Prince Charles— a fascination with those remarkable peppercorn-headed little people, the Bushmen, more generally known as the San, and the most ancient of southern African, and perhaps all African tribes. Living among the fruit trees in a hut at the bottom of his garden in the city, is Victor Pohl's close companion, a wizened and wrinkled old Bushman. At the end of each working week, winter and summer, Pohl packs up and heads out into the *veld* with his Bushman, who uses his field craft to fish and trap, and at nights, in the winter, digs a grave-like trench in a sand bank along the river, places flat rocks in the bottom, lights a fire on top, then covers the rocks with a layer of sand and thereafter his master can sleep comfortably and warmly, and out of the freezing wind. In later years this will remind me of how the first European settlers may never have been able to survive in the Canadian wilderness, especially in the winter, without the guidance and survival skills of Canada's aboriginal peoples.

In the arid regions north-west of the Cape, at the age of around seven, I had scrambled up *koppies*, disturbing rock rabbits and sun-basking lizards and blue *koggelmanders* along the way, to explore hidden caves with ancient Bushman rock paintings on their back walls. One of the most famous of the paintings in the region featured a white woman who must have been shipwrecked off one of the most inhospitable coasts in the world, centuries before. It would only be around the end of the 20th century that an ability to interpret human DNA began to lead to a better understanding of man's history and movements over the past 50,000 years. The male Y-chromosome can be used to trace genetic continuities as well as discontinuities or so-called 'markers' when variants occurred in the chromosome, literally a case of a single 'misspelling' in the code at a given moment. The misspelling is indelibly carried forward through the male line, and so those misspellings can be used to trace the routes humans had followed, by taking large numbers of blood samples in different places and among different people. In this way Australian aborigines have been traced back through DNA also found in a community on the south-west coast of India. But, most remarkably, from India back through the Middle East the given line of Y-chromosomes has been traced right back to the Bushmen of southern Africa, many of whom must have moved out from there in the face of a horrendous drought associated with the Ice Age in the north: sea levels were so low then that the coastline at the southern tip of Africa was said to have been about 40 kilometres beyond the current shores. Another stream of the same group of people who moved north ended up in the grasslands of the present-day Kazakhstan, thought to have been the originating point for a stream that eventually reached Western Europe through the Cro-Magnons. They, in turn, may have been responsible for the amazing rock paintings found in caves in France, so uncannily similar to the rock paintings I as a child explored in the caves of Bushmanland. Some historians of the Basques—that untrace-able people of northwestern Spain with their unique language—contend that the physiognomy of present-day Basques has much in common with the inferred physical features of Cro-Magnon man.

Apparently the DNA of the native peoples of North and South America (the Navajo, for example) can also be traced, through the same Y-chromosome, to those early few inhabitants of Kazakhstan, whose descendants moved to eastern Siberia before crossing over to and down the west coast of the North American continent. The original detour via Kazakhstan may also explain why the European offshoots of the Bushmen only arrived some 10,000 years later in Western Europe; something to do with having to wait for the retreat of the glaciers.

In 2007, a Cambridge-based research team found corroboration of the theory that a single group of people had left the southern part of Africa approximately 50,000 years ago and had spread far and wide. This time the researchers succeeded in correlating the genetic evidence with an exhaustive analysis of human skulls. Since then, the journal *Science* has reported the work of a psychologist at the University of Auckland in New Zealand, who traced the origin of language "by breaking down

504 world languages into their smallest components, called phonemes." Using this methodology, the researcher concluded that "human language arose only once, in southern Africa… Verbal communication then spread across the globe as humans walked out of Africa, reaching Australia and New Zealand last. This verbal spread parallels the dispersion of early human genes…" No wonder that I've always been convinced, looking at the Bushmen of southern Africa, that they must be an incredibly ancient people. And my instincts tell me that the last remnants of the tribe may still have much the same form their ancestors had 50 millennia ago.

Such unchangingness was not at all impossible when I think of my first glimpse of an ancient fish—a coelacanth, freshly caught off the Comoro Islands on the east coast of Africa—lying in a tank of formaldehyde on the lawn outside the Ichthyology Department at my old university in the Eastern Cape. Like the cockroach, the coelacanth, we were told, had not evolved in any way in the course of more than 300 million years.

The Bushmen's hunting and tracking abilities, their hunting tools, and their closeness to nature and capacity to survive in the most arid regions, are still almost unique and this, I surmise, is what must have enabled those of their ancestors who moved out, to survive on their long trek north through inhospitable and hostile environments. The way they filled and buried empty ostrich egg shells, to unobtrusively store water along their hunting routes, to be sucked out through grass straws, is just one example. Their language of clicks is also quite unique, and would have made for silent communication on the hunt. Their little poison-tipped arrows did not have flint heads. The heads were carefully crafted from bone. In Australia too, around ancient fireplaces dating back some 40,000 years—and associated with DNA evidence among aborigines—there have been findings of arrowheads of ancient bone, instead of the more common flint. Because their prey was not really as much wounded as poisoned, the Bushmen could hunt large animals, that might then still run for consider-able distances before dropping dead, and hence the Bushmen themselves had to develop into superb long distance runners. My father told me that on their farm in the Karoo a day-long race, starting at sunrise and ending at sunset, was arranged between a Bushman and a man on horseback, and that the Bushman won. When the South African military were fighting a guerilla war in Angola against Moscow-supported Cubans, they made extensive and deadly use of their Bushman trackers.

Last but not least in support of the endurance of the Bushmen is the fact that like humped camels they had a unique way of storing a very large quantity of fat—in this case in their buttocks—and so they could travel and survive for long periods of time without eating, and to some extent, without water (partly thanks also to a low rate of perspiration). The accumulation of fat was aided by their habit of eating enormous amounts of meat after a hunting kill and then falling asleep around their campfires. Distinct traces of Bushman features could be seen in the head and face of Nelson Mandela. His own people, the Xhosa, still have remnants too of the Bushman click in their language. If ancient places can be designated world heritage sites, the San should be the first to be designated, and cherished, as the modern world's true heritage people.

At night, southern Africa sits under the clearest and most wonderful display of the Milky Way. On this account alone one could understand how the San also showed a profound mystical religiosity and adopted as their principal deity, the praying mantis. Long after we left South Africa I asked my mother to buy (and send us) the still available books Victor Pohl had written. By that time he was already virtually blind and in poor health, but he and his old wife drove all the way to my mother's home to autograph the books for my benefit. Now, as I write, I hold in my hands Victor Pohl's *Farewell the Little People,* filled with poignant stories of the lives of a decimated and barely surviving tribe. He expressed the hope that his book might "help the reader to a better understanding of these little people, of whom so little is known and who are in danger of vanishing from the face of the earth..." Africa captures the imagination, and once experienced, will not let go.

From early childhood I was steeped in stories about those early seafarers—Phoenicians, and after them, Portuguese sailors—who were embarked on a quest to find a way around a vast continent. Successive explorers, probing ahead along the west coast of Africa, planted stone crosses on the coast before once again retreating, literally 'in fear and trembling.' Was it not Luiz Vaz de Camoes, in his epic poem, *The Lusciads*, who so extolled "the growth of the Portuguese nation through the art of navigation"? Some explorers hoped to find the land of the legendary Prester John, who was supposed to be a Christian ruler in an Asian land, although a very early Portuguese overland traveller claimed to have found him in Ethiopia. But, of course, the main allure was the spices of the Far East. The Cape of Good Hope (according to Sir Francis Drake, the fairest of them all) served as a way station and even as a post office, because sailors left letters under a rock, to be collected by others going in the opposite direction. The Cape was finally settled in 1652 by a Dutchman, Jan van Riebeeck, with the main objective of growing crops and rearing livestock for the benefit of passing mariners. Indelibly imprinted on my mind and in my imagination were drawings and engravings of those graceful little ships anchored at the foot of a majestic Table Mountain. For some reason they made me think of birds; white birds, like seagulls at rest. The same sight greeted my Dutch and Huguenot forefathers when they arrived at the Cape in the late 17th century, at the end of an arduous voyage. On an island in the same bay Nelson Mandela and his colleagues would be incarcerated centuries later. Happily, my childhood imagination was not impaired by any knowledge of just how hazardous and brutal those early voyages had been, when one learns that of the 671,000 Dutch sailors who left Amsterdam in those days, 266,000 never made it back.

From our histories, traditions, and forebears we derive our respective identities. A Joseph Ratzinger rarely expounded a theology that did not go back to the Book of Genesis or the Book of Exodus and to the rest of the roots of the Judaeo-Christian heritage. In his *Memory and Identity*, published in 2005, John Paul II observed that "Christ, as the Son who has come to us from the Father, presents himself to humanity with a particular patrimony, a particular heritage." There John Paul was speaking to his own people, the Polish nation, reminding them that their very identity rested on the Christian underpinnings of their culture, and how "even when the Poles were deprived of their territory and the nation was partitioned, they maintained their sense of spiritual patrimony, the culture received from their forefathers... Like individuals, then, nations are endowed with historical memory." History, he reiterated, was "the element which determines the nation's identity in the temporal dimension." He would have been mindful of how the Apostle Paul counselled Timothy "to remember what he has been taught, and to root himself firmly in the witness of his ancestors in the faith and in the Holy Scriptures."

To an enduring awareness of my Dutch and French Huguenot antecedents was added an appreciation of yet another, albeit acquired, heritage, through marriage. After all, with the Scottish common law so strongly anchored in Roman jurisprudence, was it not a precept of the Roman law of domicile that *ubi uxor, ibi domus*? (Where the wife is, is the home.) For me, a haunting refrain in Bizet's *Fair Maid of Perth* has always resonated because just a few miles outside of that most ancient of Scottish boroughs I too married a fair maiden. The wedding took place in a small pre-Reformational country church built on the very site, overlooking the valley of the River Earn, where the Scottish king Kenneth McAlpin first united the Scottish and Pictish peoples. This was not far away from where McAlpin deposited the relics of Scotland's most famous missionary, Saint Columba. McAlpin came back to die in the nearby village of Forteviot in the year 858. Outside the same village archeologists have uncovered the tomb and the redoubt of an ancient king who ruled 4,000 years ago, one and a half millennia before the Egyptians started to build the Great Pyramid of Giza. My wife was born and spent her early childhood in Macbeth country, close to Glamis Castle, and next to the local manse where a beautiful young Lady Elizabeth Bowes-Lyon (a future Queen) conducted her first public function when she came to open the church bazaar. My wife's grandparents lived in the nearby town of Forfar, on Canmore Street, where one Malcolm Canmore had his redoubt: that name, too, of Macbeth renown. He was King Malcom III, whose wife, Queen Margaret (later known as Saint Margaret) was the granddaughter of an English king, though reputedly born in Hungary. Her name is perpetuated by a small chapel in Edinburgh Castle, where the famous Stone of Destiny is now kept; the stone on which Scottish kings had been crowned since time immemorial.

And could I forget that Scottish missionaries and theologians—Murrays, McGregors, Frasers, Thoms and others—had left the proverbial indelible mark on South African church history?

By the year 1956 not the violin but the law has become my métier. Not only through the necessity of helping my father, but also because I have been greatly impressed by the performance and the courtly manner of a barrister who acted for the other side—against us—in yet another a case that has ended up in the Supreme Court. And no wonder because the same man is a future Chief Justice of South Africa.

Not all my black clients are medicine men or bogus bishops! Black people have a hard time finding legal representation in the surrounding country towns. A man would come into my office saying that he had cycled nearly a hundred miles looking for help. One of the nearest towns where this is a problem is a place called Brandfort. I have to go there to help a black widow with eight children who she could only support by running an illegal *shebeen*, or speak-easy, where not only liquor but other 'services' were on offer. She has been charged but cannot find a lawyer for a reason I will soon discover, because I'm able to secure a summary acquittal after informing the magistrate (privately, in his chambers) that unless he's amenable I shall have to present evidence that among my client's customers have been some of the most prominent white citizens of the town. One could well imagine something like that happening in the American Deep South in the heyday of segregation!

The main reason I've mentioned the dusty town of Brandfort is that it would gain much notoriety (or fame, depending on one's point of view) when Winnie Mandela, Nelson Mandela's wife, was sent there to live under house arrest.

Piet de Waal, a colleague of mine, and a good tennis player, had fallen hopelessly in love with and married a rare beauty of a girl by the name of Adéle. Eventually, he started a law practice of his own in Brandfort, where soon his comely wife struck up a friendship with a not unattractive Winnie. What a pair they must have been in that stronghold of apartheid!

Came the day when Adéle informed Piet that the time had come for steps to be taken to get Nelson out of jail. My colleague was a close friend—most likely a tennis partner—of a politician who had since become the South African Minister of Justice, one Kobie Coetzee. But now Piet had been given his marching orders. He had to prevail on Kobie. Which Adéle left him no choice but to do. History tells that Kobie did get down to work. Apparently he had to do it, initially, behind the back of the State President. That, I have reason to believe, was how the story of Mandela's return to freedom may have begun. It would not have been the first time that momentous historical developments have been triggered by the most mundane and pedestrian of circumstances. Think of the butterfly effect in chaos theory!

---

In the month of June of 1959, in the middle of a cold and rainy Cape winter, a young man—a lawyer, on holiday from up country—visits the Houses of Parliament for the first time. He's sitting in the visitors' gallery marked *Whites Only*. A thin barrier separates him from a space reserved for blacks, to his immediate left. Next to him, just across the barrier, sits an elderly man with greying hair, large of stature, and notably dignified. Down below, on the floor of the House, some kind of debate is going on. But soon the young man becomes aware of an astonishing thing. Several of the members on the government side are looking up towards the gallery and at the black visitor, making derogatory, indeed highly insulting remarks in their mother tongue, Afrikaans. The old man is clearly hurt. Slowly he gets up and walks, equally slowly, towards and down some steps. The young man is consumed with anger. After some hesitation, he jumps up and rushes down the stairs. The black man is nowhere to be seen. But then he spots him, surrounded by what looks like a small group of journalists. He elbows his way through them and comes to a standstill in front of the old man. Sir, he says, I'm an Afrikaner from the Free State. I beg you to forgive my people for what they've done in there, because they do not know what they're doing. The old man looks at him most kindly. He must be saying something but the young man is so overwrought that he fails to register the words. The old man is Chief Albert Luthuli, head of the African National Congress.

It was Luthuli, winner of a Nobel Peace Prize and a deep Christian, who had, over many years, like a John the Baptist, paved the way for Nelson Mandela. Not many years later he was to die; walking along a railway bridge near his home in the province of Natal because, being deaf, he had not heard an approaching train. An obituary in the *Cape Times* of July 29, 1967 by one Anthony Delius and titled *Luthuli the Man*, told a tale: "Inside the House Luthuli stopped to talk to a group of reporters in the passage. Suddenly a man broke into the group and announced that he was an Afrikaner from the Free State - 'Chief,' he said, 'I want to apologize to you for what White men are doing to your people inside this House.'" [5]

*Drum* was a South African illustrated magazine for blacks (with offices in Nairobi, Dar-es-Salaam, Lagos and Accra) that somehow managed to survive under the apartheid regime. The June 1959 edition covered Luthuli's visit. A highlighted heading said "Afrikaner shook hands and said: I am sorry!'" *Drum* reported that Luthuli had "attended a debate in Parliament... After he came out, an unknown Afrikaner from the country, who had also listened to the debate, came and shook Luthuli's hand and

---

5    How the threads of our lives intersect! Strange how the name of the same Anthony Delius would come back again. When I was researching material for this book, one Paul Malherbe, the son of a man who had been the Director of Military Intelligence in the wartime administration of Jan Smuts (and who had fruitlessly urged the Prime Minister to act more decisively against the *Broederbond* and other subversive organizations), was to help me in my efforts to establish the origin and the meaning of a single sheet of paper, with handwritten notes on both sides. I had discovered it among some old documents kept in a metal trunk (unopened for more than forty years). Here was a piece of paper, which—in the event, as we shall learn—would prove to have such a bearing on the pivotal moment in the history of apartheid. Paul's father had written about a woman who was a captain in Military Intelligence and who had "an intimate colleague and friend, Captain Anthony Delius, who later became a very distinguished South African author." And who was this lady who had befriended Anthony Delius? None other than Paul Malherbe's own mother.

said: 'I apologize for the things my people are doing in there.'" *Drum* added that, following Luthuli's visit, "the Congress movement, which tends to stumble along rather drowsily in the Cape, had suddenly become wide-awake and on its toes."

Here was an example of how recollections, even eyewitness accounts, can differ, as in that most exquisite of Japanese plays, *Rashomon*. And so, finally, we had Albert Luthuli's own account in his brief autobiography, *Let My People Go*: "After my glimpse of the white Parliament in action," he wrote, "I was standing in a corridor with Senator Rubin and a reporter. A young Afrikaner passed us. Impulsively he turned back, and to my astonishment gripped my hand. 'You know,' he said, 'I come from the Orange Free State. I'm ashamed of what's being said in there, I'm ashamed of what they're doing!' Then he was gone before I could reply."

If these reports showed one thing, it was the abysmal state of race relations in a country where such a relatively minor incident should receive so much publicity, even after someone's death, and if it so stuck in the memory of someone like Albert Luthuli. If they had any sense, the white 'defenders' of Christianity in southern Africa would have done well to read the public statement Luthuli issued in 1952, with its moving Christian message: where he placed his fate "in the hands of the Almighty"; where he said that he could only "pray to the Almighty to strengthen my resolve"; where he talked about "a spirit of trust and surrender to God's will"; and concluded that it was inevitable that in working for freedom "some families must take the lead and suffer: The Road to Freedom is via the CROSS."

Luthuli's African National Congress was a political movement that had been fighting for decades for the recognition of the essential dignity of the black peoples of South Africa. It was also responsible for the launching of a Freedom Charter in the very city of my birth, Bloemfontein. And, as the reader will discover, Bloemfontein was where the death knell of apartheid would be announced many years into the future.

In my (entirely fortuitous) presence...

---

If one believes in the dignity of a human being the mere thought of torture—especially physical torture—must rank with wanton abortion and the sexual abuse of children as among the most heinous actions imaginable. That someone held captive in an American detention centre at Guantanamo Bay could be subjected to water boarding, so-called, not once, not twice, but scores of times, defies characterization. If such things could be done with impunity, is there anything in human society that can still be described as unthinkable?

Into my law office limps a black man in a pitiful state. Not only is he bruised, he looks haunted. One of his eyes is swollen shut. His name is John. John Reid. He is our 'office boy'. We had discovered the theft of valuable revenue stamps meant to be used to validate certain kinds of legal documents, and had called in the police. They, against our expectations, took John away. Nothing had been heard for two days. But now John is back. John had been tortured. But not only John. Another black man by the name of Josiah Seekoei ('Hippopotamus') who worked in the same building, had been arrested at his home and taken to the same police station. As I write, I'm looking at the original affidavit signed and attested by Josiah Seekoei where he also referred to John's account of his own experience after he was returned to his shack in the black township. Their treatments had been identical. Seekoei had the presence of mind to memorize the licence number of the police car sent to pick him up, as well as the number on the door of the torture room he was taken into at police headquarters. They were handcuffed. Two white detectives first went to work on them with fists and feet. They were ordered to squat and then to sit down. A stick was pushed behind their knees and through the crooks of their arms so that they could not move. A black towel was wound around Seekoei's head and pulled through his mouth and electrical wires attached to his little fingers. They were still handcuffed. In John's case the electrical wire went around his head. Because in South Africa the electricity grid ran on 220 volts, the power was only applied in very short bursts, otherwise the victims would die. Seekoei was shocked three times, each time after he had been unable to answer the questions. Seekoei said that his hands were still painful and that he could not properly see out of his right eye. He had a headache but the *Kurra* painkillers he bought for it did not seem to help. He said he knew of "many other people" with similar experiences. The small details of Seekoei's story attested to its truth.

The head of our firm thinks it's altogether too risky for our reputation and client relations to get involved, which is strange for a man who had also confided in me that in his early youth he had communist leanings, and were communists, or even ex-communists, not supposed to be the staunchest friends of the oppressed masses? But my boss does not persist when I voice my disagreement. After fruitless efforts to secure redress I eventually sit down and write a letter to one Advocate C.R. Swart, Minister of Justice and future State President. He also has a farm outside the town of Brandfort, called *De Aap* (The Ape). With his hooded eyes he strikes me as a cruel man.

By this time I've found another corroborating witness by the name of Jakob Steenbok ('Gazelle') who suffered a similar ordeal the year before. According to his sworn statement—the original of which I'm now looking at as well—his assault included being smothered with the inner tube of a car tire (a form of torture not unlike the American use of water boarding). And so, writing to the Minister of Justice, I'm threatening public exposure, unless... Back, and surprisingly quickly, comes a letter from no less than the minister's principal private secretary. I still have it. The Attorney General of the Province, it says, has been instructed to launch criminal proceedings against the two policemen in a superior court, and I will be advised of the trial date. I have decided to testify to John's condition immediately after his release, even though the evidence would be circumstantial. Besides, for a victim's own legal representative to give evidence is, to say the least, unusual. I cannot be sure what other witnesses, if any, including the complainants, will appear: people are so intimidated. But on the day of the trial the defence, effectively acting for the state, attacks my evidence most viciously, suggesting that I had stolen the revenue stamps myself and created a diversion, putting up a smoke-screen to cover up my own complicity. Yet the most pressing question is why I had taken the step of threatening the Minister of Justice of the land. What was my motive? Was it an act of subversion? It is then that I make a fatal mistake: losing my temper. When the judge presses with the very same question on my real motive for having created so much trouble, I can no longer contain myself. "Your Honour," I burst out, "I did this because of the cancer eating this country." The exact words. Whereupon, and without waiting for permission, I leave the witness stand and walk out of the court.

On principle I shall never inquire after the outcome of the trial. In any case, the earlier proceedings have been blotted from my memory. I do not even remember which of the victims, if any, may have been called to testify. If mine was the only evidence, apart from the affidavits (which may or may not have been in the court's possession), the trial was most probably abandoned and the accused acquitted. And if so, it would have been partly my fault. I take no further interest because I have now firmly resolved to emigrate and leave this country behind, never mind 300 years of family history in a remarkable land. Besides, there is no future for me in the law. Not in this place. I had not looked for trouble. But a good lawyer should never become emotionally involved in the affairs of a client, whatever the circumstances. When he does that he brings the practice of the law into disrepute and loses his effectiveness, because at least in theory, every lawyer is still an officer of the court. Even if I became a judge one day I would still have to apply these laws. Another consideration is that my wife is pregnant and wants to have her baby in Scotland. I do not even bother to complete my apprenticeship (called 'articles') in order to qualify for admission to the bar. We shall be leaving in short order.

Only now, as I write, I notice that the affidavits were not sworn before a commissioner of oaths in our own office—itself a telling thing—but by another attorney by the name of Dennis Shuttleworth. On that name hangs an interesting story. Shuttleworth, hooked on Scientology, was a bit of an eccentric, to the point that he was shunned by most of his colleagues in the profession. He had introduced us to the good work of an organization made up mostly of war veterans, known as Toc H, and Toc H was taking an interest in the plight of the prisoners held in South Africa's maximum-security establishment for dangerous convicts who were also mentally unbalanced; mostly people convicted of violent murders and declared insane. The prison, a converted old fort, and known as the Fort, sat on a *koppie* in the centre of the city but surrounded by trees and some greenery, and (surprisingly) with its own tennis courts. On Sunday mornings my wife and I accompany Shuttleworth to the Fort, taking magazines and newspapers and tobacco along. Several of the convicts would not smoke tobacco. Sitting along a wall, they prefer to roll and smoke newspapers instead, and one of them will only smoke a newspaper with whose editorial policies he is in accord. It may have something to do with the fact that, as a mathematician, he has a brilliant and discriminating mind. We are allowed to take some of the less dangerous men outside the walls of the Fort on our own recognizance, as the saying went, for a game of tennis on the adjoining courts.

To me though, the main significance of the Fort is that, several years later, it would house a Greek by the name of Tsafendas. I had sat in the parliamentary dining room in Cape Town just half an hour before, and not many yards from where the House was about to assemble for the customary Question Period at two o'clock. The Prime Minister was already seated on the front bench on the government side, when Tsafendas, a parliamentary messenger, walked up to him, bent over slightly as if to convey a message, and thrust a dagger straight into the prime ministerial heart. The Prime Minister was South Africa's ideological father of apartheid, Dr Hendrik French Verwoerd. He died instantly, in the very seat of power.

Was there a common element in some of these stories? Yes, there was such a thread. It had to do with human dignity. Among the ways Nelson Mandela asserted his dignity was his refusal to wear shorts, the regulation prison garb. His wife Winnie Mandela's worst punishment was when she was kept stark naked in her prison cell, even when she was menstruating. Betty Moretlo, the widow, tried ever so hard to preserve her dignity under the most trying circumstances. Albert Luthuli had been deeply hurt. Even my witch doctor client felt stripped of his dignity when he was not allowed to wear the paraphernalia of his profession in court. Christ's physical suffering was as nothing compared with the mocking humiliations of the very Son of God.

Human rights, linked to notions of equality, have become the *cause célèbre* of our time; a political instrument, but also a double-edged sword. Only too often their real source has not been recognized. We have forgotten that human rights are merely a derivative, an attribute, of the fundamental dignity of a human being created in the image of God.

# CHAPTER THREE
# THE DAWN OF APARTHEID

Eric Voegelin was a political philosopher whose *New Science of Politics* was inspired by his experience of—and his search for an explanation for—the Nazi phenomenon in Hitler's Germany. If Voegelin has taught us one thing it is to beware of transformationist political leaderships: politicians whose professed aim was to wreak fundamental changes in their own societies and even the world at large (Mao Tse-tung in China or Pierre Elliott Trudeau in Canada or—although of far lesser stature—Barack Obama). In South Africa it was Dr Hendrik French Verwoerd, a childhood immigrant from the Netherlands. Before he launched himself on his political career he had studied psychology at a German university (Heidelberg) and then taught that subject at the South African university of Stellenbosch. My father was one of his students.

Here was a man who could speak logically and compellingly—though possessed of a rather thin, even strangulated voice—for hours on end, and without a note. He must have been politically ambitious from the start and seemed to have shrewdly chosen his opportunity to enter the world of politics. I never knew that my father had witnessed that moment, just two weeks before my birth.

That by itself was unusual: my father's absence from home at such a time. My parents had lost their firstborn, a little girl, to meningitis a little more than a year before. For them it was a shattering experience. Indeed, the baby's death led to a pledge that henceforth they would single-mindedly dedicate themselves to the service of the Lord. It may well have accounted for my father's subsequent development into such an outstanding preacher and evangelist. And it may well have accounted for my father's refusal of an invitation, not long after the death of Field Marshal

Smuts, to assume the leadership of the Official Opposition in the South African parliament. Jan Smuts had made the common mistake of great men of not training a worthy successor, and the one who did succeed him, was exceedingly weak and ineffective. Since my father was such an effective speaker, and understood so well the minds and the activities of the *Broederbond*, the secret delegation of politicians who arrived at our home on a sunny Free State morning must have been convinced that my father had the ability to make life impossible for the ruling Nationalists, who had only so recently come into office. And I do believe that if he had acceded, the subsequent history of my native land may well have turned out differently. After all, Jan Smuts had only lost the general election by the narrowest of margins. Many of the voters for the Nationalists had been swayed by their promise of white bread. Yes, white bread! During and in the aftermath of the war the use of refined flour was forbidden. To possess a flour sieve was a criminal offence. The Nationalists pledged to lift the restriction. Their majority was so tenuous that they resorted to all kinds of dirty tricks, of a constitutional and judicial nature, to protect their position, one of which was to disenfranchise the so-called Cape Coloureds, a term reserved for a fairly large population of people of mixed race. Another possible reason for my father's refusal was that his mother had dedicated him to the service of the Almighty even before his birth; he even saw confirmation in the fact that like his mother, he was born with a crooked little finger. In other words, he could and would not be a politician.[6]

Notwithstanding appearances and contrary to all accounts, according to my father, Dr Verwoerd was an atheist. They had stood on street corners in the university town of Stellenbosch where my father tried to convince

6    Because it was such a rather incredible development, I should add that the leader of the delegation was a senior figure in Smuts's party by the name of S.J. Marais Steyn, who happened to be the Member of Parliament for the United Party representing none other than the town of Vereeniging! The poet William Blake had famously written about a "fearful symmetry." Such might well be said of the disparate events involving Vereeniging that have cropped up in this my story. Add the strangeness of the fact that F.W. de Klerk—the man who formally and effectively brought the apartheid era to an end—should have practised as an attorney, where else than in Vereeniging.

him of the reality of the Deity. If he was an atheist he would have had to take care to hide it, otherwise his chances of political advancement would have been non-existent.

Strong ambition could also be inferred from the fact that Dr Verwoerd had prepared a schema (of which my father gave me a copy) that amounted to a psychological typology, broken into seven main categories, and useful not only for analyzing people but to know how to handle them. I had lost the document and only found it again a couple of months ago. That he was well equipped to exploit a situation I could well believe, considering the way he virtually engineered South Africa's expulsion from the (British) Commonwealth of Nations. We were living in Cambridge when he arrived in London, at Heathrow airport, for a fateful conference of heads of Commonwealth countries. Already, British Prime Minister Harold McMillan's famous "Wind of Change" speech in Cape Town in 1960, rankled bitterly with the Nationalist regime. And so, nothing could have been more provocative—especially to an emotional and emotive Canadian Prime Minister John Diefenbaker—than Verwoerd's brazen and obviously calculated declaration at the airport that apartheid was "a policy of good neighbourliness."

Not only did Dr Verwoerd specialize in psychology; he was intensely interested in sociology. Sociology he may well have seen as a stepping stone to political power. And that was why he may have chosen the so-called *Armblankevraagstuk* (the Poor Whites Problem) as his launching pad. The opportunity came when the *Broederbond* (though not in its own name) organized a national conference on white poverty, to be held in South Africa's diamond city, Kimberley, in October 1934. The strange thing was that my father never once mentioned the Kimberley Conference nor his involvement in it, and of which I had known nothing, until I started to research the nature and origin of a mysterious piece of paper that had been among other documents in a steel trunk in our basement, and that had not been opened for over 40 years. I could not remember where and how it had found its way into my possession. A single sheet had been folded and on each folded section were rough and hastily written scribbles in my father's handwriting—some of it difficult to decipher—as if written on his knee. I reckoned that he must have had an important reason for holding on to such a thing. Not only was it undated but there was no clue to either the occasion or the venue, except that it appeared to relate to a meeting of some kind. The only thing that really triggered my interest was a list of five names, one of them of Dr Verwoerd. Circumstances prevented me from asking my ailing mother whether she had any memory of my father ever having attended an important conference in which Dr Verwoerd was involved. To nail down the provenance and significance of the document took a great deal of research on my part.

Before we continue with this account—a story about the beginnings of ideological apartheid—there is something one must recognize. In one form or another, apartheid is not a phenomenon that will ever go away. Different forms of segregation, either formal or informal, are a recurring feature in societies of all stripes, sometimes under a euphemistic multiculturalist rubric. India is a classic example. Created in 1982, Canada has its own little aboriginal 'bantustan' (or homeland) for the Inuit (or Eskimo) people in the far north of the country. Called Nunavut, it has been an unmitigated disaster from almost every point of view. (Further elaborated in Chapter Five following.) Canadians have even practised a kind of reverse discrimination, because certified members of hundreds of tribal First Nations pay no income tax—even when they live and work off-reserve in the cities—and regardless of their earnings. To compound matters, many of the ruling chiefs and their cronies have awarded themselves salaries running into hundreds of thousands of dollars, all of it financed out of the billions of dollars in subsidies forked out by the taxpayer every year. And understandably, as in the New South Africa, nepotism has run rife. Only the single-minded logic and comprehensiveness, and its overtly racialist character—and yes, cruelty—of the South African version made it so unique. South Africans might be amused to learn that as late as 2011 the Canadian authorities were grappling with ways of defining and classifying indigenous Canadians of mixed race—called Métis, the equivalent of South Africa's Coloureds—who were demanding official recognition and special privileges and entitlements for themselves, along with the other aboriginal peoples. In 2015 the same conundrum cropped up when a Canadian Museum for Human Rights wanted to exempt Indians, Inuit (Eskimos), and Métis from the admission fee.

Canadians had a seemingly never-ending problem on their hands. In February 2015 they learned that "the national chief of First Nations says Aboriginal Affairs Minister Bernard Valcourt was 'ill-informed' when he spoke about how indigenous men have a lack of respect for women on reserves. 'You've got to be careful about blaming the victims again and blaming the communities,' Assembly of First Nations national chief Perry Bellegarde said in an interview Wednesday. *It's all about colonization...*'" (Emphasis added.)

---

Opponents of apartheid and even historians have either been ignorant or have taken scant notice of the story of the *Volkskongres* on White Poverty held in Kimberley between October 2 and October 5, 1934. The conference followed in the wake of a special research project, financed by the Carnegie Trust. It painted a dismal picture of the lack of proper education that went hand in hand with the poverty of large sections of the Afrikaner people. As we've noted earlier, they were not only suffering as a result of the Great Depression but the farming community especially had never fully recovered from the ravages of the Boer War. Ostensibly the conference was organized by the Dutch Reformed Church but in a speech delivered by one of the original founders of the *Broederbond* on the occasion of its 50th anniversary, he lauded the role the Bond had played in the launching of the *Volkskongres*, just as he stated, with respect to the celebrations of 1938—commemorating the Great Trek—that "God gave us the Oxwagon Trek. It was the *Broeders* who organized it. It was the *Broeders* who took the initiative. Through the grace of God the *Broeders* carried it out." They were to do the same thing when, as a sequel to the Kimberley Conference, they organized an Economic *Volkskongres* precisely five years later (almost to the day, between October 3 and 5, 1939) where, once again, "the young Dr H.F. Verwoerd, later Prime Minister, drew national attention..."

In 1934 Verwoerd was the convenor of the most important organizing committee, the Socio-Economic Committee, and it was he who was
chosen to deliver the keynote address following the official opening. The
eight resolutions he introduced were the first of many on the agenda.
One wonders how many among the audience noticed the *Broederbond*
linkage when, in his opening address, a Dutch Reformed minister, speaking on behalf of his church, dated the poverty problem to 1916, given
that the *Broederbond* itself was formed a mere two years later, in 1918.
The opening speaker then conjured up an image of two gigantic mountains which, he said, the congress was called to confront. They were the
problem of the Poor Whites, he said, and the problem of the Natives, the
black people of South Africa (both of them capitalized). Clearly, there was
more to the conference than a (nevertheless well-founded and honorably
intended) concern over white poverty.

Then followed the address by the star performer of the congress, the
young professor from Stellenbosch. As an exercise in persuasive rhetoric
the speech was unsurpassed. The speaker sought as comprehensive and
systematic an approach to the problems as human logic could conceive.
In my own literal translation from the Afrikaans, the speaker said: "We
must look openly in the face of the connection between white poverty
and the presence of coloured people and natives in the land. It is impossible to make proposals for the greater economic welfare of poor whites
without affecting the other groups in one way or another... if someone
must be unemployed: a white or a native, then, in our contemporary
society with the existing differences in standards of living, *it will be more
economic for the country if the native will be the one who is unemployed.*"
(Emphasis added.) In other words, if any group had to suffer, it would
have to be the blacks.

The speaker offered the prospect of resettling and employing the
Natives "elsewhere," on special reserves. He asked for a policy declaration to that effect because it would be in the interest of the community
as a whole. It had been necessary to look into the far future. Thus, he
said, it was the task of the congress to provide a general framework for
action, consisting of five major systemic directions, and this, amazingly,

would include measures taken for the benefit and on behalf of whites who were *not* unemployed (and not poor in any sense of the word) but in order to prevent their economic backsliding *at any time in the future*. So, to make it clear that he was not only talking of solving the existing problems of people who were already struggling with poverty, he deliberately substituted an abstraction— "white poverty" —as the issue. In other words, if anyone was white, he should never be poor, not now and not in the future. "New times," he said, "bring new problems and demand new machinery." And he underlined again that, "the two problems of poverty and the coloured problem... have been staring us in the face for decades without their having ever been tackled systematically." The speaker then proceeded to outline a range of related measures that seemed to cover every conceivable angle of social and economic life, a veritable *tour d'horizon*, and by any standard an astonishing *tour de force*.

Almost laconically the official though incomplete minutes of the congress—a copy of which I was only able to locate, not in South Africa, but in the most unlikely place imaginable, namely, in Canada in the city of Vancouver, thanks to the resources of Canada's National Library—stated that, with the exception of a few minor amendments, "all of the proposals of Professor Verwoerd were accepted." Years later a historian remarked that, "he had a great ability to marshal arguments for white privilege so as to make it appear that it was not actually the intention for whites to be the sole or even the principal beneficiaries"; listed, *inter alia*, no fewer than nineteen other related measures put forward by the speaker as an integral part of his vision; and concluded: "There was virtually nothing he left out."

Towards the very end of the Kimberley Conference there were signs that it had not escaped the delegates that a momentous turning point had been reached. It often happens that enthusiastic followers at lower echelons take a leader by his word, only to then run with the message in embarrassing ways. And so, after a speaker proposed that in certain industries there should be fixed quotas of white and black workers—and a minister of the Dutch Reformed Church not only seconded the proposal, but added that if it was not implemented whites would start to mix with coloureds and blacks—a delegate from Pretoria by the name of Abercrombie moved (in English, believe it or not) that "This Conference resolves that the future employment of the white unskilled classes, the efficiency of our people, and the welfare and prosperity of the white and native races of South Africa depend in a large measure on the complete segregation of the towns, and the gradual repatriation of all male natives" over a period of 10 years, at the rate of 10 percent a year... "Employment to be found for any redundant natives in labour colonies and on road works, etc..." A Reverend P.S.Z.Coetzee, with whom my father's path would cross again, moved that, "strict supervision be employed to prevent whites working under coloureds." Both motions were carried.

A senator with an English name voiced his disapproval of the earlier adoption of Dr Verwoerd's proposals, which had taken place in his absence, but apparently the Verwoerd motions stood. Later on, as my father's notes confirmed, a Reverend Reyneke too expressed his misgivings about the Abercrombie resolution, which, he said, "stigmatized an entire race as unhealthy, unclean, and dangerous." Yet at the same time—as my father's scribbles confirmed as well—the Reverend Reyneke took pains to assure the meeting that he had "no objection to segregation. To the contrary, he considers it to be the only solution for the Native problem." The official minutes merely noted that the Reyneke proposal provoked a "warm discussion" and eventually the Abercrombie resolution was reversed, even though Abercrombie had launched a renewed defence of his motion, insisting that "the natives should be repatriated... there were places enough in South Africa where natives could be sent." The speaker added that he was "fighting for South Africa and the children of South Africa so that when we should get a republic it should be a white republic and not a black one."

Significantly, my father's notes referred to yet another intervention—not mentioned in the official minutes—in support of the dissenting Reverend Reyneke, this time by a Dr Botha, who may have been the same person who subsequently became Prime Minister Smuts's Secretary for Education, and who expressed his doubt that the proposals were "fair and ethical." According to my father's cryptic notation, Dr Botha must have added that what was proposed constituted a "tremendous blow to the congress" and was "irresponsible."

*In light of the subsequent political history of South Africa, here, in my opinion, was the definitive turning point of the twentieth century, a moment of truth, in the life of a country and of all its peoples, and of which a single handwritten sheet of paper has borne authentic witness.*

It would not be the only time that a purported pursuit of human rights (in this case, connected with the economic and educational privations of a white minority) turned out to be a double-edged sword. That was a lesson I was yet to learn in another country and at another time far into the future.

Ever so prophetic—given the story of the following chapter—were the very words (translated here) my father attributed to the Reverend Reyneke in reference to the removal of black people from South Africa's towns and cities: *"Where would they have to go? No provision made - what about the women and families? Labour colonies? Where must they subsist?"* History would show that the reversal of the Abercrombie resolution may have been no more than a sop to conscience, or to serve appearances, because that was where events were inexorably headed with the acceptance of Dr Verwoerd's comprehensive and overarching vision.

After the 1934 conference Verwoerd went from strength to strength. He helped to edit the conference proceedings and also served as secretary of the Continuation Committee. In 1936—along with some other professors from the University of Stellenbosch—he staged a public protest in the Cape Town harbour against the landing of Jewish refugees from Germany on the good ship *Stuttgart*. (Reminiscent of how, just three years later, a Canadian prime minister, Mackenzie King, would bar the good ship *St Louis*, sending back hundreds of Jews to Europe "where many would die in the gas chambers and crematoria of the Third Reich.") One of Verwoerd's first acts on becoming the editor, in 1937, of *Die Transvaler*, an influential Afrikaans newspaper, was to publish a 4,000 word article under his own name, titled "The Jewish Question as seen from a Nationalist Party viewpoint." He needed to unify and mobilize the Afrikaners to realize his republican dream, and so—as reported by an historian— "to enforce unity in the movement he turned to the Afrikaner *Broederbond*," which he saw "as an instrument to promote his goals."

Complicit in the whole affair was an alliance between a Christian church and a secret society whose objective turned out to be nothing less than white domination. And indeed, the chairman of the congress was yet another Dutch Reformed minister with whose path my father's would cross, a Reverend Dr William Nicol. Beware political clerics! Dr Nicol had been the chairman of the *Broederbond* for a short while in the 1920s, and at some point after the 1934 congress, was destined to become the Administrator (a kind of viceroy) of the province of the Transvaal. Just how pivotal a year it was could be garnered from a report that the *Broederbond* "began recruiting political figures about 1934" although it was only on February 17, 1937 that Verwoerd himself accepted formal membership. In 1934 too, according to General Smuts's Director of Military Intelligence, Hitler sent a German professor to spy in South Africa. And it was from 1935 onwards, we learn, that a special organization "under the leadership of *Broederbonders*, studied the concept of apartheid." By the early 1960s no fewer than 848 ministers of religion were said to have become members.

Normally the word 'totalitarian' is associated with oppressive regimes. However, in the execution of Dr Verwoerd's grand vision there was something else as well, namely, a supreme manifestation of a *totalist* mind at work. Totalism was the hallmark of the political philosopher Karl Popper's "enemies of the open society." Like Hitler's 'total onslaught', and following the blueprint laid down by the 1934 congress, apartheid too would soon become an exercise in pursuit of totalism. I would yet have to discover, in another country, and many years into the future, how totalism could suffuse the mind sets of a special breed of socio-cultural and political transformationists. Although in that case of a far more sophisticated character.

In 1944, the very year my father parted ways with the Dutch Reformed Church, the Prime Minister, Field Marshal Smuts, using emergency powers to try to oust *Broederbonders* from the public service, described the *Broederbond* as a "dangerous, cunning, political, Fascist organization." Their tentacles even reached into the school board in charge of the school I attended in Bloemfontein, to the point that on account of my father's activities I was literally thrown off the school bus and thenceforth had to either walk or cycle the three miles from home to school, winter and summer. Although that story had a funny side: in primary school, boys usually went about barefoot. But not having been on the school bus I did not know that shoes were mandatory in high school, where I arrived on the first day of the school term to find that I was the only pupil among some 600 in the assembly hall who was without shoes.

The truth of the matter is that in its *essence*—and this is admittedly a provocative assertion—the Kimberley Conference was of the same genre as the Wannsee conference of January 1942, in Berlin, where it was finally determined that the Jews had to be disposed of, and how it would be done. Although in a different sense, and far less brutal, the resolutions passed at Kimberley too were aimed at the 'disposal'—or rather disposition—of an entire race, in this case black people. Not only was race a common element, but both the rise of Hitler and the rise of the doctrine of apartheid originated against a background of national poverty, deprivation and humiliation. The rise of the *Broederbond*, as did the rise of Nazism, followed an ignominious end to a war. In a way, South Africa's Treaty of Vereeniging at the end of the Anglo-Boer War had been Germany's Treaty of Versailles, except that in the former case Britain appeared more generous than she, and the rest of the western powers, would be at *Paris 1919*. It was not altogether generous because the postwar administration of Lord Milner in South Africa tried hard to stamp out the Afrikaans language, and did little to restore the shattered farm economy of the Boers. Lord Milner was so unpopular among the vanquished that when the South African constitutional convention started in the city hall of Durban in 1908, the hosts offered to cover up a portrait of Milner hanging in the room. Instead of having to carry the burden of reparations, as in the case of the Germans, the vanquished in South Africa had to give up their riches of diamonds and gold.

Born just two weeks after the Kimberley Conference, the day would come when I would find myself at the cutting edge of the execution of the vision of a German-trained professor, affecting the lives of South Africa's own *untermenschen*.

———————

Will the world ever be rid of tyranny? Here in Berlin, exactly 40 years after the Wannsee Conference, the Sunday morning dawns bright and cheerful. I've set out early to traverse as much of the Wall as I'm able to cover in one day, walking from right to left, and also to visit the Glienicke Brücke, the famous bridge on the road to Potsdam where, in the same week, important spy exchanges are taking place. First there's Checkpoint Charlie. Then the Potsdamer Platz on my right: forlorn, bleak, featureless, and lifeless, except for the odd scurrying rabbit. Years later someone will write an article about those rabbits, because they migrated to the west as soon as the wall came down! To my right too, a mound over the ruins of the Hitler bunker. Next looms the Brandenburg Gate. Red flags flutter lazily in the wind. This is most interesting. At this point the Wall is not only low, but forms a bulge, bulging out towards the West. Nothing happens for a while until an East German soldier, putting on a look of disinterest, saunters out and positions himself between the Wall and a small raised platform. But soon the reason is evident. He has interposed himself between freedom and a small group of people walking out from behind the Gate. Standing on the platform, they gaze into the distance, looking rather forlorn. They do not remain for long. But time stands still. Close by is the Reichstag, blackened, and pockmarked by artillery shells. Above the entrance, carved in stone: *Dem Deutschen Volken*. A young Jew and his wife walk up to sit down next to me, quietly. He says he will explain some things, if I'm interested. Yes, I am. He says, look at that pathway running along a grassy stretch sloping down to the River Spree, separated from the grass by a low iron fence dotted with small white plaques each carrying the name of a person, and a date. Across the water, on a watch tower, are the East German guards, the Vopos, each with a machine gun in the crook of an arm. To their left, and to my right, is a bridge. A barge chugs into sight but comes to a standstill just short of the bridge. I sense an ugliness, a darkness, an elementary evil, evil multiplied, evil intensified. Here is the face of Death, Death with a capital letter. The barge, says my companion, stops for long enough that any refugee clinging to it underwater will have sufficient time to either drown or come up. The Vopos, he says, have a grand time of it. When a refugee has desperately plunged into the river to swim across, and thinks that he has gained the safety of the west bank and freedom, the poor soul is mistaken. Not only men but women too, sometimes young girls. The Vopos wait. Only when their target has started to crawl up the grassy slope on the other side will they take aim. The body will roll back into the river. The small white plaques are silent testimony. *Here died Margarethe.* I do not know it yet, but I'm looking at the exact spot where Margaret Thatcher, reduced to tears, knelt to place a small wreath. Do you know, says my self-appointed guide, that we're sitting on top of an underground warren containing the remnants of the German High Command post of the last days? There is still a relic, he says. It's a concrete bunker but no one really knows about it because it's hidden in that small coppice you see behind us. Let's take a look. We make our way through the trees and there it is. A heavy steel plate covers the only visible opening. Dead centre in the steel plate is a jagged four-inch hole punched by a Russian shell. I put my nose to the hole. And now I have not just seen the face of Death, but have smelled the stench of Death, a dank smell that will stay with me for the rest of my life.

Later in the day I make my way back to the Schlosshotel Gerhus in the Grunewald, one of the stately houses that managed to survive the war intact. It is intimidatingly Gothic, especially in its interior. Apparently Kaiser Wilhelm had gifted the house to his lawyer. I seem to end up in houses given to their lawyers by the high and mighty. Not far outside Edinburgh is a smallish white and turreted Scottish castle-home, called Houston House, a gift to her lawyer by Mary Queen of Scots, and my favourite abode on visits to the Scottish capital. Tonight, here in Berlin, there will be a society wedding featuring a Von Weizsäcker as guest of honour, and I shall be hanging over the balcony overlooking the atrium, watching, and listening to the tribal singing someone can appreciate, who, as a child, had heard Germans sing *Lili Marlene* over Radio Zeesen. But before the day is out I also walk to the edge of the Wannsee, scene of an infamous conference held in 1942.

The very next Sunday I walk across the green meadows of Runnymede on the banks of the River Thames, to stand before the monument erected in honour of that symbol of freedom, the Magna Carta, and paid for by… the American Bar Association. That is what the inscription says. I return to my hotel on the outskirts of the nearby town of Egham, where, high on a hill, sits another monument, this one in honour of the Royal Air Force, founded by a South African serving in Britain's War Cabinet, Field Marshal Jan Christiaan Smuts. The hotel is ancient; on one side the remnants of a moat, but still adorned with black swans. Great Fosters, a gift from the sovereign to Anne Boleyn. Or was it to his or her lawyer? Tonight a group of elderly gentlemen in dinner jackets already grey-green with age, will share a meal below the minstrels' gallery in the tithe barn. They have some kind of authority over the Wimbledon tennis champion-ships and they have come to decide what to do about one John McEnroe, an American whose hallmark was the tantrums he threw on the tennis court. Welcome to the ways of the New World.

———

Years have gone by. Under blazing lights, in front of the same Brandenburg Gate, stands a Barack Obama, facing an ecstatic, spellbound crowd, their arms raised in unison. Rallying point of two successive though deceptively different totalisms. Chin out-thrust, Benito-style, a new saviour spells out his vision for a world-to-be-totally-transformed.

*Plus ça change, plus c'est la même chose…*

# CHAPTER FOUR
# THE HEART OF DARKNESS

Out there one can touch the silence, and the dark, because there are no street lights. Once or twice a dog barks in the distance. Probably out scavenging; they are scrawny at the best of times. Acrid smoke from countless open fires hangs in the air. Huddling in the corner of the room is an elderly black man, already greying, holding a *knobkerrie*, a knobbed stick, the kind the *impis* of the Zulu king Dingaan used to carry, along with their assegais and shields made out of hide. In other words, a weapon. But hardly a weapon. The old man is my bodyguard. And we are alone. Here, in the heart of the sprawling black shanty town of Nyanga, on the windswept Cape Flats outside of Cape Town, with its notorious Transit Camp and high death rates, especially among the children, and its population of 50,000 souls, I'm the only white man tonight. I had half-volunteered to act as the returning officer in an unpopular local election, conducted by my employer, a metropolitan local government authority with a rateable population of one million, and this explains the brooding silence around us and why nobody has come to cast a ballot. Sitting at a little desk, on a hard chair, I've never been so afraid in my life. Violent riots have already broken out in the black townships near the country town of Paarl, not far from where my Huguenot forefathers first settled. My employers—known as the Cape Divisional Council—are worried that the same thing may happen in their jurisdiction.

The reason I'm here is that an enlightened chief executive officer of the Council has planted me as a spy in the administrative apparatus that is now tasked with carrying out the laws passed by the central government to control the lives and the movements—and above all, the labour—of South Africa's urban blacks. The man in charge of the local operations, although nominally an employee of ours, is licensed by and responsible to the Department of Bantu Administration in Pretoria. We seem to have little control. The laws are not only numerous but extensive and extremely complex, so that my boss was able to persuade Pretoria's man that he and his staff needed my presence in their office, every working day, to help them interpret the regulations. But my real mission is to produce a report for the Council on the actual implementation of the system. And a system it is, in every sense of the word, having been finally put in place to realize the vision that was so comprehensively and pointedly spelled out by Dr Hendrik French Verwoerd in the city of Kimberley in October 1934, and where my father had scribbled those cryptic notes. In a book titled *The Afrikaners*, a historian, though sympathetic, will report that "by 1966, the final year of Verwoerd's term in office, the scheme for a white South Africa was never more forcefully pursued. All housing construction in the African townships had been frozen since the early 1960s, and in 1964 the government introduced extremely harsh influx controls that expanded the system to peri-urban areas and made possible the eradication of the so-called 'black spots'..."

This is the same system I'm now supposed to be supporting. The assignment has already lasted six months, six months that have seen me gradually going off my food, and spending sleepless nights. I've lost weight. Tonight, at around ten o'clock, we call it quits so that I can get out of here as fast as possible and drive home in our little white Fiat to an anxiously waiting wife in white suburban Cape Town. For six months I have been looking into the heart of darkness. Tonight I've paid my last dues, and can now write my report. And I shall not be surprised that in due course my employers will lock it away, that it will never be allowed to see the light of day, and that I will promise the man who had sent me—on my word of honour, and because he is a man of honour—that I have kept no copy.

Not that my other duties in local government had not been interesting. After our return from Scotland to give South Africa a second try I thought that joining the Cape Divisional Council as their Assistant Legal Adviser would represent 'clean' work, at least compared with my previous experience with the law, and also because the functions of the Council were extremely varied. In addition to the usual municipal preoccupations with roads and bridges and town planning and building permits and water services and public health, the Council was also in the business of developing amenities along one of the most beautiful coastlines in the world, where we owned and controlled a large nature reserve covering the entire southern tip of the peninsula that, in 1580, Sir Francis Drake called "the most stately thing and the fairest Cape we saw in the whole circumference of the earth." An eccentric Englishman by the name of Ernest Middlemiss was in charge of the nature reserve, and so eccentric was he that at one point he took up residence with the large troupe of baboons that made that part of the peninsula their home. Those creatures could be dangerous, as I discovered on an early Sunday morning hike on the slopes of Table Mountain when I ran into scores of hostile and barking baboons sitting on the rocks and barring my way, displaying their fearsome and ugly yellow fangs. To turn and run away could have been fatal, so there was no choice but to try to appear aggressive oneself, baring one's teeth, and walking straight through. (It also helps if one has a hat, which, with the crown clamped between one's teeth, resembles a large open mouth. It works the same way when a lion tamer points the four legs of a chair at the animal.) In Middlemiss the baboons even found a babysitter; a function he faithfully performed while the parents were out foraging.

But the real fun began with the beach business, both inside and outside of the precincts of the nature reserve. We had already built a most attractive swimming pool out into the rocks and equipped a restaurant at a place called Miller's Point, when up came the issue of... apartheid. The central government in Pretoria insisted that we segregate the public beaches under our jurisdiction, allocating separate areas to Whites, Blacks, Coloureds and people of Asian extraction. Matters were complicated enough because different government departments had a hand in the implementation of the *Reservation of Separate Amenities Act of 1953* and the provincial *Reservation of Separate Amenities by Local Authorities Ordinance of 1955*. Equally active was the Department of Community Development and a particular problem was the *Seashore Act* which fell under the jurisdiction of the Minister of Lands, who controlled the shoreline between the high- and low-water marks. We had jurisdiction over the land above the high-water mark and I cannot recall what government agency had control of the area below the low-water mark, essentially the sea itself. Now all of that was pretty complicated already, but then I was asked to attend to the problem of demarcating beaches around the perimeter of a much frequented semi-circular bay.

By that time I was already wondering whether one could make a system work against itself. *Could evil be made to serve as its own antibody?* Years later (as we shall yet see) I would come across a radical American change agent by the name of Saul Alinsky, who was a past master at such tactics. One might be lucky if one's actions did not just frustrate a system, but also exposed it to ridicule if not contempt. So I set out conscientiously and enthusiastically with the drafting of the necessary regulations, supported by elaborate maps and diagrams for the benefit not only of my Council, but also—and particularly for the benefit of—the central government agencies. The maps showed that if the beaches along a pronounced bay were to be divided into four separate sections, the demarcation lines would soon converge and then start to cross not far out to sea. I explained, formally, that many of our citizens were also strong swimmers, and in no time there would be utter chaos if Blacks started to swim into White water, Whites into Coloured water, and so forth. The law may be an ass, but it does not want to be laughed at. Along straighter beach fronts we could create buffer zones of no-man's land between the demarcated areas, but here they would not solve the problem. Or we might have to deploy beach guards to restrain ardent citizens from swimming out too far and ending up in the wrong waters. All of which gave rise to an almighty kerfuffle and anxious interdepartmental correspondence and meetings. Whether, in the end, the idea of demarcating those particular beaches was abandoned, or whether the bays were allocated to fewer groups, I cannot recall.

*Malan* was a good old French Huguenot name, as was *de Villiers*, my mother's name, both dating back to the arrival of the good ship *Zion* at the Cape of Good Hope, many months after she had set sail from the port of Texel in Holland on January 8, 1689. But George S. Malan was not just a Huguenot by descent. George was also a *witman*. Now that was something special. Just as a gentleman is not necessarily a gentle man, a *witman* (although the word meant white man) was not necessarily white. In theory, and sometimes in fact, he could be as black as your proverbial lump of coal from Newcastle. Chief Albert Luthuli—the leader of the African National Congress and Nelson Mandela's forerunner—was such a man. Eventually, in South Africa, when the tables had been turned, only black might be beautiful, but in the Year of Our Lord 1963 a *witman* was someone whom reasonable people took to be a decent and upstanding specimen of the human race. To be called a *witman* was the ultimate accolade.

Merely as a physical specimen George met all the specifications: tall, dark, handsome, well groomed and not only soft spoken but well spoken. Admittedly not your *ware Afrikaner*, your true Afrikaner, in the strict sense of the word, because George's home language was mostly English. I hasten to add that George was not dark dark; he just had the normal complexion of someone with Latin blood in him. Admittedly, even as far as a de Villiers was concerned, there were some of us who could be clearly classified with the *swart de Villierse*; the ones who had more than their fair share of black blood coursing through their veins. Indeed, it was a standing joke that with their high cheekbones and other features, the wives of two prime ministers, Dr D.F. Malan and Dr H.F. Verwoerd— both of them pioneers of apartheid—were so obviously of mixed blood. That had not deterred the Verwoerds from proudly proclaiming that not a single employee in the household or on the staff of that most beautiful of prime ministerial estates at the foot of Table Mountain, Groote Schuur, was not white.

For George Malan I had the highest respect. Not only was he a *witman*, but his heart was in the right place. As a consummate administrator of a huge metropolitan governmental authority, I believed that he too was leading a double life, because he had to keep up appearances, given that several of the councillors—at least among those elected in semi-rural wards—were avid supporters of the Nationalist regime and there may even have been *Broederbonders* among them. They were constantly looking over his shoulder, and yet George was troubled by the injustices with which he was contending every day, day after day, as an administrator.

In me George must have recognized a kindred soul, especially in the wake of my recent and extraordinary efforts at both efficient and effective beach segregation in the service of my country. Intelligent as he was, George would have cottoned on quite soon, and had no doubt helped enormously in the playing out of that little charade, without our actually having exchanged any sentiments on the matter. One afternoon, after the close of business, I was summoned to his presence and presented with an extraordinary request. To become a spy, planted in the heart of the apartheid apparatus would, of course, be an entirely voluntary enterprise on my part. No special rewards were on offer. Just an opportunity to match wits with the infidel. In other words, an offer nobody in his right mind could possibly refuse. Not a soul, not among the councilors, and not among the rest of the staff, could be apprized of the real reason for the assignment. Officially it was bruited that the great complexities in the administration of the apartheid laws needed the presence, on the spot, of a competent legal adviser. Semi-officially—although even that was not voiced explicitly, and certainly not in print—some of the councillors were worried stiff that the riots in other black townships not far away from us might spread to our jurisdiction if we did not keep a watchful eye over the way the laws were administered.

And indeed, we had already made an effort to alleviate the conditions. We had, for example, built a most impressive new community centre in our own black township, and marked by a project that gave me a sense of accomplishment on account of the kaffir beer. Kaffir beer was the accepted name for a wholesome but rather sour brew enjoyed by blacks, not only because it was mildly intoxicating unless imbibed in great volumes, but, if properly brewed, contained considerable protein and other beneficial ingredients. The trouble was that we could not supply the community with the beer because a full-blown brewery would have cost too much. At first I thought of another possible solution to our problem, namely, the fish train. The fish train was a special refrigerated and fast train used to transport fresh fish from the Cape to the Witwatersrand each day, but which, in the nature of things, always returned empty. Could we not enter into an agreement with an existing brewery up-country, so that a regular supply of kaffir beer could thus be shipped down to the Cape to meet our needs? For some reason, unfortunately, the idea did not fly. I had a brother working at the Council for Scientific and Industrial Research (CSIR) in Pretoria and was vaguely familiar with the types of scientific and technical research conducted under its auspices. But it was by pure accident that I discovered that a bright spark at the CSIR had developed a formula for *instant* kaffir beer. It consisted of a powder yielding a product that was barely distinguishable from the real thing when mixed with water and left to ferment for a short while. Naturally, customer approval had been anxiously awaited, but to our great relief the beer turned out to be acceptable, and particularly because it was so cheap.

The minutes of a gathering of administrators of black townships in the Western Cape, held in the town of Stellenbosch, were instructive. A lengthy discussion took place of the merits of brewing and selling *kafferbier* in municipal establishments, and confirmed the wisdom of our scheme. Hailing from the very town, Paarl, where the worst riots had broken out, "Mr Le Roux said that it was only now that he had seen how much delight the Bantu derived from *gemütliche* social intercourse in the beer hall and that he had realized the lack that had existed before there had been a beer hall." In Paarl they were already selling 13,000 gallons each month. In vain did the special guest, a Professor Olivier, an expert in race relations, plead that rather than running a monopoly, local authorities should allow blacks to continue to brew their own beer in the privacy of their homes. The administrator of our own township, duly licensed as he was by the central government in Pretoria, disagreed. He spoke up in support of an official monopoly, which, he said, would reduce the necessity of police raids on private premises. And still impeccably logically (as befitted any true systems-serving apparatchik) he added that it would also minimize raids being mistakenly conducted on the houses of "orderly and order-loving" blacks.

A detailed picture of the pivotal realities of the system I was now serving beggared belief. With respect to the following passages, I'm asking the reader to please stay with me. I would be surprised if anything as methodical, bureaucratic, and Kafkaesque existed back in Hitler's Germany—the historical novels of the German writer Hans Fallada notwithstanding—but reminiscent perhaps of the kind ministrations of the East German Stasi apparatus. Behold a *Government Gazette Extraordinary* boasting 87 pages of fine print. They are a set of "Bantu Labour Regulations" issued by the Department of Bantu Administration and Development (note the Development). Randomly opening it, one reads:

> 1. Mealie meal. Should the Director of Bantu Labour, after consultation with the medical officer, deem it desirable, kaffircorn or other cereal in such quantity as the said Director may approve, shall be substituted for part of the mealie-meal ration... During the months of July, August, September and October, when an orange or other approved substitute may be issued every second day, the vegetable ration may be reduced to 3 oz. per day.

This reflected the most benevolent aspect of the system, as it had been in the American Deep South, where a well-fed slave was a sensible investment. Such would be immediately recognized not only by the enlightened, but also by the prudent. As well, was it not a reflection of ones Christian duty? And who would ever have imagined that kindness could have a cruel face, or vice versa? The same enlightened approach marked the labour practices on South Africa's gold mines where the black miners were well fed and looked after medically until they developed lung diseases and were no longer useful. The enlightenment did not extend to the rest of their living conditions, because, for decade after decade, hundreds of thousands of men were closely herded in sleeping compounds, deprived of the company of their families, with the inevitable social and moral consequences, although that was well before AIDS became a problem. Yet, is it a mystery that southern Africa should have developed the world's highest rates of HIV infection?

But to return to the regulatory framework. Of particular interest is a *Handbook for the Management of District Labour Bureaux* issued by the

Chief Bantu Affairs Commissariat of Cape Town (file number N3/11/2 dated May 29, 1961) and addressed to "all Magistrates, Additional Magistrates, Assistant Magistrates and the Bantu Affairs Commissioner, Salt River." The handbook serves to assist in the execution and implementation of six major laws and government notices ("as amended") and eleven *General Circulars* issued between the years 1952 and 1960. The basic purpose is to compel *all* black men to work; to exercise strict control over the influx of blacks into urban areas; to enforce the necessary registrations, and even to list the relevant rubber stamps that are required and can be requisitioned with reference to "Article 17(1), (b), (d), (i), (j), (k), (m) and article 17 (1) (v) (b) and (c) of *Government Notice* number 1903 of 1957." "These rubber stamps are to be held under strict supervision and the last two ought to be kept under lock and key and can only be used with the consent of the head of the office." But above all, the handbook deals with *cards*: cards of all colours, related to different categories of people, namely, job seekers, those who have been placed in jobs, job seekers who have been transferred, and job seekers who have been "written off." Under each category are sub-categories, some divided into as many as four sub-sub-categories. The most prevalent cards, including "old" and "new" cards, seem to be the cards numbered B.A. 1 (A) and in strangely random order, (D), (B) or (C). When completing the monthly returns, officials are directed to draw cards from (ii), (iii) and (iv) and to transfer them to Section II, sections (i), (ii) or (iii) "as the case may be." Elsewhere, officials' attention is directed to the annual return B.A. 517 as well as to B.A. 1004 cards that have to be filed behind B.A. 84 cards. Statistics are required for the B.A. 537 annual report for which purpose a card B.A. 84 *of the applicable colour* is imperative. Particularly ominous is the sound of an attached "O" card that ought not to be issued under any circumstances to a native not in possession of a passbook, and then only (clearly underlined) in favour of natives between the ages of 15 and 16. Those who do possess their passbook should have their books endorsed in accordance with Regulation 17 (1) (I) (b) pursuant to *Government Notice* 1903 of 1957. A pin should not be used when attaching B.A. 1 to B.A. 85. Only when a native has changed from one employer to another can the slip attached to B.A. 85 be destroyed. Care should be taken to comply with paragraphs 8 and 9 of *Government Notice* 1903, except that in a proclaimed district attachment "L" of *Government Notice* 63 of 1959 must be used. Accordingly, the strips attached to B.A. 85 will gradually disappear, and there is a reminder that Attachment "D" is actually B.A. 1004. B.A. 1 and 84 must be kept in the same drawer as the B.A. 85 strips, and so forth. Detailed instructions refer to the proper completion of Return B.A. 86, and transfers should be handled by reference to paragraph 4 of *General Circular* Number 47 of 1957 as amended by *General Circular* Number 7 of 1958. Details of transfers can be recorded on the back of form B.A. 86. Special attention is drawn to paragraph 16 of *Government Notice* 1903 of 1957 with respect to endorsements made by virtue of subparagraphs (i) and (v) of sub-regulation (1) of Regulation 17, and so forth. If any employers on farms refuse to cooperate form N.L. 24 should be sent to them, by virtue of Article 35 of Act 18 of 1936 read along with Regulation 135 of *Government Notice* 494/37 within a period to be determined by the Magistrate. And so forth.

Now apart from all of this there is, of course, the overarching Section 10 (1) of *Act 25 of 1945* (as amended) wherewith I shall be most concerned in my new capacity as the appointed legal adviser to the administration. Equally relevant is Section 11 and the Regulations promulgated by *Government Notice* No. 63 of the 9th January, 1959, including Chapter (v), Regulation 2 (1) (a), (b) and (c). Not to mention the *Bantu Laws Amendment Act No. 76 of 1963*, *Government Notice* No. 1032 of 1949, as well as *Government Notice* No. 6164 of 1959 ("See Regulation 1 thereof"). Besides reference to the *Act on Urban Bantu Councils, No. 79 of 1961*, I am supposedly cognizant of *thirty-two* other major pieces of legislation enacted at different times between 1911 and 1959.

I'm now well set to carry out my responsibilities as the legal adviser, placed *in situ*, to help with the smooth operation of South Africa's most indispensable and most critical transformative apparatus. Speaking of cards, what I shall best remember—of all the colours—are the darkish pink ones. They are clearly in greatest demand, even more than the blue, white and green cards. My main bible is a thick tome, namely, the aforementioned *Native Urban Areas Act 25 of 1945* (as amended), with commentaries—as befits any bible—and it's a sobering thought that some of it predated the advent of systematic apartheid. Actually, my focus is not so much on the laws and the regulations themselves—about them we can do very little, if anything—as on the way they have been, and are being, carried out, and more particularly, on a practice known as 'endorsing out'. But at night I dream of cards.

So the problem is about implementation. Laws may be one thing, but how they are applied, or not applied, quite another. And especially where those who carry them out enjoy an unfettered discretion. One day, living and working in faraway Canada, I shall really come to appreciate how vital *implementation* is to the most *avant-garde* and resolute of political transformationists, where *praxis* and the means and the method must take precedence over everything else. The root of the problem we are now facing was well expressed by Dr Verwoerd when he was still the Minister of Native Affairs and not yet prime minister in the land. He emphasized that "the task of the urban authority is to carry out the policy of the country... The interpretation of that policy is in the hands of the Native Administrator who is a municipal official. He has obligations towards his employer, but he has certain statutory duties to fulfill and when he carries out his statutory duties, he does so in his own discretion and is not subject to orders from anyone else... He is licensed by the Minister... and the purpose of that provision is that he must carry out the policy of the State. If he does not do so, the State is entitled to withdraw his licence... The State determines native policy and the local authorities carry it out."

The position could not have been made any clearer. Thirty years after my father witnessed the same Dr Verwoerd's pivotal enunciation of his vision for apartheid, I find myself in the centre of a sprawling black urban shanty town, placed there to witness and to report on the *operational* ful-fillment of the key provision of that dream, namely, the forcible removal of black people, one by one by one, from urban areas to uninhabitable, jobless, and godforsaken patches of earth. More than just an echo of that hardly contested resolution at the Kimberley Conference of 1934 that foresaw a ten-year process after which there would be no blacks left in urban South Africa. But of course, there are millions of them *and that will never happen because their cheap labour is far too much in demand.* (As would also transpire in the United States, facing the dilemma of what to do about the millions of illegal Hispanic immigrant workers on whose, often cheap, labour substantial parts of the economy—and especially in the agricultural and hospitality sectors—were said to depend. Would those illegal workers ever be deported, never mind the rule of law?)

The effect of the South African system is to reduce urban blacks to mere interchangeable labour units, pawns *that* (not *who*) can be shunted hither and thither, and the moment they become redundant or undesirable (or merely fall ill or out of favour with an employer), can be summarily sent away and thereafter left to their own devices, wherever they may end up, and probably starve. The fact that the white regime will never expel the black work force from the urban areas merely underscores the essential hypocrisy of apartheid (just as the exploitation of cheap Chinese labour by North American and European companies would make nonsense of human rights pretensions). Essential to the system is to keep the work force in a perpetual state of rootlessness, and to ruthlessly weed out labour units that, for one reason or another, are considered dysfunctional. Systems, by definition, cannot brook irregularities. At that issue we shall be looking in due course.

Even the 'immorality' laws, which descend like a ton of bricks on any white who has had sexual relations with a black—and even more brutally on any black man who has similarly transgressed with a white woman—have been belied by the frequency with which white men (Afrikaners in particular) continue to consort with black women. One suspects a natural proclivity to do so, given the substantial numbers of the Coloured Afrikaans-speaking population of the Cape. On occasion even white cabinet ministers are implicated. But the first realization of the truth about the *bona fides* of apartheid came to me when still a young student. This was when the government rejected the recommendations of a special commission of inquiry chaired by a respected economist: the Tomlinson Commission. The report spelled out the cost and the financial sacrifices that would be entailed by a genuine effort to make the various *bantustans* (black reserves) economically viable. I had studied the report in considerable detail, and was able to draw my own conclusions about the reality of the situation. And, of course, there is always a certain sense of disappointment when people show their lack of *bona fides*, and especially when one is young and idealistic.

Meanwhile, and more tragic than 'mere' expulsion, is the way families are broken up, husbands and wives separated from one another and their children, lives utterly ruined. Forsooth, the Reverend Reyneke's plaintive questions at that Kimberley Conference were nothing but farsighted. It's bad enough to be a non-person, but to be both a non-person and to have literally nowhere to go, is to be consigned to a living hell. Some years ago, in a law office in another city, and before our first emigration from the country, I had made notes on a piece of paper about events I witnessed in the course of a single day: Tuesday, November 11, 1958. It was then that I first became aware of people who literally had nowhere to go. "Nowhere to go" became a refrain in the lives of individuals. Jantjie of De Bloem was given just seven days to leave the place where he was living, but for him "there was no accommodation in the location." I had jotted down the words "Nowhere to go." The police told Simon from De Bloem that he was a crook and that they would beat him up, and now he had "Nowhere to go." Tobo Moxosa, also known as Jimmy the Bull Fighter, tried to assuage the white Native Commissioner by bending down and wiping the Commissioner's shoes with his handkerchief, in a gesture of submission, but to no avail. The mere thought of it can make one weep. Jantjie and Simon and Tobo had become disposable. The introduction to Chief Albert Luthuli's autobiography told the story of Luthuli's interest in a squatter who had been evicted by white landowners: "His eviction… at once made it illegal for this man and his family to be *anywhere*: squatting elsewhere was unlawful, and neither reserve nor city would have him … There was no legal answer, nowhere to go."

---

Jesus said to him, "The foxes have holes, and the birds of the sky have nests, but the son of man has nowhere to lay down his head."

---

I'm now sitting in the very heart of a system whose main function it is, or so it seems, to dispose of people, consigning them to nowhere. The disposal of undesirables—in that case by simply liquidating them, and very systematically too—was the objective of the Wannsee Conference of 1942, *except where, once again, their labour was in demand.* Here we are looking at a different form of disposal, the logical outcome of another conference, held in another place and at another time, where my own father made those scribbles. It has become my assignment and my desire to put a spoke into this wheel, and to do it for people who have nowhere to go. They are completely at the mercy of the state.

In its most benevolent form, statism has deteriorated to the point where its very essence seems to lie in the state appropriating and controlling things that used to be in the private domain, in order to be seen to be giving back the benefits, but with strings attached. In some countries rights formerly enjoyed under common law, for centuries, are appropriated through the agency of governmental Charters of Rights and Freedoms, so that the same rights and freedoms can be dispensed back to a grateful people (and more easily qualified) with or without the help of the courts.

*But above all, the state grants permissions.* Having appropriated the public square unto itself, the state issues licences and permits. In the land of apartheid a black person cannot live, cannot exist, unless in possession of a permit. Officially known as a reference book, everybody knows it as the pass book, or more simply, the pass. Without the pass in his hand a black man has no identity; he may as well not exist.

There are other less formal forms of passes. When I was still wet behind the ears and my parents were not at home, old Koos—already grey and a longtime faithful worker—had to come to me to ask for a signed note to certify that he had permission to leave our premises to go to the nearest shop to buy sugar and salt, or to visit his auntie on the other side of town. Old Koos would have called it "a false policy," his favourite expression. Everything in old Koos's universe smacking of some or other irregularity, something that should not be, was a "false policy." Watering our trees at the wrong time was a false policy. Riding a bicycle with flat tires was a false policy. Even too cold a winter morning, or too hot an afternoon, was by itself a false policy. Maybe Creation itself, being what it appeared to be, especially to a black man, was the ultimate false policy. In this respect old Koos could have been the original Gnostic. Old Koos had learned to live with false policies every day of his life. At least he was still able to recognize the real ones and call them by their name.

If old Koos were here today he would have known that I am now confronted with another and very real false policy, looking it in the face, *and looking into the faces*, day by day. The way I look into a face, Cardinal Ratzinger wrote, "is decisive for my own humanity... The moral drama, the decision for good or evil, begins with our eyes, when we choose whether or not to look at the face of the other... the look I freely direct to the other is decisive for my own dignity too." When a black man or woman has to be consigned to limbo under Section 10 or Section 12 of *Act 25 of 1945* (as amended) he or she will be "summarily endorsed out." Those are the words. One is "summarily endorsed out" by a simple entry in one's pass book and one must then "prepare to leave the area." Simple as that. Sounds better than being "written off," which may also happen, judging from one particular regulation.

For the next six months I have to sit in the general office in the administrative building in the heart of the township, observing a steady stream of black people, men and women, but mostly men, coming and going, day after day—some handcuffed, accompanied by police—and many of them just standing there either in stoic resignation, or in distress. The way people stand, just as the way they walk, can speak volumes. They come for various purposes, and for everybody there seems to be a card in the system. Shades of the East German Stasi. Much rubber stamping takes place. Depending on what I'm able to observe and deduce, I have the authority to ask to see cards that have just been drawn and processed. My main interest is in those pink cards, the ones receiving entries pertaining to "endorsements out." I cannot now recall individual cases, not only because there were so many of them, but because I was obliged to keep no copy of my reports, where large numbers of them had been individually cited, and the circumstances described and analyzed. The worst cases are those of families broken up, and husbands separated from wives, to be sent in different directions, most of them back to some unspecified destination in the black 'homelands'. But I shall be keeping copies of the minutes of the meetings of the Cape Divisional Council where the chief executive officer will be reporting, albeit verbally, on the gist of my findings, and copies of 'briefs to counsel', seeking legal opinions to help us to justify, to the central government, some of the remedial actions being contemplated.

Of some of the correspondence I still have copies, as well as a copy of one particular legal opinion. A young barrister, a former university colleague of mine—and a Rhodes Scholar—worked long and hard and assiduously, drafting his legal opinions, when he realized what I was trying to do. One was always to wonder why he too eventually left the legal profession, when he became a professor of English literature. From these proceedings, correspondences and legal documents a fair amount can be deduced. Nonetheless, one episode in particular has stuck in my memory. For the rest, the whole thing is like a bad dream. A thin, poorish-looking white man, speaking in a high-pitched and whining drawl, comes in to lodge a formal complaint with the office. He says he's a dairy farmer and much dependent on his black labour. "There was a disturbance among my workers, I admit, and I did call the police to help to sort things out, but things were not so bad, really. The police had no reason to shoot them. This is most unfair. My cows are in distress and what am I to do? Now I have no workers. When can I have my replacements?"

The chief executive officer's carefully measured and understated introduction of my report to the Council speaks volumes: "I have carried out a departmental investigation and review of the Council's Bantu Administration, and I have found that certain policy matters required the attention of the Council. The Bantu laws administered by this Council are indeed complex and the proper administration of these Laws at all levels of administration has become most difficult, particularly in regard to the interpretation thereof..." Among the Resolutions the Council then adopts, two in particular stand out.

The first, in dry prose but pregnant with meaning, and quite far-reaching, pertains to "the 'endorsing out' of married female Bantu." George Malan recommends "that no married female Bantu woman be endorsed out of the proclaimed area on a mere technicality and that the Manager of Bantu Administration be required to submit to Council each month a list... stating full reasons for the action taken, and secondly, that the Council adopts it, as its policy, to preserve a Bantu marriage wherever this is permissible in law and that all applications for permission to remain in the area under Section 12 be approved, and where such approval is not desired to be given by the responsible official at Nyanga, the reasons for such refusal be reported to Council each month." The Council amends the motion so as to apply to women "who are to be endorsed out of the area separately from their husbands."

The second Resolution, backed by our legal opinions, and even more crucial in its implications (because it directly defies Dr Verwoerd's statement about the status and powers of an administrator licensed by the central government) applies to "the position of Manager of Bantu Administration," the central government's agent, the one with the power to sign off on all of the 'endorsements': "This official is an exclusive employee of the Divisional Council of the Cape and who is only responsible to the Divisional Council and it would be grossly irregular for him, as an employee of Council, to accept instructions from any other person or body without the Council's prior approval. To a certain extent the Manager is also responsible to the Minister of Bantu Administration and Development (not as Manager but only to the extent to which the Divisional Council itself is responsible to the Central Government). This is an important proviso. It means that the Manager may not take private instructions from the Government as to its policy or on any matter without the prior approval of the Council. For instance, the Manager may not interpret Government policy on his own and give instructions accordingly, unless authority thereto is given by Council. This safeguard is essential, e.g., it may happen that Government policy is illegally (or rather cannot be legally) enforced."

The gloves are off. My work has not been in vain. At least two major objectives have been secured. It will now be much more difficult, and in most cases impossible, for the apartheid regime to break up black families in our area. And secondly, and most important, and with good legal backing, we've succeeded in not only hamstringing but in fact wresting control of a key element of the administration of the apartheid laws in our area from the central government's apparatchik, and thus from the apartheid regime itself. But we have not been able to do very much about the raw statistics on the graphs I've procured from the Medical Officer of Health, drawn in dramatic red and black bars. Those very graphs are before me now, as I write. They show the extraordinarily high rates of tuberculosis and of children with their distended stomachs, dying of *kwashiorkor* in the Transit Camp, so aptly named for the lives of a rootless and homeless people.

---

In the aftermath of this experience there was also time to think about the problem of means and ends. When do ends justify questionable means? I thought about those harrowing months in the black township of Nyanga, where I was working under false pretenses, sitting a few feet away from where families were being broken up in front of my eyes by officials who were unthinking at best and utterly ruthless at worst. The office manager was a brute of a man and the subject of a joke I shared with the Medical Officer of Health, who said that whenever Mr S. was sent for his annual medical check-up they had to use an extra powerful X-ray machine to penetrate his tissues because he was so thick-skinned. In his work at least, this man may well have been an example of Dr Verwoerd's doctoral thesis on the blunting of the human emotions. What was I to do? I probably had it within my power or persuasive abilities to step in and put a stop to a particularly bad transaction, and even if the separation was 'legal', then on the pretext that it was illegal, if only on the facts of the case. But I was an undercover agent with a larger responsibility, and if I had done that, I might well have blown my cover. In this case the means to the achievement of a higher purpose was an act of omission, a deliberate dereliction of what some may have considered a fundamental moral duty.

The most moving account I have ever read on the means-ends dilemma is in a novel by the Japanese writer Shusaku Endo. In his masterpiece, *Silence,* Endo tells the story of a Catholic missionary in Japan by the name of Rodrigues who has been witnessing the most horrible torture of Japanese Christians who could have escaped their fate if they stepped upon and trampled on a *fumie,* a portrait of the Madonna and Child engraved on a bronze plate. More Christians are brought to Rodrigues, who is told that if he himself stepped on the *fumie,* their lives would be spared. For a time Rodrigues steadfastly refuses to commit such an act of apostasy, and many more Christians go on to suffer as a consequence. Eventually, facing the entreaties of another priest, Rodrigues raises his foot over the *fumie.* The foot begins to suffer a dull, heavy pain. He is about to do the unthinkable. And then the Christ in bronze speaks to him and tells him to "Trample! Trample!" He places his foot on the bronze plate and at that moment the cock crows. Philip Yancey's account of this story in the course of a short overview of the life of Shusaku Endo was titled *Japan's Faithful Judas.* By an act of betrayal of his own faith—a faith that forbade him from desecrating an image of the Mother Mary and the Son of God—Father Rodrigues has done the will of God. And he may well have earned the calumny of other Christians, who may have looked upon him as not only a traitor but a coward.

---

I realize that having shot my bolt, so to speak, I shall henceforth be a marked man, that there is not much more I can do, and that the time has come to move on. In our own small corner of the world we have, for once, grappled with and bearded the infidel, even if only with temporary effect.

Thinking that a career in the business world will be a 'cleaner' way of life, I manage to find a managerial job in an agricultural cooperative with 30,000 farmer members. Not only are we the biggest processors of fruit and vegetables in the southern hemisphere, we also export to more than 70 countries. But increasingly convinced that for the sake of my family we shall have to emigrate once again, and since it was unlikely that I could count on my legal qualifications to find work abroad, I go back to university (as a part-time student) and after three years earn a Master of Business Administration degree. Meanwhile, to further bolster my chances of gainful employment in North America (on which I have now set my sights), I land an appointment as the company secretary, legal counsel, and manager of office services of the southern African subsidiary of the Mobil Oil Corporation of New York.

Unfortunately, once an ideology permeates a society, there can be no escape. Even the corporate world turns out to be anything but 'clean' from a human rights point of view. Almost all of the nearly 100 employees in Mobil's office services department at head office who are in my care, are black or of mixed race, and there *are* problems. The American authorities have announced the so-called Sullivan Principles. They govern the ethical responsibilities of American employers in South Africa. Mobil's chief honcho, the big Chairman himself, is coming from New York to check on our performance. The director in charge of the personnel department collars two of my employees and carefully coaches them so that when they meet the big man they will know what to say. Our black staff are subject to the government's influx control regulations (of which I already know everything!) and there is one old man, dignified and already greying, who has worked for us for years but has not seen his family back in the black homelands for nearly a decade, because he's been afraid that if he left the urban area and came back, he may be "endorsed out." Which is not unlikely. I take his plight to the board of directors to ask if the company would use its influence with the government to secure a guarantee, and also pay the old man's travel expenses. After all, our chief executive officer often plays golf with government ministers. My request is flatly refused. It would create a precedent.

Almost three years have passed. My wife and two children have already left the country. I've been busy selling our house, car, and most household effects. And I've asked the same old man who was prevented from visiting his family in a South African 'homeland' to lend a hand. This is my last evening, before the removers come, in the beautiful tree-lined suburb of Newlands nestled under the southern slopes of Table Mountain, and not far from the famous botanical gardens of Kirstenbosch. I've asked the old man to do one more thing for me. On our front verandah, under our 200-year old oak tree—so wide that its branches overhung both edges of the property—and in full view of the (white) neighbours in our upper-class suburb, I lay on our bamboo dining table with its glass top a starched table cloth, and napkins, and our best crockery and silver. He has never seen anything like it in all his life. In the black township outside the city he most likely lives in a hovel. Then I prepare a meal and serve it to him. There's no need for either of us to say anything. He's a wise old man. He knows that I know that he knows...

———————

I cannot remember the circumstances behind a one-page letter, long forgotten, and just discovered, that must have found its way into a file. On a single blue sheet of flimsy and stained writing paper, it must have come from one of our black staff, written when he landed in a hospital in the middle of South Africa's arid region of the Karoo; a man by the name of William Guta:

> I was very glad when I received your letter it was a great rejoice and exated being knowing that there are some one behind me to whom are great in Company to remember me in time like this, but now I am little better all Pain are going and also I regain booth my [indecipherable] Just waiting for the good days what Dr going to say, About money I need R8.60c to pay my Hospital fees before I left here [indecipherable] may God Blessed you, mr., thank you very much what have you Don for me I am yrs. Servant...

Whenever I read this letter, I'm in tears.

———————

And thus, in 1970, after just two or three of my years with Mobil, we finally leave—this time for good—the country where my forefathers have lived and worked (and sometimes fought) for almost three centuries.

### Cobblestones

More than ever before is it clear to me that 'Africa is for the Africans' and not only on demographic grounds. Even after a sojourn of hundreds of years the Portuguese settlers will be summarily booted out of both Angola and Mozambique. If ever the writing has been on the wall...

1. The Directors of the Chamber Hoorn of the United East India Company who sent my forefathers to the Cape of Good Hope in 1689 (Westfries Museum, Hoorn, The Netherlands)

2. Me with my Parents, 1935.

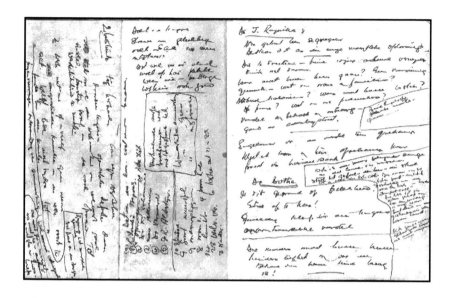

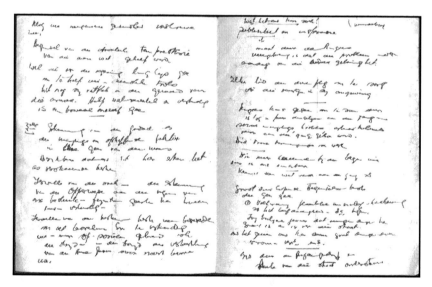

3 & 4 (above & below). My father's cryptic notes
taken at the Kimberley Conference, 1934 (The de Vos-de
Villiers Family Collection, Archives and Manuscripts
Dept., Pitts Theology Library, Emory University).

5. Jan Christiaan Smuts (1870 – 1950). The portrait that hung on the wall of my study throughout my university years.

6. Walt Whitman's *Leaves of Grass*, a major influence on the philosophy of Jan Smuts (Small, Maynard and Company: Boston, 1905).

7. My father's rescue at Vereeniging (The de Vos-de
Villiers Family Collection, Archives and Manuscripts
Dept., Pitts Theology Library, Emory University).

8. My client the medicine man

9. A Scottish Wedding.

10. "Rebuilding the Proud Tower," Canadian Museum for Human Rights, Winnipeg, under construction (Bryan Scott, Winnipeg)

11. Kenneth Hamilton

# PART TWO

# CHAPTER FIVE
# NEW HORIZONS

Emigrating to Canada wasn't easy. The decision to go there may have been influenced by the fact that quite a few of my professors at the Cape Town Graduate School of Business used their summer breaks from McMaster University in Ontario to teach in South Africa, and who could blame them, given the climate and the beauty of the Cape? We also thought—mistakenly, as it turned out—that since Canada was an English-speaking and founding member of the Commonwealth, and Ottawa only six hours' flight away from London, we would still feel in touch with Europe. South Africa had remained closer to Britain than to any other European country (even The Netherlands) in sport, in the news, and (notwithstanding apartheid and the political gulf) in the cultural domain (including that indispensable element: a shared sense of humour).

We were astonished that it was impossible to apply for Canadian immigration from South Africa. To please the apartheid regime the Canadian government had closed down its immigration facilities, telling all applicants to apply in Beirut, a continent away! They might as well have told them to apply in Outer Mongolia. I wasted months on fruitless correspondence with Beirut. The reason was that the South African government was particularly exercised on account of a brain drain to Canada, especially from within the skilled and professional mixed-race cadres. So we were forced to first emigrate to Scotland, from where we were able to apply on the strength of our British (dual) citizenship and British residency. This took additional months of virtual homelessness and even then the process might have taken longer had it not just so happened that the Canadian immigration officer in Glasgow had shared a curling game with my Scottish father-in-law!

## Cobblestones

As we sailed on the *Empress of Canada* into the interior of the country on the mighty St Lawrence River, I stood behind the river pilot, noticing that most of the triangulations on his chart were drawn on one silvery church steeple after another, strung along the river banks. One could be excused for thinking that the country was religious, but this was Quebec, a society that—having foresworn its Christian heritage—was already paganized in the wake of its own cultural revolution. Not that the New Europe would be much different in that respect, notwithstanding the sight of those beautiful Gothic cathedrals, and so much so that a new Pope would make it his life's hope to re-evangelize the historical heartland of Christianity.

As soon as we docked in Montreal, the second-largest French-speaking city in the world, and had our car unloaded, we should have realized that we were in a society already in the grip of its own peculiar solitudes, because nowhere was a road sign to be seen to the nation's capital, Ottawa, only two hours' driving away. Soon I was to read—and at first greatly impressed by—Pierre Elliott Trudeau's highly polemical *Federalism and the French Canadians,* where he excoriated Quebec nationalism. But my enthusiasm was to evaporate when I came to better comprehend the philosophy and alternative world views of a man who, as the progenitor of a new Constitution, was destined to become not only Canada's new Father of Confederation but also the spiritual father of a New Society. For Prime Minister Trudeau (a one-world dreamer, like his American counterpart Barack Obama) even nationalism in general was a dirty word. Of course, I had just come from another society where nationalism had gone off the rails but that did not mean that I did not have an ingrained appreciation of the aspirations—especially the cultural and linguistic aspirations—of a people or peoples who wanted to safeguard their own common identity and achieve a measure of self-determination in a homogenizing world. Thus I thought I recognized remarkable parallels between the history and development of my own people—the Afrikaners of southern Africa—and that of the Quebeçois. It even included the degree to which churches played such a strong role in the development of the respective cultures (for better or for worse, one might add). When eventually I had the privilege of being taught French, at government expense, to the point of being rated fully bilingual, I would come to appreciate the haunting songs of Quebec's most popular folk singers, with their remarkable inflections. And in fact a French Canadian was the Canadian politician I would come to most admire and respect. He was, among other attributes, steeped in a knowledge of the history of his own people.

We had made the transition and there was no looking back. But there would be a brief return.

———————

It is nineteen years later, and I find myself once again—and for the first time since our departure—in the country and the city of my birth. I've come to visit my aging mother. This is the month of October (the most beautiful of all, in the lyrical words of an early Afrikaans poet) and precisely 55 years from the month of October when I was born and when my father returned from a congress where systematic apartheid too was born. Destiny has brought me back, but at this moment I do not know it as I approach the dusty brown sandstone city hall of Bloemfontein, across the street from the very building—the old *Raadsaal*—where my great-grandfather had presided over the legislative assembly of the Republic of the Orange Free State. All around, in the dark, among the shrubs and the trees, are black-clad policemen hanging on to fearsome Alsatian dogs on leashes. An ugly scene. They are here to guard the State President, F.W. de Klerk, who will be speaking tonight; a man who had a law practice in the town of Vereeniging where, on an equally dark night, my father had been so brutally assaulted. Here now is the scene of another congress, a congress of the National Party of the Orange Free State. Presiding over the meeting will be one Kobie Coetzee, the Minister of Justice, the same Kobie Coetzee who was prevailed upon by an erstwhile colleague of mine to start the work that would eventually lead to the release of Nelson Mandela.

This appears to be a closed meeting, closed to the general public. Delegates are registering and issued with name tags at the main entrance, but I manage to persuade an official that he cannot possibly bar an

95

Afrikaner who has come all the way from Canada, from being with his own people. But how could I not have been here, and how could I have been excluded, because tonight, still unbeknownst to me, I shall be witnessing the beginning of the end of apartheid, just as my father had witnessed the birth of ideological apartheid at another congress at another time and in another place, not that many miles from here. Unbeknownst to the audience as well because they are still singing heartily:

*Afrikaners Landgenote.*
*Land van die Vaders.*
*Uit die Chaos van die Eeue.*
*Lied van Jong Suid-Afrika.*
*Vrystaatse Volkslied.*
*Sarie Marais...*

They sing of their past. They sing of their hopes for the future. But tonight they will also be singing the swan song of apartheid.

Just as the 1934 congress was opened by a minister of the Dutch Reformed Church, here too, a Reverend Strydom opens the proceedings with *Skriflesing en Gebed,* a reading from Scripture followed by a prayer. He prays with palpable sincerity. Does he know what's coming? As he reads, his President looks up at him with great intensity. And now, as he finishes his prayer, the State President acknowledges him and bows his own head, as if in prayer himself. He rises to speak. His wife, sitting primly behind him, looks most unhappy. (Eventually she will be murdered by her own domestic servant in her apartment in the beach resort town of Bloubergstrand near Cape Town.) The President tells his people that he has a hard message for them. They have to steel themselves. Political meetings of this kind are normally exuberant, even boisterous, but now the hall sinks into a deathly silence. We've come to the end of the road, he says. Apartheid is no longer viable. Not only is it no longer viable; it has been unjust. It has offended the law of God. We will have to change. This country will have to change. We have no other choice. We will have to extend our hand to the black man and embrace him as our brother. We shall have to share power. We have arrived at a turning point in the life of this country, in the life of our people. May God, in his infinite mercy, help us.

Nobody stirs. Nobody speaks. It is the end, or rather, it is the beginning of the end. And for some, the beginning of a new beginning.

---

I have already mentioned the parallels between the Afrikaners and the Quebeçois. But imagine my astonishment—considering that I had just recently arrived from apartheid South Africa, and was a 'Boer' to boot—when I was invited to join a governmental project team who were tasked with a fundamental redesign of the legal and administrative framework for Canada's aboriginal peoples, and whose lives were dominated by the so-called Indian Act. I would be the director in charge of the formal drafting of the requisite legislation! The government had already published a White Paper, proposing to rewrite what was in fact the linchpin of the country's aboriginal regime. The plan was to abolish the Department of Indian and Northern Affairs within five years; to transfer jurisdiction to provinces and municipalities; and to essentially terminate the special status of Canada's Indian and Inuit peoples, so that they might begin to be incorporated and perhaps assimilated in (what still remained of) 'mainstream' Canada. The move would also have affected the treaties governing aboriginal lands. All of which, of course, was the right thing to do, given the dysfunctional state of the Canadian aboriginal scene. But the plan was soon abandoned because the Indians themselves fought back vigorously with their own Red Paper. It meant that they did not want to be emancipated. Their band councils were doing very well feeding at the public trough, and in fact there was a humongous problem with corruption in all its forms. Also, not unlike the South African blacks who burned their pass books and then felt lost without them, could it be that the Canadian treaty Indians too could not face the prospect of having to begin to stand on their own feet?

More than 40 years later the situation had worsened. The government was in the thick of mounting aboriginal land claims, so that at one point, in the province of British Columbia, for example, it was said that the total extent of the land claims exceeded the size of the province itself. In the capital city of Ottawa the very site of the Canadian Parliament was the subject of an Indian land claim. A large and ambitious housing development on Crown land near an upscale section of the city was frozen by yet another land claim, so that the responsible government agency had to dissolve the bureaucratic apparatus that would have been in charge of the project.

Here, in a somewhat different context, we might as well add to the sorry story of Canada's northern homeland, already encountered in Chapter Three. Apart from the sheer cost of keeping it going, the suicide rate was extraordinary, by any standard, either domestic or international. On a *per capita* basis there were more suicides in Nunavut than deaths *from all causes* in the Iraq War. The abuse of powerful narcotics (including opiates) was endemic in all too many aboriginal settlements. Apart from suffering from the usual chronic social and health problems that marked literally hundreds of Indian bands, both large and small, Nunavut had close to zero economic viability. By way of subsidy, each inhabitant cost the Canadian taxpayer $40,000 a year, and they were still living in misery. All in all Canada was spending *at least* $12 billion (some say nearer to $15 billion), year after year, on maintaining its First Nations in conditions which, for the vast majority, appeared to be unremittingly miserable.

Anyway, these were among the lessons that were still lying in the future. We had landed in Montreal on June 5, 1970. I had little inkling of the learning curve that was still ahead.

# CHAPTER SIX
# A VERY STRANGE SOCIETY

"I hope I've sufficiently drilled home the notion that, as a practitioner, my thinking is rooted in the belief that you cannot go from books to problems, but the reverse, from problems to books."

Nassim Nicholas Taleb, *The Black Swan*

In 1967 the American writer Allen Drury (who had written *Advise and Consent)* gave an insightful account of the realities of a people caught in the grip of an ideology. As we noted earlier, in *A Very Strange Society* he passed little comment of his own. Instead, he simply left people in the land of apartheid to speak for themselves. I had already lived and worked in four quite different cultures on two continents, and now finally ended up on a third continent and in a country that seemed to be even stranger than the one Allen Drury portrayed.

Because it did not take long to discover—although difficult to understand—that Canada appeared to be not so much a society as a non-society. More often than not Canadians defined themselves in terms of what they were *not*. They were *not* European. They had already largely discarded their Anglo-Scottish heritage. And above all, they were *not* American. The closest approximation may have been the Argentinians of European descent, after so many years still feeling lost between two civilizations, or at least cultures. Canada felt as if it was an island adrift, like Gulliver's flying island of Laputa, suspended between heaven and earth. Well into the 21st century anti-Americanism would remain the essential card any political party would have to play to assure an apparently insecure and skittish populace of its eligibility to govern. In the general election of 2006 an American ambassador had to resort to a most undiplomatic public speech to ask Canadians to "please keep America off your ballots" only to find renewed anti-American breast thumping by the prime minister of the day, proclaiming that "I am the Prime Minister of Canada, and I shall stand up and fight for my country." His immediate francophone predecessor played the same card with spectacular success, bolstered with his own trademark and inimitably loud way of expressing his bottomless love for Canada. His successor, in a new 'Conservative' government, had to use his very first press conference to put the American ambassador in his place on the issue of Arctic sovereignty. When still in opposition in parliament he had to write a special refutation of an article published by an enthusiastic observer at the American Cato Institute who thought he saw in the Conservative leader a potential friend of the United States. Admittedly, the arrival of Barack Obama on the international political stage had a distinctly muting effect on anti-American attitudes in Canada, as it did in other parts of the world, but it was not possible to predict how long that would last. But one had to acknowledge that this anti-Americanism was more prevalent among the intelligentsia and the socio-political opinion leaderships than among the ordinary working people of the land.

More important was that without a discernible identity of their own—other than an identity of non-identity, one might say—Canadians, some observed, had become *tabula rasa* (a blank slate) offering a unique oppor-tunity for socio-cultural experimentation for anyone so minded.

This was not news to Canadians. Not only the people, but the country itself was seen as a convenient blank. But let them, or at least their opinion leaders, speak for themselves. In *This is My Country, What's Yours? A Literary Atlas of Canada*, Noah Richler (son of the famous Mordecai) inquired exhaustively into the minds of a variety of Canadian writers, both past and present. "Any place," Richler said, "is only a landscape until it is animated by the stories that provide its identity, or to use a term that is more popular today, its 'psycho-geography'... The Canadian conviction that the country is a Nowhere has been a trait of its psycho-geography since the earliest days of its settlement." When Richler asked a contemporary writer whether 'Canada as Nowhere' was an exciting place for her, she said that she loved the idea of the country being undefined. Another notable writer, Margaret Atwood (by many regarded as a literary icon), opined that "we are Somewhere, but also Nowhere" and that one of the appeals of Canada as a Nowhere was "like the blank sheet of paper that is every writer's wildest dream and worst nightmare because it is exactly what you choose to put on it. The space is yours to fill."

Ditto, I would add, for Canada's self-appointed socio-politico-cultural shapers and transformationists. It has been thus for a long time, but especially since the year 1967 when a new Pied Piper by the name of Pierre Elliott Trudeau started to play his tune. In a later chapter, and in a different context, we shall revisit the ways in which Canadian change agents, deliberately and literally, invoked the usefulness of Canada as *tabula rasa*.

---

"J'ai surtout l'impression d'être au milieu de nulle part... où il n'ya aucune route et dont je n'ai aucune carte."
Arni Thorarinson, *Le Septième fils*

---

And so it may well have been more than just symbolic that Ottawa was the only capital city in the world with a huge Experimental Farm, known by that name, in its very centre. (Indeed, when we've arrived at the end of this story we might well ask whether Canada-as-experimental-farm was not of the same ilk as George Orwell's *Animal Farm*, except that the former was a lot more sophisticated.) Governments and bureaucracies—battening on a regime of heavy taxation in innumerable forms and at seemingly innumerable levels—loomed extraordinarily large, not only in fact, but also in the popular psyche. Indeed, in bureaucratic legalese the overriding federal constitutional power was known as POGG (*Peace, Order, and Good Government*). The status and achievements of POGG far outstripped the American *Life, Liberty, and the Pursuit of Happiness*. Given their *tabula rasa,* no surprise then to find numerous official white papers and other, often glossily printed, and ideology-intensive policy prescriptions, literally presented, in their very titles, as having been conceived 'for Canadians'. Admittedly one of the earliest, published in 1961 and titled *Social Purpose for Canada,* did not originate with government; but one notes that the editorial committee included the future Prime Minister Trudeau himself. The essays in the book were directed at Canadians who "were being lulled into accepting a glitter of prosperity which covered a reality of purposelessness, mediocrity and inequity..." The book claimed to be in the tradition of a similar work published in 1935 by the League for Social Reconstruction, titled *Social Planning for Canada.* The chief editor's contribution was "Democratic Socialist Policies for Canada."

After Trudeau's accession to power there would flow a veritable stream of prescriptive and directive instruments 'for Canadians'. A foreign policy 'for Canadians'. A defence policy 'for Canadians'. A communications policy 'for Canadians'. It would have been surprising if there had not been an official dietary policy 'for Canadians' although that was bound to come sooner or later. But perhaps the ultimate example of an artifact produced 'for Canadians' (whether they liked it or not) would have to be a Charter of Rights and Freedoms that was wrapped in a new Constitution for the country, and then patriated (brought home) to Canada from the jurisdiction of the British Parliament. That the Charter was not the handiwork of Canadians for themselves is also mentioned in a later chapter, the reason being that Trudeau and his ilk knew full well that if they first brought home the Constitution and then attempted to persuade Canadians of the merits of adopting such a charter, there would have been little chance of success. How could Canadians look such a gift horse in the mouth if it was actually described as "the People's Package"? (*Timeo Danaos et dona ferentes.* "Beware the Greeks when they bear gifts.")

The strangest thing was that hardly any utterance about anything in the public arena referred to people in one or other capacity, or to the public in general. All too frequently the reference would be to 'Canadians', as if the people were separated from themselves, or at least from those who were issuing the prescriptions for the better health and well-being of one and all. By contrast, in other societies where we had lived, in daily discourse, allusions might generally be to 'we' or to 'us' or to 'the public' or to people in the applicable capacity or category, such as 'voters', 'taxpayers', 'workers', 'consumers', or 'immigrants' where it would be taken for granted that they were Americans, or British, or Scottish, or French, or German, or whatever. Not that there was not much talk in Canada of 'community, community' where, on closer examination, no real community existed. A construct in people's minds, and perhaps not even meant to have intrinsic meaning.

The country seemed to be almost congenitally fractured, not only by its regionalisms and provincialisms, but especially by the policies and practices of a legislatively and even constitutionally entrenched multiculturalism. The historical analogy of Varronic Rome before its downfall was irresistible. In the Rome of the ancient scholar and writer Marcius Terentius Varro (116 BC - 27 BC) multiculturalism had developed a religio-ideological character. Rome had become a city of multiple gods. In Canada, multifariousness had become god. Lacking a core identity, in *The Patriot Game* expatriate British journalist Peter Brimelow described Canada as "a mere geographical expression." This was before he moved to New York. With their fast-expanding Hispanic influx, and their linguistic demands, Americans would have been well advised to take account of the Canadian experiment, and so would the Dutch, the French, the Germans, and the British with their own multiculturalist fracturings. The crowning symbolic glory of Canadian multiculturalism was the appointment of a politically correct and comely black immigrant from Haiti as the country's Governor General. She, ironically, had previously made a speech in which she roundly denounced multiculturalism, but it must have escaped the attention of a smitten Prime Minister when he selected her for the post.

Living in a milieu of nowhereness was a strange experience. The best way to describe it was a sense that one was living in a state of internal hollowness; a hollowness that was both personal and communal, not unlike the feeling of having eaten without ever feeling satisfied. (Already the Canadian economy itself was described as having been hollowed out by virtue of the fact that as soon as a Canadian business, whether large or small, became successful—and often heavily subsidized by taxpayers—it was sold out to foreign investors and thereafter controlled from abroad. Frequently, smaller innovative firms with highly developed new technologies, found that after they had been taken over, they were stripped of their technologies and the related know-how, in order for those assets to be exploited, and create jobs, in other jurisdictions. I ought to know, because I was one of three people who were most directly involved in setting up and staffing Canada's Foreign Investment Review Agency, which was explicitly designed to try to counter these problems. For a short while I served as the agency's first director of legal policy and surveillance.)

For the country's non-identity, *multiculturalism* was the chosen label. There cannot be many, if indeed any, western countries that have legislatively entrenched that condition, as it was when parliament passed the Canadian Multiculturalism Act of 1988. Indirectly it was already entrenched in Trudeau's new Constitution. Whereas Canadians were constantly commending their own polity as a model for a new world, Europeans may have been right when—by the end of the first decade of the 21$^{st}$ century—in one country after another, they had started to raise serious doubts about the extent to which they themselves had fallen prey to multiculturalism in one form or another. None of those countries had emulated the United States in describing itself as a melting pot.

Worsening the situation was the fact that, like Canada, those same countries had slowly but surely shed themselves of their Christian heritage and identity. European Muslims told Pope Benedict that what most disappointed—even frightened—them, was having to live in the midst of societies that no longer respected their own Christian antecedents. Communally, what glue had been left, had slowly dissolved. Meanwhile, the universality, ubiquitousness and resourcefulness of the internet greatly exacerbated the breaching—and in some cases the virtual disappearance—of the political and cultural boundaries that had also helped to preserve and nurture national identities. Instead the 'open' world was in fact becoming a closed system, in the form of a self-contained and reverberating sphere of ephemeral, fickle, constantly shifting, often random, and purely atomistic encounters among individuals of one stripe or another, like a single colony of ants whose restless members make only the briefest of physical contacts with one another before moving on. As a child I used to watch those ants, and their behaviour, on the South African *veld*. But at least the ants made physical contact. In January 2011 Pope Benedict felt constrained to warn that internet-based interactions among individuals were no substitute for face–to-face communication. "It is important always to remember," he said, "that virtual contact cannot and must not take the place of direct human contact with people at every level of our lives." Even in the world's proverbial melting pot, the United States of America, there was a feeling that the world view of a Barack Obama was pointing them in the same direction. A *weltanschaung* he had so dramatically expressed before a crowd of Germans.

So to me, Canada would become more and more of a puzzle. After all, puzzlement has been a starting point in many a journey of discovery. Think of the writer E.F. Schumacher's *Guide for the Perplexed*. Even more pertinent—as I would discover with its publication in 2010—were the very first words in the British journalist and writer Melanie Phillips' *The World Turned Upside Down*. "This book," she said, "arose from a sense of perplexity and cultural disorientation. It appears to me that much of public discourse has departed sharply from reality. Self-evident common sense appears to have turned on its head." For me, Canada became the trigger for a peculiar learning experience, gradually yielding insights—with wider application—I most likely could not have gained anywhere else than in this self-appointed and continually self-described "microcosm of, and model for the world."

One also became aware of a progression, wholly inductive in nature—a process of 'theory' being culled from practice—and not deduced from *a priori* principles or based on what other observers may have said or written: a process I came to describe as "steadily backing into theory." Because understanding requires frameworks. Even science, as the philosopher Thomas Kuhn so persuasively argued, cannot do without paradigms. This learning experience was not unlike the process Eric Voegelin had gone through, with his exposure to, and puzzlement by, the Nazi phenomenon. And so this process, even as most of it will be descriptive of the activities of others, continued to be the story of my journey, and not theirs. The other striking thing was that without those previous experiences in another country, far to the south, this process of discovery might not have been possible in the first place. And some of the parallels would be nothing but thought-provoking.

---

We're invited to a weekend retreat on this rocky outcrop, a small island in the Rideau Lakes to the south-west of Ottawa, called Grindstone. We arrive in a rowing boat. The guest of honour is an American of uncertain provenance. He seems to be an activist of one sort or another. The other guests are mostly an assortment of government officials, one of them—as I shall later discover—an active speaker and consultant to government departments. We're gathered under tall trees, mostly white pines with their soft-green needles. More than a century ago they dominated the landscape. Here they're casting a brooding presence. There's something elemental about the setting, something vaguely pagan. The novelist Margaret Atwood saw the Canadian landscape as "strangely threatening - a place that swallows up things." In her story, "*Death by Landscape,*" she says that "nature does just that." Everyone seems to defer to an elderly, long-haired and rather untidy woman, a kind of Earth Mother. As far as my wife and I are concerned, we are babes in the wood, because it turns out that this has been our very first encounter with people whom we shall, in due course, recognize as disciples of a widespread New Age cult, except, in this case, of a political stripe. But for the moment we do not know that. Except that on the last evening, when the faithful have gathered in a circle to share their respective experiences of a soulful weekend, I feel constrained to express misgivings. Admittedly a discordant note, and one feels badly about it. Everybody has come across as so well-meaning, so my reaction must be intuitive. Not that the topics for discussion have been esoteric. Not at all. They were focused almost entirely on public affairs.

---

In May of 1964 an already middle-aged French-Canadian lawyer (and future prime minister) by the name of Pierre Elliott Trudeau co-authored a manifesto, translated into English by a future prime ministerial assistant who would become the most senior of the civil servants in the federal government. Trudeau would not have been the first change agent in history to have announced his intentions well in advance. *An Appeal for Realism in Politics* was the title. But his future actions would show a remarkable conflation of realism and dream. "Canada, today," the manifesto proclaimed, "is a country in search of a purpose." This was his clarion call; his mission and that of his closest acolytes. To my mind it merited careful reading because of some of the most basic themes it contained, themes that will be surfacing time and again in the rest of this story:

"It is an affirmation of faith in man, and it is on the basis of human criteria that we demand policies better adapted to our world and our times. This is our only motivation... First, there is the juridical and geographical fact called Canada. We do not attach to its existence any sacred or eternal meaning, but it is a historical fact... We reject the idea of a 'national state' as obsolete... In fact - and this is our second reason - the most valid trends today are toward more enlightened humanism, toward various forms of political, social and economic universalism... If Canadians cannot make a success of a country such as theirs, how can they contribute in any way to the elaboration of humanism, to the formulation of the international political structures of tomorrow... The challenge presented to us consists in defining and implementing a policy with precise objectives, practicable and based on the universal attributes of man... Planning is largely a technical problem... We must start to analyze reality and establish priorities in terms of the precise tasks to be accomplished."

Eric Voegelin would have been amused. Considering that "enlightened humanism" was at the very core of an immanentist world spirit—whose meaning we shall yet examine—here is probably one of the most insightful sentences Voegelin had ever written (emphasis added):

*With radical immanentization, the dream world has blended into the real world terminologically; the obsession of replacing the world of reality by the transfigured dream world has become the obsession of the one world in which the dreamers adopt the vocabulary of reality, while changing its meaning as if the dream were reality.*

Anyway, here, in a nutshell, was a program. And here, in sum, were the operative elements: A country in search of a purpose (*tabula rasa* again). An 'elaboration' of enlightened humanism. Universalism. Planning, and practical ways of achieving objectives. The dream, by all means. But also the methods of implementing the dream. Actually—and this was the interesting thing, and to be more fully explored later in this narrative— the methods, the means, would come first. That was the element that was so distinctive of the Canadian apparition. The only other notable practitioners of a similar ideological but particularly means-based philosophy in the world of politics were Vladimir Lenin and Chairman Mao. (Even Pope Benedict, in his Encyclical *Spe Salvi*, was moved to recognize how "Lenin must have realized that the writings of the master (Marx) gave no indication as to how to proceed.") On the same wavelength, as we shall see, were the beliefs and tactics of Barack Obama's political mentor, Saul Alinsky. The political philosopher David Mitrany's theory of functionalism—which we still have to address—was of the same means-driven ilk. Except for his experience of Nazism in action, Voegelin too was an academic, and this may be why he had missed the means-focused proclivities of the modern political Gnostic. He had not been able or inclined to relate his observations to contemporary, post-Nazi, real-life examples, which, naturally, gave an opening to his many critics. To these topics our story will be returning shortly.

---

When we disembarked in Montreal the country was still in the lingering afterglow of Expo 67, a world exhibition. That was also the year when Trudeau burst upon and immediately dominated the political landscape. Here was a new charismatic figure, seemingly capable of inducing an almost hysterical sense of excitement among voters, both young and old. *Man and his World* had been the theme of the Montreal exhibition, with its dominant geodesic globe symbolizing and underscoring the fact that, as in the case of Barack Obama's agenda for change, the new leader's program was not just a program 'for Canadians,' but also 'for the world.' It would turn out to be a program of transformation, both personal and collective. And it would be active.

In South Africa the apartheid regime's election promises included white bread, after the war-time ban on the use of sifted flour. But like a Moses of old who not only brought the people manna, but came down from the mountain with the Law, the Canadian Moses, Pierre Elliott Trudeau—who would lead his people out of the bondage of British rule by patriating the Canadian Constitution from the Parliament at Westminster—came down from Mount Royal (*Outremont* was the name of his parliamentary constituency in Montreal) with a different set of tablets in the form of an Omnibus Law Reform Bill designed to release the people from the straitjacket of outdated personal moralities by removing the legal constraints on abortion and homosexual practices, besides eliminating obstacles to divorce. That was how he first made his mark as a rooky Minister of Justice in Ottawa.

Among feminists and other active change agents it has been customary to proclaim that "the personal is political, and the political, personal." And that would also turn out to be a central feature of the Canadian transformation project. Fundamental changes would have to be both personal and collective, private as well as public. *The operative processes would be interactive and mutually reinforcing.* But it would be quite a while before I would begin to appreciate the ways in which a country could be subjected to such shaping aspirations, and what it might mean for the world at large. As a member of the so-called Group of Seven countries (subsequently expanded to Eight until Russia fell out of favour) Canada considered itself a major player on the world stage and made much of its influence as a leading member in both the (British) Commonwealth and the *francophonie*. One could not have imagined, let alone foreseen, a more interesting and a more challenging learning environment.

> **Transform** *vt* **1 a:** to change completely or essentially in
> composition or structure (more than just a change of form):
> **syn metamorphose:** to change one thing into another or
> different thing: **transmute:** suggests an elemental change
> (the alchemists believed that base metals could be *transmuted*
> into gold by such a process)

---

*You take a particularly deep breath and discover that you are floating effort-*
*lessly above the ground. You float around the tree and see what was behind*
*you, opposite the seascape... In the crater is the clearest lake you have ever*
*seen... You descend to the island... On this island, beneath a small, old bonsai-*
*like tree, a clear, cool spring bubbles forth from the roots and cascades down to*
*the lake. You lie on the ground and peer into the roots at the very source, and*
*when your eyes adjust to the darkness, you see something in the depths. What*
*is it? Remember whatever you see. Study it. And then let it go. Drink from the*
*spring, move away from the tree... Try to fix the impressions from your journey*
*in your external consciousness, then immediately write or draw your impres-*
*sions and images... Simply repeat the exercise daily... It is actually easier than*
*it may seem, since all you really have to do is to 'imagine' a breakthrough.*

Soon the author of the handbook and the much longer self-hypnotic
session from which this brief extract has been taken, shifts to the broader
political scene: *Central projects, in this sense, are means of focusing the ener-*
*gies of a population during an evolutionary transition to a higher level of*
*culture.* In other words, a cultural revolution. The objective is to transform "man and his world."

The author hails from California. A former professor of engineering-
economic systems at Stanford, he works out of the Stanford Research
Institute, besides serving as the President of the Institute for Noetic
Sciences. One of his books is titled *Global Mind Change: The Promise*
*of the 21ˢᵗ Century.* I'm more interested that Dr Willis Harman consults
for the Canadian government. A large government department whose
mandate it is to be actively involved in the country's foreign aid programs,

spending massive amounts of money, and spreading 'Canadian values' at the same time, employs him to put every senior manager and every manager of the numerous field offices in other parts of the world, through intensive training courses. Transformation has to take place on two levels: the personal and the public (or rather, political). Personal transformation is a prerequisite to effectiveness on the political level, where truly 'magical' transformations can be achieved. The personal is political, and the political, personal. In this way the effectiveness not only of the senior managers but also the program managers in the field can be greatly enhanced.

Incredible as it may sound, these government officials were being asked, and taught, to deliberately dream the impossible, and to consciously seek to eliminate the boundaries between reality and dream. New Agers would recognize it as a sophisticated and systematized variant of 'visualization.' I came across other instances of active change agents preaching the same strange imperative of pursuing the impossible, and I would therefore be instantly alerted when, in 2010, Samuel Moyn published his *Last Utopia: Human Rights in History*, where he explained how "the idea of rights has seized hold of the utopian imagination." A reviewer observed that according to Moyn "*a project is utopian when it can be known in advance that its central objective cannot be realized. This may be because these aims are impossible in any human society, or because they cannot be achieved in particular communities in any future that can reasonably be anticipated.*" (Emphasis added.) The communist agenda of a Karl Marx belonged to the first category. Examples of the second category were the attempt to convert Iraq into a liberal democracy, or to make Afghanistan into a modern state where, among other objectives, women would be liberated. Moyn conceded that the pursuit of the impossible was "too much a part of the modern Western tradition ever to be truly renounced. That the idea of utopianism will disappear is itself a utopian dream."

This is something we must take on board because it did not just involve Canadians. Almost by definition utopias have always been impossibilities. Which was why, in his *Rules for Radicals*, Barack Obama's mentor in Chicago, Saul Alinsky, talked about "our wished-for fantasy of the world as it should be." Alinsky had published his *Rules* shortly before his death in 1972. Here and elsewhere in this text I refer to Alinsky as Obama's 'mentor.' Fact is that Obama never personally met Alinsky, but at the age of 23 the Alinsky team hired him to organize the residents on the South Side of Chicago "while learning and applying Alinsky's philosophy of street-level democracy." And for several years Obama himself taught workshops on the Alinsky method. An enduring image in my mind is of a picture of Obama standing before a blackboard. Left-handedly (amazing how many politicians are left-handed!) he had drawn a diagram under the general heading of Power Acquisition; written in capital letters. Below were interconnected blocks, listing Corporations, Banks, Utilities, and something else that was not decipherable. Eventually, as President of the United States, Obama appointed, as his Secretary of State, Hillary Clinton. She had devoted her honours thesis at Wellesley College to Alinsky, having interviewed him in person. After she graduated Alinsky offered her a job, but the offer was not taken up.

No recent agenda of impossibilities could possibly compete with Barack Obama's euphorically received 2008 speech in Berlin, as well as similar utterances in other venues. Obama was literally going to change, not only America, but the world. "This is the moment," he cried out no fewer than sixteen times in front of the Brandenburg Gate, when the promised process of change would begin to "build new bridges across the globe"; "defeat terror and dry up the well of extremism that supports it"; "rout the traffickers who sell drugs on your streets"; and "renew the goal of a world without nuclear weapons." His incantations also encompassed "trade that is free and fair for all"; "a new dawn in the Middle East"; and a call "to come together to save the planet"; "to give our children back their future"; and "to stand as one." This meant that "the walls between races and tribes; natives and immigrants; Christian and Muslim and Jew cannot stand. These now are the walls we must tear down." How many encirclements and blowings of trumpets had it taken to bring down the walls of Jericho? Elsewhere Obama announced that his election would also be the moment when the oceans of the world would cease to rise. By himself trotting out objectives and outcomes that were so patently impossible of achievement by any politically practicable measure, was it Obama's way of signalling that the "change" he was advocating was of an entirely different stripe? We shall be in a better position to answer this question when we've considered the transformationist's interest in fundamentally changing the *processes* of change.

Nevertheless we have to avoid the temptation, and the mistake, of appearing to regard an Obama—the individual—as other than a passing phenomenon, needing to be mindful of the Venerable Bede's metaphor of our human fleetingness, when he wrote: "Then comes a swallow flying across the hall; he enters by one door, and leaves by another. The brief moment that he is within the hall is pleasant to him; he feels not rain nor cheerless winter weather; but the moment is brief, and he passes from winter to winter." No, as in the case of a Canadian Trudeau, we should be interested in Obama only as representative of a certain (thankfully infrequently) recurrent type; the truly activist and charismatic political utopian. On this score British people might be reminded of a recent prime minister of their own who set as his goal the *abolition* of world poverty... except that he was anything but charismatic!

Samuel Moyn was absolutely right. Their brand of utopianism would never cease to manifest itself, if only intermittently, charging crowds with energy, and raising expectations that—in the cold light of day, and in retrospect—would be seen to have been nothing other than ridiculous. A reviewer remarked, however, that "like many writers on utopian movements today, Moyn shrinks from attacking *the impulse that inspires them.*" (Emphasis added.) This too was correct. Yes, one was soon to realize that a more profound, and more problematic, impulse seemed to be at work; an impulse of very much older *provenance,* as it would turn out.

It is not enough, either, to examine such utopianist outbreaks in the abstract. As important as—or even more important than—the question of *what kinds of people (political leaders in particular)* purvey such dreams, is the need to identify and to try to understand *the means and the methods* employed by the ones who are seriously committed to implementing their dreams. Among those, of considerable interest might be the rare ones who appeared to have actually succeeded, if only in part. But even success, however defined or measured, was still a subsidiary element. Because of a further complication. Because it transpires—as we have noted else-where—that the most sophisticated and problematic practitioners of such arts and techniques, *are not really interested in outcomes*. After all, why would you care about outcomes if you are in pursuit of impossibilities? Their interest lies in the launching and exploitation, and the manipulative opportunities of transformational *processes*. Transformation for the sake of transformation? Changingness as religion. "Change" was the overbearing and repetitive mantra of Obama's election campaign and one might quip that after his spending excesses that were to take the national debt to such unimaginably high levels, it would leave American voters—not to mention the next generation—with but small change in their pockets.

As thought-provoking as the foregoing tales is a semi-public meeting where Canada's Under-Secretary of Foreign Affairs pays tribute to Willis Harman's life-changing influence on himself. On my knee I make hand-written notes on a piece of paper, folded several times over, as my father had done at a certain conference in South Africa so many years ago, a conference with such distinct socio-political transformative objectives. In due course the speaker, to whom I'm now listening, will be based in Washington D.C. as a virtually permanent Canadian representative on the board of one of the foremost international decision-making agencies in the world. There seems to be a connection between this event, the activities of a Transformation Research Network, and a report commissioned by no fewer than seven major Canadian government departments as well as two departments in the government of the province of Alberta. The report commends Willis Harman's work in the department first cited above, noting that "to date, over 100 of the senior people have spent three to four weeks in groups of about 35 wrestling with the way the world is changing" and that the training sessions would "eventually include the top 200 people in the organization." But, the report warns, it will be necessary to move to the "third stage." The third stage is meant to extend the depth of one's understanding. Here, as in the medieval monk Joachim of Fiore's Age of Aquarius, thirdness is in! "Finally," we learn, "one moves beyond strategic planning and policy analysis and even departmental mission statements, to underlying questions of societal purpose and even more deeply to the underlying sense of the nature of the earth and of the human." 'Man and his world' again. This objective demands an "increasing integration between one's public and private life and integration among one's mental, emotional, moral, spiritual and physical dimensions. As Wilfred Smith puts it so beautifully, 'one must become a different sort of person.'" Transformation plus! Whether the Canadian taxpayer is receiving value for his money is a different question.

I've landed in a more than strange society, and my learning curve has already steepened. This must surely be the most interesting and potentially exciting of the countries we have lived in thus far. After all, it was also in Ottawa where the Cold War had started.

———————

Before me, as I write, are two sheets of paper; two single-spaced typed pages. They came from an old lady, Margaret MacDougall, the widow of a Canadian judge. Not long before her death she had entrusted them to my wife. Margaret, in turn, had received them from a woman who had worked for her husband (the judge) and had become her friend. The woman's name was Fernande Coulson. Fernande used to work in the office of the Canadian Crown Attorney in Ottawa. She wrote that on September 5, 1945, the Assizes of the Supreme Court of Ontario opened at 2 p.m., and shortly before that hour her boss, Crown Attorney Raoul Mercier, left the office with indictments to present to a Grand Jury.

> ...I was alone in the office.
> Shortly after 2 p.m., a man and a woman (who was about 7 months pregnant) entered my office and the man said that they wished to apply for Canadian citizenship. I asked him for his 'Landed Immigrant' card, when he informed me that their name was Gouzenko, that he was not landed as an immigrant because he had defected from the Russian embassy the night before with his wife and young boy, that he had been working at the embassy as a Cipher Clerk and that he had taken with him piles of documents to prove that Canadians were spying for Russia. He told me that he

was desperate, that he wanted protection, and quickly, as he feared for their lives. He further told me that before coming to me he had been to the Ottawa newspaper The Journal, told them his story, but that they had refused to help him. From there, he had gone to the RCMP where they also turned him down.

I knew that Eddie O'Meara, a newspaper reporter for The Journal, was in the building, I ran out of my office, found Eddie and asked him to come to my office and see what Gouzenko had (inside his jacket pocket - bulging - and inside the old-fashioned handbag that his wife carried and which I could see was very thick). He came down, I closeted with him with the Gouzenkos in Mr. Mercier's office. A few minutes later they emerged from Mr. Mercier's office, and I asked O'Meara if what Gouzenko claimed was true. His answer was 'Yes, but we can't touch it', and he left.

I decided to call the C.I.B. section of the RCMP as I knew many officers and requested that they send an officer to my office to investigate the matter. One came shortly thereafter. I again closeted with him with the Gouzenkos. He saw what they had and when they came out I asked O'Meara [the officer] if what I had been told by Gouzenko was true. He said, 'Yes, but we can't touch it.'

I was getting desperate. His wife was crying and every few minutes his wife would interrupt and speak to Gouzenko in Russian. I asked him what she was saying and he said that she wanted to know what we were talking about, what I was saying to him (she could not understand or speak English). He could speak it enough to be understood.

Realizing that this was a matter of national importance and safety, I decided to call the Prime Minister's office, which I did, and spoke to Sam Gobeil, his personal secretary. I told him who I had in my office and what had transpired until then. He asked me for my telephone number and promised that he would call be back shortly. He did, and all he said to me was, 'Do you wish to listen to good advice?' I said, 'What advice?'. He said, 'Have nothing more to say to that man, have nothing more to do with him, kick him out of your office as soon as you can.' I said, 'Thank you!!' I was seething.

I then called the French newspaper Le Droit, even though I felt that I probably would not get help from them, and their answer was the same, 'We can't touch it'.

Then I suddenly thought of Inspector Leopold, whom I knew well. He was in charge of the anti-subversive element section of the RCMP, and his office was in the Confederation Building, corner of Bank and Wellington. I called him, told him who was in my office, what they were looking for, what they did, and that I felt that something had to be done, that he needed protection, and quickly, otherwise I feared for their lives. I finally convinced him and he agreed to see them the following morning at 9.30 in his office. I then wrote Leopold's name and address on a piece of paper, also the date and the time of the appointment, and explained it clearly to Gouzenko. By this time, it was 5.15 p.m. Before leaving, Gouzenko begged me to keep his papers with me, but I was afraid, especially after having been told by the Prime Minister what Gobeil had relayed to me, and also knowing that Gouzenko had to have them when he went to see Leopold. I watched the two of them from the window of my office when they boarded a street car at the corner of Daly and Nicholas, wondering if they would make it back to their apartment on Somerset Street West.

Fernande Coulson then describes what she learned later about the way the Russians tried to break into the Gouzenkos' apartment that night, but were chased away by the neighbours, who in turn called the city police.

From September 5th, 1945, to February 6th, 1946, I heard nothing of what had happened to Gouzenko until the news story was announced on the radio the evening of February 6th, 1946, (10 o clock news). What had happened to the

Gouzenkos from the time they left my office on September 5th, 1945, was confirmed to me by Constable Walsh.

On February 7th, 1946, Mr. Mercier called the Prime Minister's secretary and asked him if he remembered the phone call he had had from me on September 5th, 1945. Gobeil answered, 'What phone call?'. Mr. Mercier said, 'The phone call that my secretary made to you'. Gobeil said, 'No, I don't remember'. Mr. Mercier was furious, as he well knew that I had not made it up. A few minutes later, Gobeil phoned and said to Mr. Mercier, 'About that certain phone call, forget it was ever made'. When Mr. Mercier repeated to me what Gobeil had said, I said, 'Forget? No, never.' The rest is history.

In the fullness of time it transpired that Prime Minister Mackenzie King entered in his own diary the following comment, which explained the general clamp-down that must have originated with him: "I thought we should be extremely careful in becoming a party to any course of action which would link the govt. of Canada up with this matter in a manner which might cause Russia to feel that we had performed an unfriendly act. That to seek to gather information in an underhanded way would make clear that we did not trust the (Russian) Embassy... My own feeling is that the individual has incurred the displeasure of the Embassy and is really seeking to shield himself." A historian commented that "King was not about to allow a Soviet code clerk to disrupt the cordial diplomacy that had characterized Ottawa's relations with Moscow." And King (believe it or not) did not particularly care whether "the man was apprehended by Soviet authorities or committed suicide." The other interesting thing is that whole sections of King's diaries covering the crucial period in November and December 1945 have gone missing and that "those are the only missing months in the 57 years that King kept a diary." The historian in question thought "they may have been destroyed because they reflected badly on King's judgment." Or on the country?

———

Fernande Coulson died, in Ottawa, on November 12, 2007, at the age of 93. I'm glad I did not miss the short obituary. No mention was made of the most outstanding, memorable, and courageous achievement of a lifetime.

In John le Carré's *The Russia House*, Nicholas P. Landau makes the rounds of no fewer than four ministries in Whitehall on a warm Sunday morning in a futile effort to hand over notebooks he has smuggled out of Moscow; a highly secret set of documents containing vital information related to the national security, in this case on the subject of nuclear armaments. At the Defence Ministry he is frogmarched to the door. Eventually, at the Foreign Office (his last desperate port of call) he is told to come back during the week, but then pushes past the security desk and manages to leave the notebooks with one Palmer, an effete minion who happened to be the duty officer that afternoon. Palmer had "a nice time with the notebooks. For two nights and one and a half days. Because he found them so amusing." Meanwhile poor Niki Landau lives in fear of his life. Did John le Carré have Igor Gouzenko in mind when he penned this story?

There's a saying that to understand a country one has to ask oneself what is unthinkable in or about it. And so one had to start to wonder what was unthinkable about a country that seemed to be happily governed for 22 years by a man (albeit a staunch Presbyterian) whose Spiritualist proclivities would lead him to only make important decisions when the hands of the clock stood at ten minutes to two. At other times, as someone observed: "If you are reading this article at, say, 7:35 or 6:30, Mackenzie King would be very impressed, because he was obsessed by the position of the hands on a clock; when they were in alignment, timing was propitious and King made note of this almost daily." On May 7, 1945, shortly before the Prime Minister was informed of the German surrender in the Second World War, "King had a vision of capturing two white rabbits on a train. These, he later surmised, were symbolic of the German surrender to the Americans and Soviets." When his beloved dog was giving up the ghost he asked it to convey a message from him to his (King's) deceased mother.

But it was the Prime Minister's anxiety to not unduly upset Iosif Vissarionovich Dzhugashvili (a.k.a. Joseph Stalin) in the Gouzenko affair that should perhaps be tied to his admiration for another leader cut from similar cloth, Herr Adolf Schickelgruber. That we can learn from a biography of Lady Aberdeen, the wife of a Canadian Governor General. Being a 'mystic' himself, King told Lady Aberdeen that he intended to travel to Berlin "on a divinely inspired mission to avert war" because he had heard Hitler described as a mystic. "To King this meant that an other-worldly bond could be established, a great portent... saying he would seek to assure Hitler that Canada and other parts of the Empire desired nothing more than 'friendly relations all round.'" King told members of the British cabinet of his intentions, but to Lady Aberdeen he confessed his "higher purpose." King maintained that he had received a message from the dead, from none other than former British Prime Minister William Gladstone, in which he was "urged to have a heart-to-heart talk with Hitler." Hitler was a fellow psychic and since "Hitler belonged to this elect he knew the Nazi dictator must be inherently a good person. How could it be otherwise?" Fortified by a cable sent to him with a prophetic verse from the Bible, "For He shall give His angels charge over thee," King departed for Berlin. Hitler received him at the Hindenburg Palace, where King impressed on Hitler the symbolism of the fact that he, King, was born in a Canadian town by the name of Berlin (later renamed Kitchener). "He saw in Hitler a humble, sincere man dedicated to the welfare of his people and mankind. Hitler had 'a sort of appealing and affectionate look in his eyes... a calm, passive man, deeply and thoughtfully in earnest... He is distinctly a mystic... He is particularly strong on beauty, loves flowers and will spend more of the money of the State on gardens and flowers than on most other things.'"

But some fearful symmetries come in threes, and I was yet to discover—this time not from books—the admiration of yet another Canadian prime minister for the great Chairman Mao Tse-tung (or Zedong) and his Cultural Revolution, and similarly impressed by the great wisdom reflected by the face of yet another mass murderer. There are hat-tricks in the game of cricket, but in the life of a nation: Stalin + Hitler

+ Mao Tse-tung? As far as Canada was concerned, nothing appeared to be unthinkable.

I'm also beginning to learn another lesson, best expressed as: *Beware of the professors!*[7] Not just any professors, but the rare ones who have moved from theory into the world of *praxis*; political *praxis*. Not the ones who are content with only trying to transform the minds of their students, but professors bent on transforming 'man and his world' actively, and preferably by gaining access to the levers of power. One might say the same to the Americans who had, for the first time, put a professor into the White House. Professor Hendrik French Verwoerd had embarked on a fundamental transformation of an entire country, but he had no designs on the world beyond its borders. Granted that, like Professor Willis Harman, he harnessed the art and craft of psychological manipulation (or at least persuasion), but, unlike Professor Harman, he was no humanist. Professor Harman is. He is much esteemed and celebrated in Humanist circles (capitalized) —especially in California—and highly lauded by the Association for Humanistic Psychology. Professor Pierre Elliott Trudeau, on the other hand, has been identified by many as a philosopher-king, but not as a professorial ruler which, of course, he became; he too, like Obama, had been a law professor. He is not only a Humanist but he has also co-published a manifesto that went well beyond the strictly Humanist dimension. This is quite rare: professors do not normally do such a thing. Of course Professor Harman has not been that far removed from the odd manifesto either: both the *Humanist Manifesto I* and its successor, the *Humanist Manifesto II,* originated in California. (Much later the leadership of Trudeau's Liberal Party will pass into the hands of a Professor Stéphane Dion of Quebec, assisted by the Party's deputy leader, Professor Michael Ignatieff from Harvard, destined to take over the party leadership himself from Professor Dion.)

Yet another professor looms large in the administrative entourage of Professor Trudeau: a certain Professor Ivan Head. He hails from the province of Alberta. For many years he will almost single-handedly

---

7    Niall Ferguson, the historian, recounts how "with astonishing prescience (Edmund) Burke warned against the utopianism of 'the professors'…"

define and indeed steer Canada's foreign policies, reporting directly to Professor Trudeau, and thus largely by-passing (to its extreme chagrin) the Canadian Department of Foreign Affairs. Eventually he will be put in charge of a rather unique crown corporation, apparently specially created for him, with practically unlimited funds at its disposal. The International Development Research Centre (IDRC) is essentially beyond the central controls to which ordinary government agencies are subject. On paper, IDRC is meant to help the Third World with practical, and preferably inexpensive, develop-mental technologies, but there is more than meets the eye, as I shall discover.

Equally intriguing (albeit not an active politician or bureaucrat) is a Professor David Mitrany, who was holding sway at the London School of Economics when Professor Trudeau was studying at the same institution. It has always been assumed that at the LSE, Professor Trudeau fell under the influence of that famous socialist, Professor Harold Laski, but I suspect that few people, if any, have tied Professor Trudeau to the teachings of Professor Mitrany. I might not have discovered Professor Mitrany but for my short tenure as a Visiting Scholar at the University of North Carolina at Chapel Hill, and from where several of his books had been published. Professor Mitrany will loom fairly large in my understanding of how political transformationist agendas could best be carried out. Professor Mitrany was first and foremost a peace activist, and so is Professor Ivan Head, although outshone in that department by a world-circling peace offensive conducted by Professor Trudeau. Therefore it was not impossible that Professor Head too had sat at the feet of Professor Mitrany, if not literally, then at least in spirit.

Forsooth, Canada has become a particular attractor—like those 'strange attractors' discovered in the newly-developing science of fractals—to hyperactive social activists, including yet another professor, Johan Galtung, who teaches peace studies at the University of Hawaii. Equally prolifically and prominently attracted to the Canadian scene is one Professor Richard A. Falk, who has taught both in California and at Princeton. Speaking at a meeting of the United Nations Association in Ottawa, Falk cited one Mohammed Azhar Ali Kahn on how "Canada can contribute to a better world order, by not being a junior partner in a larger imperial enterprise, but in having the courage to face reality in a constructive and challenging way." A variant on Professor Trudeau's "call for realism?"

Several other global change agents, who have started to orbit into the (chaos-theoretical) basin of the Canadian 'strange attractor', are assembled under the wings of one Professor Immanuel (in this case not God with Us but rather, I might suggest—and with good reason—God help Us) Wallerstein. Their works are published out of Montreal by Black Rose Books. They represent the 'party of movement', as against the 'party of order', which they associate with outdated "Europo-centric constructions of social reality." It is a matter, they say, "of seizing the chance because it involves aggressive state action that takes advantage of the weakened political position of core countries and the weakened economic position of domestic opponents..." Several of them make a particular point of invoking the new social experiment generally known as the Chinese Cultural Revolution. Professor Galtung's attraction to Canada leaves nothing to be desired when he proclaims that "in the years ahead a primary priority... is to assure that domestic, change-oriented, progressive elites understand the relevance of the larger world setting to their more specific and local programs of reforms. Thus movements associated with the status of women, minority rights, labor reform, population policy, environmental protection, and consumer protection need to be linked to an interpretation of the total world order..." just as Professor Wallerstein sees no alternative but "to seek to transform the system as a whole." This element of totalism (invoking Professor Trudeau's invocation of universalism) is reflected, I seem to notice, by the frequent use of the word 'larger.'

'Consciousness-raising' has to begin, as Professor Harman is trying to do, at the personal level, especially among the progressive elites. After that, the personal will extend to the political at the domestic level, and finally, the domestic level becomes the launching pad for consciousness-raising on a global scale, thereby seeking to bring about a New World Order. One Joseph Chilton Pearce has already stressed modern man's need to define an "adequately big world picture", and how that, in turn, depends on "an adequately large image of man." In fact, claims Pearce, if we "challenge constructs of mind and reality" we shall see the first "crack in the cosmic egg."

Already well into the 21ˢᵗ century yet another Canadian prime minister will proclaim Canada's role as "the conscience of the world." And he will, much to the annoyance of some Americans, berate that country for ignoring the "world conscience." But in case one has been inclined to suspect that these people are no more than a small claque of mostly foreign eccentrics, one is pulled up short by a paper presented at a meeting of the Canadian Political Science Association by Professor Elizabeth Smythe of the Department of Political Science at the University of Western Ontario. She quotes both Professor Galtung and Professor Wallerstein at considerable length. They all agree, she says, on "placing Canada within the category of a semi-periphery or go-between country", and therefore a useful launching pad for any enterprise to transform the "world-wide system." Nothing more, nothing less. We still have to discover, in due course, what Chairman Mao had to say about Canada's semi-peripheral status.

This is why it is so noticeable that the Mexicans have already got the message, and particularly with respect to the role Canada will be playing in the global transformation. Both Houses of the Canadian parliament have convened to hear an address by His Excellency José Lopez Portillo, President of Mexico, after Prime Minister Trudeau had remarked that "I have been greatly impressed by your country's growing stature in the global community... Canada welcomes your country's determination to use its stature..." President Portillo rises to the occasion. He observes that Canadian and Mexican energy resources should be exploited "within a system of total responsibility on the part of mankind" and that "Canada is close to us and is inevitably linked to our destiny." But this is what really attracts my attention (as, years hence, will the pronouncements of Barack Obama):

> ...our aim is to transform [the world]. We have little time left in which to do this, but we cannot renounce our commitment to forge the roads along which the new forces of life will march.

So there was a cornucopia of 'big talk' of a transforming and transformed world. In his celebrated speech at the Mansion House (seat of the
Mayor of the City of London) in March of 1975, Trudeau called for "the
maintenance of equilibrium among all our activities, whatever their nature
[and] *an equitable distribution, worldwide, of resources and opportunities.*"
(Emphasis added, given, once again, in this instance, the invocation of an
objectively impossible dream.) "The proper discharge of those functions,"
the speaker added, "calls for more than tinkering with the present system.
*The processes required must be global in scope and universal in application.*"
(Emphasis added.) Yet another impossible dream, of the same genre as
Obama's invocations in Berlin, 30 years in the future. Six years later, on
his way to a conference in Mexico City, Trudeau once again referred to his
Mansion House speech and when asked why he was not sending a trade
minister or even a foreign affairs minister to the conference, he explained
that they did not have "the coverage that the Prime Minister has *and
therefore the influence he has on Canadian public opinion.*" My emphasis
again, partly to underline the way this pronouncement also related to the
reverse influence that deliberately pursued international diplomatic escapades were supposed to have on the domestic transformational process.
This was just one of the tools in the hands of the political and cultural
transformationist. Later on we shall be taking a close look at a variety of
such devices.

By way of another example, a vigorous international campaign—
mainly aimed at garnering the support and the votes of sympathetic Third
World and other socialist regimes, but meant to have an impact on the
leading western industrial states—was launched in an effort to weaken
the international treaties governing and protecting the patent and trade
mark rights enjoyed by industrial enterprises. The ability to protect and
control its core technologies and its trademarks has been, and will always
be, at the very heart of the competitiveness of any business and especially
now, in this highly information- and knowledge-intensive age. That's why
those interests go under the generic name of industrial and intellectual
property rights. Without getting those treaties amended first it would not
have been possible for the Canadian change agents to amend the domestic laws, changes that would have made it easier for the state to compel

businesses to do its bidding. The campaign to change those property rights had been in the works for nearly a decade, but fortunately (thanks to some rather extraordinary measures) it was thwarted in the end. (More can be told about this episode, were it not for the fact that the penalties for breaches of the Official Secrets Act can be exceptionally severe.)

In other words, one was looking at a deliberate setting up of a reciprocal or oscillating function between various domestic and international initiatives, with the express intent of boosting transformational processes *in both directions.* More recently, when Barack Obama was touting a quest to fundamentally change both America *and* the world, could he have had a similar kind of process in mind? (Think of the New Age embrace of the symbol of the rhizome, a horizontal plant root form which, uniquely, grows simultaneously at and from both ends. I should know, because we have a thriving bed of the virtually indestructible *Geranium macrorhizum* in our garden.) Thus, on his trip to Mexico City, referring to "international problems" and "Canadian problems", Trudeau added that they "are interdependent and both can be solved only one with the help of the other." In the following year, 1982, the Prime Minister invoked the Catholic theologian Teilhard de Chardin's talk of "a much more intense process of planetization." What was "required today... [was] a brand new incarnation" and the transformation of the world into a "really organic society" reflecting a "universal moral order."

We were seeing a certain way of thinking, affirmed in different ways and in different situations. Oscillating positive feedback processes would be made to shift between the domestic and foreign domains, and thereby help to bring about the desired transformations of 'man and his world.' But how would such transformations be brought about, in general? It was all about process: the deliberate harnessing of *process* and (as yet unspecified) *processes.* Process was and would be both creative and transformative. Indeed, if surprisingly, process by itself was capable of creating new goals and objectives. Process was all. *The challenge was to get the requisite processes going.* It would not do to wait for the gradualisms of evolution to reveal themselves. No, the transformative processes had to be driven, and driven by a new breed of single-minded, determined and resourceful politicians and bureaucrats who had come to dominate the affairs of yet another 'very strange society.'

———————

"Sometimes - history needs a push."

Vladimir Lenin

———————

Granted that there was nothing particularly new about an apotheosis of process. The same thought had already surfaced most famously in the works of the British philosopher Alfred North Whitehead, as well as in the domain of modernist theology, where even God himself became process, or subject to process. Buddhism was already credited as "the most comprehensive process philosophy and religion." But quite apart from the fact that many political New Agers harboured pronounced Buddhist proclivities, they also held in high esteem such as the Austrian astrophysicist Eric Jantsch's *Self-Organizing Universe,* where he expounded a new vision of a world that was entirely "process-oriented" and where the emphasis was wholly on "the becoming;" a world constituting a system of "coherent, evolving, interactive processes..." Both realms—the religious and the secular—had to be transformative of both 'man and his world,' except that in the latter case salvation lay entirely in process. Or so it appeared. And so it seemed to me that to properly understand another strange society, a society with such extraordinary and often bizarre utterances coming from leading lights in the public arena—and with their evident commitment to bringing about not just social change but fundamental process-oriented transformations of 'man and his world'—it was necessary to first look into the significance of process itself.

For Alfred North Whitehead process was everything. Process was the basic reality. A great influence on Whitehead was the philosopher Samuel Alexander, for whom God was "in continual process of becoming via the evolution of the world." One of the most influential and populist prophetesses of the New Age was Marilyn Ferguson, and especially on account of her book with its telling sub-title *The Aquarian Conspiracy: Personal and Social Transformation in the 1980s*. Ferguson reminded her readers that even Buckminster Fuller (originator of Canada's geodesic globe) "tried to capture the sense of God as process":

> Yes, God is a verb,
> the most active, connoting the vast harmonic
> reordering the universe
> from unleashed chaos of energy.

Ferguson added the following emphasis to her claim that "the importance of process is another discovery. Goals and end-points matter less... Means *are* ends. The journey is the destination." In like vein did the New Age physicist Fritjof Capra see nature as not having any inherent stability, but merely the stability of a "dynamic balance," remarkably similar to Trudeau's call for "the maintenance of an equilibrium among all our activities, whatever their nature..." And in the same way did the British theoretical physicist, David Bohm—much acclaimed by New Agers— contend that the world could only live in harmony "if the world view itself takes part in an unending process of development, evolution, and unfoldment, which fits as part of the universal process that is the ground of all existence." During my tenure as a Science Advisor at the Science Council of Canada, Bohm was one of its guest speakers. He too must have been attracted by the Canadian Enlightenment. Equally popular in New Age circles—as well as at the Science Council of Canada—was the Russian-born naturalized Belgian physicist Ilya Prigogine, winner of the Nobel Prize for physics in 1977. His theories were infused with the idea of creative processes and flux, and it was notable how much of his thought had been influenced by Whitehead's *Process and Reality*. Process also played a pivotal role in Karl Marx's anatomy of the revolution: people-in-process, so to speak, produced the necessary ideas, but then "conscious intervention (was) necessary to give shape to the process of change."

The same mode of thought invaded the domain of *psychology*. Capra himself alluded to the "new psychology" in which the focus "is now shifting from psychological structures to the underlying processes," and added that "a special kind of group therapy, which was not developed by psychotherapists but grew out of the women's movement, is practiced in political consciousness-raising groups." And it was on the same score that the Christian psychologist Paul C. Vitz, in one of his critiques, cited Carl Rogers' theory that in the life of an individual "much the more significant continuum is from fixity to changingness, from rigid structure to flow, from stasis to process" until a person "has become an integrated process of changingness." To the point of being dissolved in the All? (Psychology is the subject of Chapter Ten, following.)

Nor did the field of *law* escape, as I learned, listening to yet another distinguished visitor to the Canadian capital in the person of Laurence H. Tribe, Professor of Law at Harvard, who wrote about "means-ends fluidity" because, he said, "people lack clearly articulated ends and values at any given time." Their inchoate values, according to Tribe, were only crystallized "into distinct preferences or criteria of choice... through the concrete process of seeking means to attain them..." The ends held by individuals or groups were shaped, *inter alia*, by "the processes of choice they adopt." In other words, here too, both goals and ends were products of process.

In the world of *theology* a much-quoted and prolific American bishop by the name of John Spong was utterly persuaded by the Catholic Hans Küng's conviction that "God does not operate on the world from above or from outside but from within. God acts in the world process... God is the source, the center, and the goal of the world process." Immanence in full flower; a phenomenon that will be the subject of one of the concluding chapters of this book. Process was central, too, to the Humanist world of Willis Harman and to the first and second *Humanist Manifestos* with their fundamental affirmation that "man has emerged as the result of a continuous process."

In the field of *management*, not irrelevant either was a study by the Asian Institute of Management on the differences between Western and Asian organizations and the way Asian organizations were said to arrive at decisions. "No specific goals were observable." A Japanese company was both a functional and a communal group, and that for the latter "existence is a goal in itself." In the kinship community "the goal is the community itself so that the work goals can be as fluid and as many as the community's needs dictate."

Nobody would deny that such process-dominated ways could be productive, but a problem would arise—especially in a Western society—if a particular person or a particular elite were to seek to deliberately design or exploit process and processes that, in their eyes at least, would be a means whereby a fundamental transformation of society—or of the way people thought—could be brought about. But to what end?

As I would discover, there was much to be learned about both the philosophy and the various ways of exploiting process and processes, but it was necessary to start by trying to understand the motivations and the activities of a cast of characters whose discourse was utterly suffused with active, transitive words like 'shape,' 'to shape,' and 'shaping.' Were 'man and his world' but as clay in the hands of the shapers? Transformation did not just embrace substantive changes —changes in character, composition or nature, and indeed "changing one thing into another" as in alchemy—but in the first instance it was about changes in form, which is where, apparently, 'shaping' really came into its own. And not only form *but the very frameworks within which individuals and societies oriented themselves*, frameworks that were indispensable, as would be explained by Canada's 2007 Templeton Prize winner, Charles Taylor (to whom we shall return in due course). The same principle was implicit in the epistemology of Alasdair MacIntyre (a British philosopher) and Michael Polanyi (a Hungarian-British polymath), namely, that it is not possible to acquire any knowledge whatsoever except within the framework of a tradition. Thus, in the eyes of the political utopians, *the frameworks themselves* had to be the subject of *induced* processes of change. Stability at any level of existence was anathema in a world without constants.

Now we are moving on to an even higher level of activity: meta-change. Thus, as William Friedland (Dean of Social Sciences at the University of California) contended, just as the very frameworks had to be transformed, *the process itself had to be shaped*. "Conscious intervention is necessary," he said, "to give shape to the process of change." This is a most important qualification. It is of the same genre as a concomitant belief, in the religious domain, that not only the *content* of faith had to be transformed, but the very notion and essence of faith itself, of faith as faith. Such is the language of the genuine transformationist. Friedland was an expert in "community studies and sociology" but not, like Barack Obama, an active community organizer.

Protean man was a creature who constantly changed his form. Proteus was the old god of the sea who could change his shape at will. At least he only changed himself. He was not out to change others, and least of all the world at large.

We may then ask: If process is so important, what does it spell in the hands of the socio-cultural and political transformationist? Especially pertinent for our purpose is that it is still not enough to know that *process* has so occupied his mind as well as the minds of an assortment of philosophers, psychologists, physicists, lawyers, theologians and New Age gurus. It signifies that we should have to look more closely at the *ways* in which such processes can and have been exploited, and that will be addressed when we take a look at 'transformationists at work'—the subject of the next chapter—and especially in a subsequent chapter devoted to 'the means and the method.'

"Live the questions now. Perhaps you will then gradually, without noticing it, live along some distant day into the answer."

Rainer Maria Rilke,
*Letter to a Young Poet*

# CHAPTER SEVEN
# TRANSFORMATIONISTS
# AT WORK

"We are five days away from fundamentally transforming the United States of America."

Barack Obama, election eve, 2008

**Rodomontade:** arrogant boasting or blustering, ranting talk. Origin: Fr < *rodomont*, braggadocio, after *Rodomonte*, boastful Saracen leader in Ariosto's *Orlando Furioso*

We should first take a step back. Two kinds of change agent have made themselves manifest. Comparatively rare are the ones who—when they find themselves in a position to do so—are happy to act boldly, whether successfully or not. They look to seize the moment.

The other kind serve to provoke. They incite from the sidelines, like cheer-leaders egging on players on the field. They're attracted to the real actors like wasps around a honeypot.

If a change agent is also charismatic, he becomes like one of those strange attractors found in chaos theory. Come to think of it, the metaphor of chaos theory is particularly apt, when active change agents also embrace the promises of anarchy.

Historical precedents for the business of visualizing the reshaping of 'man and his world' have not gone a-begging. Long ago Friedrich Nietzsche created the Superman, an artist who could shape the human race according to his will: "Man is for him an un-form, a material, an ugly stone that needs a sculptor." H.G. Wells recounted Lenin's dictum that "the Russian people are by habit and tradition traders and individualists; their very souls must be remolded if this new world is to be achieved." Benito Mussolini put it more crudely when he said that the state "necessarily transforms people even in their physical aspect." In his preface to the Party bible, *Organisations Buch der NSDP*, Herr Adolf Schickelgruber wrote that "the state can only be a means for reaching a goal, the work of the German renaissance is not in a change of form of the German Reich or its constitution. It is a case of… reshaping of the people."

The eponymous cultural revolutionist, the great Chairman himself, Mao Tse-tung, devoted a lifetime to "using revolutionary practice as an instrument for re-shaping mental attitudes… by changing people's mentality through indoctrination and study, one could also change objective social reality." As recalled by Yale Professor Charles E. Lindblom, Chairman Mao, like Lenin, spoke of the need to "remold people to their very souls." A fellow Communist, Fidel Castro, said something similar about "the formation of the new man." "Persuasive efforts (had) to be reserved for inducing personality transformation and for motivating major tasks," added Lindblom, in commenting on Castro.

With his pronounced interest in Canadian affairs, Willis Harman would have been jealous, just as he admired the way the Buddhist yogis of Tibet developed control over their own dreams so that they "became a step in a much grander process of soul shaping." At least on the face of it "soul shaping" came closer to the theological domain—and given the way Canadian shapers looked upon Latin American developments—they may well have noticed a five-volume work by one Juan Luis Segundo, *A Theology for Artisans of a New Humanity,* as well as the works of the Jesuit and neo-Marxist Paolo Freire, for whom the "Cultural Revolution takes the total society to be reconstructed, including all human activities, as the object of its remolding action." As well—and not surprisingly—Immanuel Wallerstein, with his fascination for the Canadian eruption, observed, with respect to "the eastern European countries, China, North Korea, Vietnam, and Cuba", that each of these countries "has sought to remold the social psychology of its citizens, that is, to create 'socialist man' in one form or another." Richard Falk—who, like Wallerstein, latched on to the Canadian phenomenon with agility—was persuaded that "a consensus favorable to drastic global reform must initially be shaped simultaneously in various national arenas throughout the world... the next stage of the discourse would proceed to the *shape of a new system of world order.*" (Emphasis added.)

In similar fashion Robert J. Lifton of Harvard claimed that "I have evolved a concept of 'Protean man,' named, of course, after that intriguing figure of Greek mythology renowned for his shape-shifting;" commented on how "the inner life of individuals shapes itself;" and pointed out how a "shared history plays an increasingly important part in shaping the self-process." With his congenital aversion to cultural and political manipulators, the political philosopher Karl Popper excoriated a kind of social engineering aimed at "remodeling the 'whole of society'" and controlling "the historical forces that mould the future of the developing society." With so much touting of shaping in vogue, Leszek Kolakowski (the Polish historian of ideas) warned that the decline of historical awareness was fostering a manipulative and rationalist view of society; a society that was "in principle" malleable.

And then there was Barack Obama. I asked myself what *he* was after when I recalled my father's advice to be always alert to the need to "read between the lines," whether written or spoken. My dreams of *my* father were markedly different from *his* dreams of *his* father! That Obama was a self-confessed transformationist in pursuit of fundamental "change" everybody who fell for his extraordinary invocations knew very well. But how many have asked themselves about the mindset behind it? Granted that he did not directly and overtly address the necessary re-shaping of individuals. He had more in common with the advocates of changing the entire "system of world order." And so, in his appearance at the Brandenburg Gate, when he called upon the "people of the world" he concluded by exhorting them to join him in "remaking the world once again." Long ago Alexis de Tocqueville foresaw the apotheosis of *totalism* when he commented on the American belief in the essential unity of all mankind. About democratic man he wrote: "Not content with the discovery that there is nothing in the world but a creation and a Creator, he seeks to expand and simplify his conception by including God and the universe in one great whole." When totalism becomes a religion...

As for particular Canadian 'shapers'—other than political leaders or prominent bureaucrats in government—take one ubiquitous Canadian change agent who I shall simply identify as X. He is a prolific adviser to assorted government agencies. I see him sitting on his own in the lounge of a prominent hotel in Ottawa with a legal writing pad in front of him, clearly immersed in deep thought. He writes slowly, but not as slowly as the novelist John Updike was observed as doing by someone who sat next to him on a bench in London's Hyde Park. Consider the following gems of wisdom flowing from X's pen, when he refers to the "inter-penetration of human consciousness and environment, of the double-fitting process by means of which we shape our world and, in turn, are shaped by it... Rather we change the shape of our consciousness because it dawns on us that the continued use of the present form of consciousness will continually lead to failure." At issue is not only the "shape of the soul" but the shape of consciousness itself.

Now for the clincher: In his own words, X makes no bones about it that what is required is not just a world fit to live in, *"but people fit to live with."* (Emphasis added.) Later we shall refer to the political scientist Sheldon S. Wolin's observation about how exponents of 'group think' distinguish between 'functional' and 'dysfunctional' individuals in their midst, but it was Sir Karl Popper—in a 1944 essay on social engineering—who wrote about the program of the Utopianist, that "it substitutes for his demand that we build a new society, fit for men and women to live in, the demand that we 'mould' these men and women to fit into his new society." Popper did not live long enough to also learn from such as X about a need for "people fit to live with." Intolerance—to put it mildly—is a subject yet to be addressed, and more properly when we come to look into "systems and the systems mind." Suffice it to say that the mind of the shaper seems to be not at all averse to a high degree of compulsion.

At a public meeting held in a church, X makes fun of an "outdated Catholic Pope" and proposes that the churches too gear up for "shaping a new culture." (The only advice he can offer the Pope, he says, is "tough Charlie.") More interesting is his listing of examples of major Canadian organizations (of which there are fourteen in all, he says) that are "already coming on board." Canadians, he insists, have to be "introduced to their own spirit" and then teach other Canadians to "follow the spirits."

Shaping was an active thing, as the President of the Canadian International Development Agency—a government agency which, like Professor Ivan Head's IDRC, had a distinct international mandate with programs aimed at shaping other malleable societies—pointed out in a speech delivered in 1982. "Our choice," he said, "is between taking constructive action to shape the course of events, or sitting back and letting change take place without our intervention." This meant that at least our shapers were not Darwinian, just as the scientists who went on the warpath against global warming, seemed to have forgotten or overlooked the role of evolutionary adaptation, which was supposedly an effective response to the most adverse of circumstances; and, in any case, would have left fitter humans in its wake!

The same activist element distinguished Prime Minister Trudeau's Mansion House speech, where he observed that "the history of mankind has been shaped in large measure by men and women who have acted as architects of social organization." Here, too, social organization was not the product of a natural evolution; it was a construct. Evidently Darwinian beliefs—usually so ardently espoused—could be easily suspended when circumstances so dictated! A major influence on Trudeau had been the Quebec socialist poet, Frank R. Scott, the title of whose biography, *The Politics of the Imagination*, written by one Sandra Djwa, may not have been far removed from the incantations of a Willis Harman. One of the chapters in Djwa's study was titled "*A Search for Form.*" Scott, too, contributed to a veritable industry of prescriptions 'for Canadians' or 'for Canada' when he wrote an article on *A Policy of Neutrality for Canada*. At a symposium held in 1981 Trudeau professed that "Frank taught me everything I know." It was Scott who apparently brought Trudeau (in his own words) to realize that the law was "an instrument of social control." Referring to Scott and Trudeau, Scott's biographer believed that "both held at the back of their minds a conception of the lawmaker-politician as philosopher-king with the power of bringing into being the ideal state, 'the state as a work of art.' Many of these early views Trudeau carried into his fifteen years in power as prime minister of Canada. Indirectly, in the next two decades, Scott may have helped shape the future of Canada..."

Even so, pride of place in the shaping business remained with Trudeau; he who had written, in 1968, that the Canadian brand of federalism "could become a brilliant prototype for the moulding of tomorrow's civilization." When, in praise of Canadian federalism, Prime Minister Laurier wrote to General Smuts in the wake of Sir Henry de Villiers's visit, he had not gone nearly that far! With all the shaping in evidence, no wonder that in due course even Trudeau's socialist compatriot, the philosopher Charles Taylor, and winner of the 2007 Templeton Prize—a prize awarded for "Progress Toward Research or Discoveries about Spiritual Realities"—developed an allergy to manifestations of 'instrumentalism' in the affairs of men.

Why not give the last word on the shaping syndrome to a man of wisdom? In his *Abolition of Man* C.S. Lewis talked about "the Conditioners" and the "Man-moulders" of a new age. Previously, said Lewis, they had been largely subject to their own teachings: "It was but old birds teaching young birds to fly. This will be changed... Judgments of value are to be produced in the pupil as part of the conditioning." The Conditioners became the designers of their own values. And those would be the values driving the enterprise of shaping 'man and his world.'

At this point one might ask just what kind of society did these totalist shapers have in mind? Certainly and decidedly not one that was cognisant, let alone reflective, of any Christian heritage. We might consider a few examples.

Once upon a time there was a woman by the name of Elisabeth Mann Borgese, daughter of the writer Thomas Mann. She edited, and wrote an introduction for, a book titled *Self-Management: New Dimensions to Democracy*. Highly active in the negotiations leading to the international treaty known as the Law of the Sea, she was recognized for her efforts—because Canada had its own designs and put extraordinary diplomatic resources into the process over many years—when Prime Minister Trudeau specially created and endowed an institute in the Canadian maritime provinces for her to manage, and mainly with Third World beneficiaries in mind. With Canada's ostensible (and often ostentatious) concern for the Third World, it was Trudeau's way of rewarding the Third World countries—many of them not even bordering on the sea, as we've already noted—whose votes Canada cultivated in its opposition to the professed interests of the major maritime powers. The United States and Britain in particular had strong misgivings over a possible threat the Law of the Sea might pose to the freedom of the high seas, and more pertinently, to navigational rights through strategic straits.

Already, evidence of a Chinese interest in maritime choke points was beginning to build. In 2010 the Chinese started to construct a very large port facility in Sri Lanka, which—according to the writer and geopolitical analyst Robert Kaplan—would give a fast growing Chinese navy a distinct advantage by way of exerting control, or at least influence, over events in the Indian Ocean basin. As a former South African, and seeing so many signs of Chinese incursions all over the African continent, I could easily foresee an active Chinese presence at the southernmost tip of Africa, the Cape of Good Hope. Given the vulnerability of the Suez Canal, and its inability to handle the largest (so-called Capesize) vessels, a more strategic maritime choke point would be hard to imagine, other than perhaps the Straits of Malacca.

Just as a new Canadian Charter of Rights and Freedoms was designed to replace ancient rights already enjoyed under the common law (see below), the United Nations Convention on the Law of the Sea served to replace centuries-old customary international law. Two contributors to an article in the February 2012 edition of an American journal, *The Diplomat*, pointed out that customary international law had always "protected the traditionally expansive understanding of freedom of the seas," whereas "China is trying to curtail that access, fence off its peripheral waters, and deny to other maritime nations the freedom of navigation they have long and lawfully enjoyed." The writers then explained why the United States would be at a distinct disadvantage if it were to ratify the Convention, instead of continuing to rely on and abide by customary law. On both fronts—domestic and international—charters replacing ancient rights and freedoms were favourite devices in transformationist hands. I should have mentioned that a reincarnation of Alger Hiss (the Soviet agent who held President Roosevelt's hand at the disastrous Yalta conference at the end of the Second World War) served as the right-hand man of the chairman of the chief Law of the Sea negotiating committee. Not long afterwards the same man was unmasked as a KGB agent and was only arrested at the airport in the nick of time on his way back to Moscow.

If C.S. Lewis could have read Borgese's contribution to *Self-Management*, he would have been intrigued to discover that the self-managing society would be yet another vehicle for the Conditioners, and it would not be Christian. Borgese said as much. "Finally," she proclaimed, "we will live in an order no longer dominated by Judeo-Grecian-Roman values. The new life-style will be infused with an admixture of Oriental values." Up to now, she added, "we have been living in a hierarchical, vertical order; in a closed order, based on property, power, and sovereignty," and she felt compelled to literally reiterate: "...in an order dominated by Western, Judeo-Grecian-Roman values." One of the characteristics of the new order, she said, would be a brand new set of values; self-designed values in the self-managing society, a society not subject to any external or higher norms.

One way to try to 'remould' a society—and of particular appeal to lawyers like Trudeau—was to rewrite or amend a country's constitution and to embed in the constitution stipulations that were very difficult to change. Americans certainly know about the importance of constitutions. In a chapter still to come there's mention of how Prime Minister Trudeau had returned from a visit to Tibet, absolutely determined to run for office once again and to give Canadians their Charter. This would be the centrepiece of a new constitution for the country. In the event it was rammed through the legislative process with breathtaking "boldness and imagination," an expression employed by one of the main actors in the process.

Trudeau's obsession with his Charter, to the virtual exclusion of everything else, was sufficient to raise any reasonably sensitive antennae. I should know because, as part of the constitution-making exercise, I served on a special interdepartmental task force mandated to look into the division of the economic powers between and among the central and provincial governments. To this end we examined the constitutions of other industrialized western democracies, and the way the development and application of the American 'trade and commerce' power had succeeded in knitting the American economy into a single and efficient unit. This was a crucial concern in light of the persistently low productivity of the Canadian economy. Among the dismal statistics was the fact that in the decade preceding the year 2010, Canadian labor productivity had only grown at an annual rate of 0.8%. Thus no wonder that the standard of living of Canadians was consistently as much as 30% below the American. In fact, the *per capita* income in the poorest of the American states was said to be higher than the *per capita* income of the Canadian population as a whole. More trade barriers existed among the Canadian provinces than among the member countries of the European Union! But soon the work on the division of the economic powers was abandoned because of the prime minister's singular concentration on his main objective (which was fully consonant with the Maoist-Gramscian doctrine that notwithstanding Karl Marx, it was not the economic but the cultural superstructure on which the revolution would be built.)

Now consider the new preamble to the new Canadian Constitution and hark back to Elisabeth Mann Borgese's self-managing society. Not much, if anything, was left of the country's Judaeo-Christian heritage. *If self-managing Canadians could not be subject to higher authorities of any kind then it would also have to be reflected in the pivotal new Charter of Rights and Freedoms enacted in 1982.* And indeed, a definitive shift could be detected between the original Canadian Bill of Rights of 1960 and

Prime Minister Trudeau's new Charter. In their respective preambles, both instruments professed that Canada was "founded upon principles that acknowledge/recognize the supremacy of God," but in 1960 the human rights and fundamental freedoms embodied in the Bill were clearly said to have *derived* from the governing principles.

Not so in 1982, where there was a strange disjunct between the words of the preamble and the rights and freedoms thereafter enumerated. The 1982 Charter, having started with the words "Whereas Canada is founded upon principles that recognize the supremacy of God and the rule of law" then jumps straight into the first section of the instrument, as follows: "The Canadian Charter of Rights and Freedoms guarantees the rights and freedoms set out in it subject only to such reasonable limits prescribed by law as can be demonstrably justified in a free and democratic society." *But no linkage.* The preamble hangs suspended in mid-air. An empty slogan. And in fact a contradiction, if one thought about it. No mention of the rights and freedoms being derivative in any way, and any limits on them were likewise not subject to external norms of any kind. What limits there might be, would be purely a function of fickle public (or judicial) opinion. Elisabeth Mann Borgese would have been happy.

Not surprisingly a rejection of the Godhead as an external authority, in favour of self-management, would soon go hand in hand with a rejection of external norms of any kind, at least with respect to both public and private morality. This lack of recognition of external—let alone higher—norms could not have been more dramatically shown than by a 2005 Supreme Court decision. The court ruled that the most egregious and disgusting group sex activities performed in swingers' clubs could not be regulated by any law, civil or criminal, unless they directly affected and caused demonstrable harm to others, which, in this case, the Court said, they did not, because they were taking place behind closed doors. And the harm the participants were inflicting upon themselves was irrelevant as well. (However, this did not prevent the state from preventing Canadians from harming themselves when it came to smoking; driving cars without wearing seat belts; sailing in boats without wearing flotation vests; and riding bicycles without wearing headgear.) That the broader public knew about those activities and that society at large could be harmed by the mere fact of public knowledge that such activities were taking place with impunity, was not a consideration either. Except that it was encouraging that five years later the Attorney General of British Columbia did argue in court that polygamy should not be legalized because such a decision would "harm the moral fabric and democratic essence of society."

The important thing to understand here is that when the Court applied the harmfulness test it also decided that *the activities under scrutiny were not subject to any community standards of decency and morality.* One could not help but wonder whether one of the reasons for the decision was that, in a disintegrating society, there was no longer a community out there whose standards *could* be gauged. But of norms of rightness and wrongness in the light of "principles recognizing the supremacy of God"—and thus the laws of God or even natural law or, for that matter, the laws of nature—nary a word. In a way, the self-managing society had lost control of itself!

Representative democracy was bound to be the next casualty. Thus the most telling thing about the new Canadian Constitution was the way it took away the authority of Parliament, except for a limited recognition and protection of parliamentary sovereignty by virtue of a last-minute addition of a Notwithstanding Clause, which permitted legislatures to set aside or override court decisions that would otherwise be binding on the legislative branch. But such measures would only be valid for a maximum of five years, and the *status quo* would be automatically reinstated, unless the clause was once again and expressly invoked. In practice it turned out that there was hardly a politician in the land who had the courage to have recourse to the Notwithstanding Clause, thereby signifying a *de facto* acceptance of the abandonment of the sovereignty of a democratically elected parliament. Regrettably, under the tutelage of the European Union and the European Human Rights Court, Britain (the cradle of the Westminster model of parliamentary government) was going the same way. Canada is a rare example of a country where a political and cultural transformationist actually succeeded in achieving fundamental changes, thanks to a legislative instrument he managed to ram through not only the Canadian but also the British Parliament, as we shall see later in this saga. Given the division of powers in the United States, it was less likely that Barack Obama would manage to do the same. Through time the Charter would become Canada's primary and most potent instrument in the hands of the molders and the shapers.

What can happen when parliaments deliberately deprive themselves of some of their most fundamental responsibilities? In Canada, legislators of all parties were quite happy to have an abortion system not subject to any rules or regulations of any kind, though satisfied that taxpayers, through the public health system, should foot the cost of carrying out those 'procedures.' Even if they wanted to impose restrictions on the abortion industry, the Charter would make it impossible. In fact the legislators soon gave up because, when they were invited by the Supreme Court to define and write the rules governing the institution of marriage (as distinct from civil unions) parliament declined to do so. In 1984 my oldest childhood friend (a friendship dating to our sojourn in Durban, back in South Africa, in the early 1940s) delivered the Frederick William Atherton Lecture at Harvard, where he contended that "the supremacy of parliament is perhaps the most crucial element of the Westminster system of government... Parliament was vested with supremacy solely to shield and promote the fundamental rights and freedoms of those whom it represented. In its proper historical context, therefore, parliamentary sovereignty *is* the Bill of Rights in the Westminster system of government." (That was, of course, before the British legislators too reneged on their most fundamental privileges and responsibilities.)

By contrast, the American people were still relatively fortunate in their enjoyment of representative democracy and *responsible* government. Richard C. Halverson, Chaplain to the United States Senate, had written a book titled *No Greater Power*. The foreword came from the Reverend Billy Graham. About the rights of a sovereign people, a people "endowed by the Creator with certain unalienable rights", Halverson said: "Take Creator God out of the formula, and the whole structure collapses." Many commentators would agree with the British political theorist John Dunn's greatly understated conclusion, namely, that "with the disappearance of a determinate external locus of authority conceptually impervious to human whim... claims of purely individual right become markedly less imposing." More than just an echo of something British Prime Minister Margaret Thatcher wrote in her foreword to a book titled *Christianity and Conservatism*: "Not for 2000 years has it been possible for society to exclude or eliminate Christ from its social or political life without a terrible social or political consequence."

As for the Creator being effectively excluded from constitutions, Europe was in the same boat. Thus Pope Benedict was acutely aware that "in the debate about the preamble to the European Constitution" the Constitution omitted any reference to either God or "the Christian roots of Europe." He went so far as to make a most revealing assertion, namely, that "the Muslims... feel threatened, not by the foundations of our Christian morality, *but by the cynicism of a secularized culture that denies its own foundations.*" (Emphasis added.) In other words, Muslims felt unsafe under regimes that were traitors to their own spiritual heritage! The Pope wondered whether any culture could even lay claim to being a culture if "it does not need any roots outside itself." Almost in desperation, it seemed, he called upon Europeans to at least try to live *as if God existed.* This by itself was an astonishing turn of phrase because previously, the Europeans of the Enlightenment had boasted of their own self-made norms *etsi Deus non daretur* (even if God did not exist). But that, at least, still implied an acceptance of the reality of the Godhead, whereas Pope Benedict's proposal looked like an acceptance of a regrettable fact: a congenital and fundamental European atheism. No wonder that elsewhere he should have observed laconically that "the world is what it is." Only after I had written these words did I discover that Kenneth Hamilton had said something very similar in 1965, in his *Revolt Against Heaven,* in a final chapter devoted to the theology of Dietrich Bonhoeffer: "To live in the world *etsi Deus non daretur* was not to be without theological orientation. It included an understanding," said Hamilton, "of what it was to live 'before God' even while living 'without God.'" In other words, there was a big difference between living *as if God existed*, and living in accordance with self-made norms but on the implied assumption that God did exist.

145

Towards the end of this book we shall be looking at the perennial contest between immanentists and transcendentalists. Here, with respect to the Canadian and the European refusals (in John Dunn's words) to submit to any "determinate external locus of authority"—in the Canadian case not even communal standards of decency—we have an excellent example of how a rejection of the transcendent already manifested itself on different levels of society.

A spirit of rebelliousness against higher authorities was, of course, not new under the sun. To speak only of rebellions was one thing—if only because they mostly came and went—but a more congenial and ingrained rebelliousness quite another, because there was something more permanent, more endemic, about it. The French Revolution was the supreme historical example of atheistic rebellious man. Modern fascism itself, argued the American writer Gene Veith—in a book by that title—was a "resistance to transcendence." In her analysis titled *The Gnostic Gospels*, Elaine Pagels told of how Clement, the Bishop of Rome, complained about the willfulness and the rebelliousness of the Gnostic heretics against the laws and the rule of God. One might well speculate whether the principal father of the new Canadian constitution, Pierre Elliott Trudeau, sought to put into place an instrument which largely reflected his own self-willed rebelliousness against authority of any kind; something that had already manifested itself in his earliest years.

Indeed, it was generally accepted that by and large, Trudeau was a law unto himself. With Voegelin, one might well ask what kind of 'pneumopathology' would have been at work in this case. In his seminal *Federalism and the French Canadians*, Trudeau alluded to the way the journal he and like-minded colleagues had founded—with its telling title of *Cité Libre*—practised "systematic scepticism in the face of established dogmatism, and having practised it as regards most of our traditional institutions, we should hardly be surprised if a new generation should turn it against one of the establishments we ourselves have spared: the Canadian state." *Cité Libre,* he claimed, "became a rallying point for progressive action and writing" as a result of which "bossism collapsed, blind traditionalism crumbled, the Church was challenged, new forces were unleashed...

The dogmatism of Church and State, of tradition, of the nation had been defeated," and most interestingly (shades of Lenin), "The Family itself had lost its power over young men and young women..." "In 1960," he added, "everything was becoming possible in Quebec, even revolution."

As for that other cultural revolutionist, Chairman Mao, Charles E. Lindblom (who taught political science and economics at Yale) recounted that Mao too was determined that men had to be "made less responsive to the appeals of family, union, church, employer, landlord and other associations." He too, like Lenin before him, was noticeably exercised by the power of religion, hence the first cultural revolutionary slogan of May 1919: "Down with Confucius!" Only in 2011 were the Chinese authorities bold enough to erect a 31-foot bronze statue of Confucius on the east side of Tiananmen Square, thereby greatly upsetting the Maoists. The revolution, according to Mao, demanded the dismantling of the "superstructure" of "the ensemble of ideas, habits, customs and behavior—philosophical, legal, religious, political, artistic, literary—in any given society, and the institutions through which they function." And so he made fun of the gods, asking the peasants: "Will you believe in the gods or in the peasant association?" They knit their brows, he said, when they imagine "it all depends on the will of Heaven and think... Who knows if Heaven wills it or not?" Trudeau's version of the same sentiment was his excoriation of people who, as he wrote contemptuously, "...believed that authority might well be left to descend from God in God's good time and God's good way."

Obama's mentor, Alinsky, had a more oblique way of commending the same kind of rebelliousness, when he wrote: "Lest we forget at least an over-the-shoulder acknowledgement to the very first radical: from our legends, mythology, and history... the first radical known to man who rebelled against the establishment and did it so effectively that he at least won his own kingdom - Lucifer."

There were other notable parallels in the respective lives of Mao and Trudeau. Like Trudeau's father, Mao's father, according to Alain Bouc, "had gradually become rich." In other words, they had grown up

147

privileged. Like the young Trudeau, whose "adolescent combativeness had pushed back at ecclesiastical as well as every other kind of authority", the young Mao too stood out on account of his youthful obstreperousness and lack of respect for authority: "Even in primary school, say the old peasants of Shaoshan who knew him, he would refuse to stand when reciting his lessons. 'Why,' he would ask the old master, 'must I stand up if you are sitting down?'" Towards the end of this book, and as I have already suggested, we shall have to address the question of *just what kinds of people* are behind particular ways of thinking and acting. It is not an idle question.

Equally noteworthy was how Trudeau based his initial popularity on an omnibus law reform bill (already mentioned in a previous chapter) whose main purpose was to promote easier divorce, legalize abortion, and decriminalize sodomy. He was commended in the House of Commons for having gone beyond the recommendations of a parliamentary committee by adding "the marriage breakdown concept to the grounds for divorce" and was profusely thanked by a member of parliament who wanted to "compliment the Minister of Justice, a member of the swinging set, if I may say so, for bringing in the legislation." Mao Tse-tung too kicked off his own political career in not dissimilar fashion, when, soon after his December 1949 trip to Moscow to sign a friendship treaty, he initiated a marriage law that was revolutionary at the time when it "gave women legal equality and ended their enslavement of thousands of years." Biographers Clarkson and McCall described the omnibus law reform move as "the breakthrough that marked Trudeau's public emergence as the purveyor of the new" and that "it had an electrifying effect on the public imagination... Here was a man who was willing to declare himself in opposition to the established order" and that Canada need no longer be "a museum of outmoded ideas." Hail to rebelliousness! With respect to women's rights, a not dissimilar tactic came from an electioneering Barack Obama, when he promised Planned Parenthood that the very first legislative measure he would want to sign if elected president, would be designed to override the right of any American state to place restrictions on abortion. In 2012 he even attempted to force Catholic institutions to supply their employees, through insurance not only with contraceptive but also abortion-inducing "health care" products.

It did not take long before my interest in these matters began to focus on Trudeau's determination to give Canadians a new Constitution, given that front and foremost was a plan to entrench a Charter of Rights and Freedoms in such a way that henceforth—and for a variety of reasons—the Constitution would be practically unamendable in respect of anything that was remotely contentious and of general application across Canada. What was going on?

Even so it would take quite a while to realize that one of the principal preoccupations, a priority, of the Canadian shapers of 'man and his world'—and a supreme example of how process could be exploited—would be the constitutional escapade. In fact, here was an instance where process itself could be shaped, quite apart from the shaping that process, in turn, could be counted upon to achieve. In the end the resulting transformations were nothing but profound. And this was one case where it would be possible to point to real-world outcomes, as distinct from indulging in generalizations, misgivings and prognostications.

The shapers were at it once again. Just ten years after the constitutional exercise, a Canadian law professor was to write a book titled *Most Dangerous Branch: How the Supreme Court of Canada Has Undermined Our Law and Our Democracy*. And in a study of "The Supreme Court as the Vanguard of the Intelligentsia: The Charter Movement as Postmaterialist Politics" two Calgary-based professors observed that:

> ...the achievement of true democracy will first require a period of purification through social reconstruction by a vanguard of purifiers... Willing to abandon democracy now in the name of more perfect democracy in the future, the modern transformatory project can succeed only by setting aside the constitutionalist ideal of limited government... Charter victories become political resources to shape public opinion.

They could not have said it better. Others had finally cottoned on to the peculiar interests and accomplishments of the shapers, molders and conditioners. In February 2004 the following lament surfaced in the *Ottawa Citizen*:

> In his recently published book... Canadian law professor Robert Martin argues that judges make social policy and legislators fear challenging them. Canada's top court is so highly politicized, says Martin, who teaches constitutional law at the University of Western Ontario, that it has abandoned legal principles in making its decisions, preferring instead to decide matters—such as the 1995 decision to unilaterally add homosexuals to the list of protected classes contained in the Charter—on the basis of "values" that reflect the judges' personal preferences. Such activism not only usurps the tradition of parliamentary supremacy, but offends fundamental principles of democracy since the judges were never elected to make social policy. As Martin states: 'Canada may be the first country in the world to have experienced a judicial coup d'etat.'

By 2015 the Court had decreed alarming Charter-dictated changes not only in the law governing contracts but also in the country's labour laws. In the latter case (thanks to Madam Justice Rosalie Abella, who wrote the judgment for the Court, and who we shall meet again) governments could no longer prohibit public servants from going on strike. One wondered about the possible impact if the group in question were also responsible for maintaining essential services. A fundamental Court-dictated change in the laws of contract prompted a legal scholar to observe that "law is settled rules. Its value is letting us know where we stand... But we need to know what the law is before we act." Out of the window—it would appear—went the age-old principle of *acta sunt servanda* (contracts have to be honoured). The need for stability is behind the fact that courts generally respect judicial precedents, but in February 2015 yet another legal scholar observed that "recent decisions of the Supreme Court have shown a remarkable disregard for precedent. The law is obviously not unchanging, but unjustified departure from precedent risks undermining the Court's role as an arbiter. In each case, we can ask: Is this disregard justified?" If that was the only thing that was being undermined in the Canadian polity!

The law, and the judicial system, are supposed to be a stabilizing force in society, but what about the role of a country's constitution? I suppose my interest was also aroused by the fact that the poet and teacher F.R. Scott (who had taught Trudeau "everything I know") not only fingered the law as a primary tool for transforming society, but said the same with respect to constitutions. *But, surely, constitutions are not normally—if ever—written for the purpose of transforming societies! Rather, are they not written for the purpose of stabilizing societies?*

In short, and particularly when I too was involved in the process, the whole Charter business was both troublesome and troubling. I had come from a country where ideological obsessions led to abuses of the rule of law, and where only a judiciary schooled and rooted in the fundamental principles of the common law was able to stand up to the ideologues, until, eventually, to overcome the judicial obstacles, the government literally packed the highest court of the land with new and sympathetic judges. The debates in the Canadian Parliament on the new Constitution had already reached a late stage so that there was a sense of urgency with which I sat down to write a long and closely argued quasi-legal opinion. Near us lived a senior member of the caucus of the official 'Conservative' opposition party in the House of Commons (whom I had never met before, nor would meet afterwards) and in whose mailbox I then dropped the document. The question, I wrote, was "whether the Charter is calculated to override, replace or remove such rights and freedoms that exist or may exist in the Dominion of Canada, including the vast body of rights and freedoms which constitute the unwritten part of the existing Canadian constitution. On the face of it, the Joint Resolution purports not to infringe on such other rights and freedoms..."

This is not the place to revisit the document, given its length and complexity, but looking it over after so many years, I may be excused for still being struck by its cogency. Yet that was not enough. I had to seize on a particular interest to be able to gain sufficient traction—abstractions are never very useful—having already drawn attention to the fact that the representatives of the native peoples of Canada were not persuaded that the stated guarantees in the proposed constitution would safeguard their own pre-existing entitlements, and in that case the government was quite willing to add to a new proposed section in an explicit recognition of Indian rights. My wife and I had been active in the pro-life movement and I knew that the member of parliament to whom I gave my statement was also strongly pro-life. Why the pro-life element was relevant is explained by the following account.

And so I wrote another memorandum (also dropped in the neighbour's mailbox) and perhaps too dramatically titled *A last warning*; a warning that "the proposed changes may be calculated to (i) deny the sovereignty of parliament; (ii) extinguish or disable important unwritten parts of the Canadian constitution; (iii) remove the historical basis upon which the liberties and the fundamental rights of Canadians have rested, and (iv) open up the way for further fundamental changes over which neither the people nor the Parliament of Canada may have any control."

Following several related arguments, the document observed that:

> ...the Charter of Rights would give guidance to the Courts as well... The first thing that must be grasped... is that in the new regime proposed for Canada, the freedoms and rights of Canadians will be almost wholly related to their status as *citizens*, no longer their status as persons, in the sense that their fundamental rights and freedoms will flow from an instrument of state. The moment when freedoms and rights are rooted in a formal act of State, they become creatures of *public law*...

The document also pointed to the offered guarantee that nothing in the Charter would be construed as denying any rights or freedoms that may exist in Canada, but this, I argued, was misleading for a number of reasons, one of which was that "it only promises not to deny the *existence* of other rights and freedoms, but in so doing, does not guarantee that those other rights and freedoms will be able to compete with the rights and freedoms contained within the Charter." Rights were always in competition with one another. And in this regard I mentioned a last-minute provision slipped into the wording, namely, that "the Constitution of Canada is the supreme law of Canada, and any law that is inconsistent with the provisions of the Constitution is... of no force and effect." I also remarked that other constitutions contained similar provisions but that in the United States, for example, "the supremacy of the Constitution is coupled with the safeguard of a rigid division of powers; in Canada... the effective power will lie with the Executive, the bureaucracy and the Courts, and they will be armed with a supreme law, *including* the Charter."

Besides, the 1960 Canadian Bill of Rights had only been concerned with *procedural* safeguards, meaning that people could not be deprived of their rights *"except by due process of law."* (Emphases added.) This encompassed the ancient principles or rules of natural justice, including the age-old and tried judiciary rules of evidence and procedure. Instead, the new Charter used strange language. It stipulated that nobody could be deprived of the enumerated rights *"except in accordance with the principles of fundamental justice."* (Emphases added.) Neither the concept of "fundamental justice" nor its possible sources was explained, let alone defined. One of the problems I foresaw was that this new and novel provision might be construed, not in a procedural way, but in a substantive way, particularly when the Charter were to lead to the creation of new "positive" rights. So should one be surprised that eventually Canada's numerous human rights tribunals would function without being held, in any way, even to the (procedural) rules of natural justice? In South African parlance, one could well say that one could drive the proverbial oxwagon through the new instrument of law.

Finally, the legal opinion reached my main objective:

> Although freedom is indivisible, certain rights are more important than others. They are the ones that are

fundamental to a free society, more particularly a society that places first and foremost the inherent dignity of individuals as persons, and that values the capacity of persons to assert their individuality and their privacy *against* the State. The inviolability of honestly acquired property is such a necessary personal interest; even the word itself conveys a sense of distinctiveness and uniqueness. Another basic freedom, is the freedom to live. This freedom is also one of the most fundamental reasons for the legitimacy of the State, even a State which may not acknowledge the authority of a Creator of life. The primary purpose of the community, as State, is to protect those who are weak and defenceless, including the 'widows and the orphans' and especially the future generation - the children. It is of the *essence* of the State that it shall be the protector of people, of those who cannot protect themselves. A State which fails to fulfill *this* function is not worthy of survival, it is illegitimate. And a State which voluntarily *relinquishes* this duty does not deserve to endure, let alone prosper. We made the point, at the beginning, that the issues raised in this document are of general application and that they may affect any number of interests.

"But we have at least one major interest at heart, and that is the so-called right to life. If the Canadian Parliament relinquishes its future *ability* to protect the unborn, it will have abandoned the one function without which the State of Canada cannot uphold its dignity. Legal opinions differ on the important question as to whether the Charter is 'neutral' in this regard, and whether Parliament may be disabled from preventing the gross abuses that have been invited by the enactment of the omnibus amendments to the Criminal Code, in 1969. It is not acceptable that there should be any doubt whatsoever about the future freedom of the Canadian Parliament to make amends for the misdeed of 1969, and if there should be room even for only *one* amendment, the purpose of this document is to prevail upon our elected representatives to include a categorical affirmation of this *prerogative* in any new Constitution.

In the concluding paragraph of the document I even raised the question "whether our elected representatives are *entitled* to relinquish their fundamental responsibilities to the people."

----

On April 4, 1990 the Belgian parliament declared King Baudouin "unable to reign," because he refused to give Royal Assent to the abortion laws approved by the Belgian parliament. The next day, after the bill had become law, the king was reinstated. He had effectively abdicated for one day.

> *To His Excellency the Ambassador*
> *Embassy of Belgium, Ottawa:*
>
> *I should deem it a singular favour if you could, at your convenience, convey to His Majesty, the King of the Belgians, the heartfelt felicitations and admiration of my family. This refers to His Majesty's act of abdication on a matter of conscience and principle. In this regard His Majesty expressed the highest duty of a Head of State, and of all government, namely, to guard the interests of the weak and the defenceless. This was an act of legitimization of the state for which all citizens must be deeply grateful. If ever there was a doubt about the circumstances surrounding the abdication of His Majesty's predecessor (and I express no judgment) the recent action of your King confers honour on the people of your country.*
>
> *Yours sincerely,*
> *Dirk J. de Vos*

## Cobblestones

*Cabinet du Roi*

*I have the honour to acknowledge your letter addressed to H.M.
the King concerning the respect for human life. The King greatly
valued the feelings you expressed to him and has instructed me to
convey to you his thanks and appreciation.*

*Yours sincerely,*
*J. van Ypersele*
*Chef du Cabinet of the King of the Belgians*

––––––––––

On November 18, 1981 the government gave notice of a motion covering
the final version of the new Constitution. It took special care to guarantee
that nothing in the new instrument "would abrogate or derogate from
any right, privilege or obligation with respect to the English and French
languages." It took special care to enunciate a similar guarantee with
respect to "aboriginal, treaty or other rights and freedoms that pertain to
the aboriginal peoples of Canada." Nor would anything in the constitution be construed as abrogating from "any rights or privileges... in respect
of denominational, separate or dissentient schools." *But the government
summarily rejected an amendment that would merely have preserved, for the
future, and without prejudging the issue, the prerogative of parliament to
address a matter of life and death; the life and death of a child yet to be born.*

On November 27, 1981 David Crombie, the diminutive Member of
Parliament for Rosedale (for whom my wife worked when he was first
elected to parliament after a remarkable stint as the mayor of the city of
Toronto) stood up and said:

"Mr. Speaker, I would like to propose and speak to the following
motion: That the proposed Constitution Act 1981 be amended by adding
after Clause 31 of Part 1 the following new clause:

*32. Nothing in this charter affects the authority of Parliament to legislate in respect of abortion."*

In vain did Crombie reiterate that nothing in the amendment was intended, or could be construed, as an attempt to prejudge the issue. Whereupon, the Right Hon. P.E. Trudeau (Prime Minister) rose to oppose the motion, and gave the *false* assurance, in the course of a lengthy discourse, that "under the constitution the House retains the right to amend the Criminal Code, which is the statute affecting the issue of abortion." Another member of parliament drew attention to the fact that on April 23, 1981 (*little more than a week after I dropped my second memorandum in a neighbourly mailbox*) a similar motion had been put forward and was lost by a vote of 175 to 93.

And so the official minutes of parliament recorded that "The House divided on the amendment (Mr Crombie) which was negatived on the following division: YEAS: 61, NAYS: 129."

The die was cast. November 27, 1981 would forever be marked as a day of infamy in the history of the Canadian polity. And not only of infamy, but of betrayal.

Not prepared to give up, I then incorporated the gist of my previous legal opinions in a single document and made my way to the United Kingdom, on my own, where I met with the leadership of the British pro-life movement. They, in turn, undertook to alert British politicians and even found the most unlikely of allies in the far-left and radical Mr Anthony Wedgwood Benn because at least Mr Benn, they said, believed in representative democracy! I thought there was one last chance to put a spoke in the wheel of the Canadian Charter of Rights and Freedoms, if only on behalf of the unborn, on the argument that it would be *ultra vires*—beyond the competency of—the Parliament at Westminster to create another constitution under the Westminster form of representative government for a parliament that would not only not be sovereign, but by not being sovereign, was antithetical to the most basic principle of representative democracy. To reduce the argument to the absurd, one might as well ask whether Westminster would have the competency to convert Canada into a one-man dictatorship, or even to convert the government of the United Kingdom itself into a dictatorship. In other words, there was one basic and inherent constraint on a Westminster form of government that even a sovereign parliament such as the one of Great Britain did not, by definition, have the power to vitiate. At that time, in Britain even the highest court of the land, the Judicial Committee of Her Majesty's Privy Council, remained an integral part of the parliament and the government of the United Kingdom. Before the British parliament was to yield much of its sovereignty to instruments of the European Union, the country was not ruled by judges, and least of all by judges enjoying legislative power, as they would henceforth do in Canada.

Not even Magna Carta was entrenched in the (unwritten) British Constitution. Prime Minister Margaret Thatcher was said to have been furious at the way the patriation of the Constitution was being used to piggy-back Trudeau's Charter. This was confirmed again when, in April 2012, Canadians were celebrating the 30th anniversary of the event, and when it was recalled that in one of her first speeches after she had taken office, Mrs. Thatcher had explained that her government was determined "to return to one of the first principles which have traditionally governed our political life… The paramountcy of parliament for the protection of fundamental rights." According to the historian Frédéric Bastien, in his book *The Battle of London: Trudeau, Thatcher and the Fight for Canada's Constitution*, Mrs Thatcher exclaimed: "But now you want a Westminster Parliament to pass a Bill of Rights. Someone is certain to ask why the Canadian Parliament could not pass the Bill of Rights for themselves once the Constitution has been patriated." In an earlier chapter I gave the most likely reason for Trudeau's insistence that Westminster should legislate his Charter, thereby presenting Canadians with a *fait accompli*. A whiff here of an undemocratic *coup d'etat*? And yes, indeed—according to Bastien—the British High Commissioner, Sir John Ford, confirmed that once the patriated Constitution was in Canadian hands, so to speak, "it would be very difficult to secure the adoption of a Bill of Rights."

Of course there was no guarantee that Canadian parliamentarians would have the intestinal fortitude to grapple with questions related to even one of the most fundamental rights, namely, that of the unborn, even after the Supreme Court virtually invited them to deal with the horror of third-trimester abortions. And thus, in the same month of April, 2012, all three political parties vigorously opposed a private member's motion for a parliamentary committee to examine the question of whether an unborn child was a human being. A newspaper reported that the motion had "caused a furor in the House." The same failure occurred when parliamentarians did not respond when the Supreme Court confirmed their prerogative to define the fundamental institution of marriage.

No wonder, before long the Canadian Supreme Court started to 'read into' the Charter of Rights and Freedoms *provisions that the Canadian parliament itself had expressly excluded.* In effect, the Canadian courts were telling parliament what it ought to have done and also, on more than one occasion, were giving it orders as to what it should be doing in the future, even to the extent of imposing time limits. A friend of mine had gone to see British parliamentarian Enoch Powell at his home in London, and at my request made use of the opportunity to test my thesis on Powell, who immediately saw the point and agreed that the argument was well-founded. The Canadian Charter of Rights and Freedoms, inasmuch as it deprived the Canadian Parliament of its sovereignty, would, if enacted by the parliament of the United Kingdom, be *ultra vires* that parliament. The new Canadian Constitution would be unlawful, and a government governing by virtue of it, illegitimate. It could, of course, govern by force, or sadly, thanks to public apathy. As the saying goes, in the end we get the governments we deserve. Lawless governments for lawless or apathetic people.

And so there unfolded in the British House of Commons the same debate we had seen in the Canadian House of Commons, as well as in the course of the previous and exhaustive proceedings of a joint House of Commons and Senate Committee. A British member of parliament by the name of Dale Campbell-Savours moved an identical motion to the one that had been put forward in Canada, to the effect that nothing in the new Canadian Constitution would "affect the authority of Parliament to legislate in respect of abortion." The wording suggested that he must have had access to the documents I had submitted to the leadership of the British pro-life movement. (In his dogged determination, Campbell-Savours even proposed two additional motions related to a section that provided for a First Ministers Conference to be held in Canada within one year after the Charter came into effect, to discuss the rights of the aboriginal peoples, and he wanted a provision that the rights of the unborn child would be included in the same conference agenda.) The British debate, in both quality and intensity, stood head and shoulders above the comparable proceedings in the Canadian legislature. In the end it became so urgent that Mr Campbell-Savours, showing extraordinary resilience and persistence, was expelled from the House. To his eternal credit. In the preceding Canadian debates no protagonist had even come close to being expelled from the House of Commons.

On the more general principle of the abandonment of parliamentary sovereignty in Canada, the talented Mr Enoch Powell argued both lengthily and cogently. He went on to claim that "as we go through the Bill, my fear deepens that we are engaged, largely innocently, in perpetrating a fraud. The fraud consists in persuading large numbers of people and interests in Canada that our passing this Bill will entrench—whatever meaning may be attached to that—certain rights on their part and will entrench certain portions of the future constitution... The case against the Bill is that it is participation in a deceit." In fact, a triple deception was in the making, except that no cock was on hand to crow twice.

First, there was the arguably false impression that the Canadian Constitution was actually being patriated (removed from British to Canadian jurisdiction) in the sense that no longer would the British parliament have the capacity to legislate for Canada. All the British legislation did was to undertake to *desist* from legislating for Canada in the future, when, as we know, *no parliament can bind a subsequent parliament*. In addition, well into the next century the founding province of Quebec—one of the two original partners of Confederation—had yet to sign on to the new Constitution, so that one had to wonder on what basis it would be functioning within the Canadian polity. Second, there was the pretense that the Canadian Parliament, in the words of the Canadian prime minister, would retain the prerogative to legislate on abortion under the rubric of the Criminal Code. And third, there was Mr Powell's well-argued contention that if Canadians thought their precious fundamental rights were actually protected, they were sorely mistaken. Should it therefore have been cause for astonishment that notwithstanding the Charter of Rights and Freedoms, Canada's human rights tribunals would soon be in a position, with apparent impunity, to ride roughshod over the rights and freedoms of Canadian individuals who dared to offend the country's group-based political correctnesses? Eventually this would also become a problem in Britain itself. And since the British Parliament had so conspired with the Canadian in betraying the interests of the unborn, this might well be regarded as a case of divine justice.

If the people behind the Charter had any sense, and perhaps *bona fides*, they might have paid attention to Chapter 106 of the 1968 report of the Ontario Royal Commission of Inquiry into Civil Rights, headed by former Chief Justice J.C. McRuer. It dealt at length with "The Appropriate Blending of Parliamentary and Judicial Supremacy in the Constitution: The Need for Integration and Completeness." There the purpose and the proper place of a limited and not too strongly entrenched code of human rights under a Westminster system of representative government was incisively, exhaustively, and wisely analyzed. The report noted that the Trudeau cohorts were already aiming at a wide-ranging and strongly entrenched Charter of Human Rights, and had, *inter alia*, in favouring some features of the American model with its strong Supreme Court, failed to acknowledge the important differences between the respective systems of government. Even today the protagonists of expanded codes are given to copying or importing various international codes and treaties, but as Mr Justice McRuer pointed out, those international codes and treaties are not embedded in any system of representative democracy with its peculiar checks and balances and safeguards, and therefore those codifiers had no choice but to resort to courts and judicial instruments for their implementation and enforcement and even expansion. This was something the Canadian political system did not need.

Just as my Dutch forefathers witnessed the destruction of the Roman-Dutch system of common law by the imposition of Napoleon's *Code Civil*, the same straitjacketed and supremely humanist French Revolutionary influence extended into Canada, via Quebec. And with the practical difficulties built into the Canadian constitutional amending formula, Canadians would be locked, seemingly forever, in their own transformative straitjacket. 'Straitjacketed' struck me as singularly apposite in an Ottawa where the main parliamentary and bureaucratic apparatuses sat under green copper-clad roofs, just as they did in Quebec, reminiscent of the custom in my native South Africa where green roofs were reserved for institutions housing the mentally disturbed. The pity was that in the event the leaders of the New South Africa decided to copy the Canadian Charter of Rights and Freedoms in their own Constitution, thanks to the ministrations—heavily underwritten by Canadian taxpayers—of phalanxes of Canadian advisers and consultants, convinced, as always, that Canadian models are invariably models for the rest of the world.

In one respect the South Africans were ahead of the Canadians, however, when they formally added sexual orientation to the forbidden forms of discrimination, whereas Canadian homosexuals had to wait for their Supreme Court to read a similar provision into the Canadian instrument. As I have already mentioned, when it came to same-sex 'marriages', with the Supreme Court actually giving the Canadian Parliament a chance to define marriage in the conventional way, the legislators once again shirked the opportunity, and indeed responsibility, because care had been taken to ensure that a sufficient number of members of parliament were not allowed by their party leaders to cast a free vote. *Evidently a Charter of Rights and Freedoms did not include a right for the people's own representatives to vote freely, not even on a matter of conscience,* as this vote was supposed to be! Such a freedom was actually a foundational feature of the kind of representative democracy Mr Justice McRuer described. So much therefore too for freedom of conscience in a country whose most recent prime minister proclaimed it "the conscience of the world."

They say the gods laugh, but I'm not so sure. The Canadian Charter experience would provide yet another invaluable backdrop to my still

inchoate understanding of the philosophical and operational characteristics of a determined and single minded man- and world-transformative politics.

As for the anatomy of the transformationist, the concluding chapters
of this memoir go into these matters in greater depth, but this is one
chapter where a brief summary may be in order. From what we've seen so
far, the mind of the transformationist reveals:

1. An ardent shaper of people (collectively and individually) and
   exploiter of processes
2. Not only a totalist, but an intolerant enforcer
3. A congenitally rebellious spirit; and (concomitantly)
4. A denier of transcendent realities (and quite often, of the authority
   of the Godhead itself)

"Since Justin Trudeau became Liberal leader, there has been an unflinching belief among party supporters that the mission to redeem Canada and remake the country would, inevitably, have a happy ending."

John Ivison,
*The National Post*

# CHAPTER EIGHT
# GROUPS, GROUPISM,
# AND GROUPISTS

"The National Party is committed to the principle of group recognition. Own schools, own institutions with exclusive decision-making authority in respect of own affairs, and effective protection of commensurate group rights are the essential means by which the National Party wishes to ensure group security."

South African Minister of National Education
and future State President F.W. de Klerk

"The idea of a charter thus acquired politically significant backing from new political forces, organized on a group basis, whose political emergence was part of broader changes in Canadian society."

Royal Commission on the Economic Union and
Development Prospects for Canada

"...the groups now seek vigorous implementation tantalized by a legis-lative framework."

Rosalie S. Abella,
Ontario Law Reform Commission
and future Supreme Court Justice

Our job is making all groups who come to this country... feel at home... and be Canadians.

Conservative Prime Minister Stephen Harper

Imagine the wonderment, coming from the land of apartheid, where we even had Group Areas Acts reserving separate residential and creation areas for members of different groups, while certain jobs were reserved for members of yet another group—the white population—when I discovered that in Canada the rights of individuals were classified as civil liberties but that human rights were collective. *For all intents and purposes they were group rights.*[8]

That human rights were group rights would be made doubly clear by one Rosalie Silberman Abella, a future Supreme Court Justice—and still on the Supreme Court in 2015—writing on "Equality and Human Rights in Canada: Coping with the New Isms." In fact, a commentator on Abella's work insisted that "a distinction between civil liberties and human rights is critical..."

In a speech, Ms Abella explained that Canada differed from the United States, "whose individualism", she said, "promoted assimilation." Because Canada, from its beginning, allowed "two groups, the French and the English", to "remain distinct and unassimilated, and yet... of equal worth and entitlement," she said (albeit rather obscurely) "we in Canada have always conceded that *the right to integrate based on differences* has as much legal and political integrity as the right to assimilate." (Emphasis added.) "Those who assert that groups *and the individuals in them* have no right to a unique identity or to protection from enforced assimilation," she added, "are those who contradict history." (Emphases added.) *The South African doctrine of "separate but equal status" for "distinct groups" could not have been more effectively restated!* Even South Africa's ideological father of apartheid, Hendrik French Verwoerd, would have been jealous of Ms Abella's sophisticated formulation. None of the American melting pot for Canadians! Ms Abella could also have referred to yet another 'group', namely, the country's own little Inuit *bantustan* in the north, called Nunavut, that would have qualified for the vision of her South African forerunner.

---

8    In South Africa complications did arise when it became necessary to accommodate foreign businessmen who were not European, such as the Japanese. But not to be daunted, to enable them to stay in white hotels, they were given the temporary status of "honorary whites."

Except for a twist to Ms Abella's diagnosis: human rights based on one's membership of a group only came into play if, in practice, *somebody* decided that the group in question were (or had been, at some point in the past) victims of unequal or 'unjust' treatment. It did not seem to matter whether the disparity occurred in the present or in the past (or frankly, purely in people's minds). In some instances it could be the distant past. This was typically the case (and not only in Canada) with respect to many so-called affirmative action programs.

Was this any different from a reminder by Harry Ferns—a former communist infiltrator in the Canadian Department of External Affairs, before he recanted and accepted a professorship post in a British university—that "implicit in Marx's doctrines and analysis of society was the conclusion that suffering is unequally distributed" and that there were classes in society "which suffered from exploitation and oppression?" In Canada one merely needed to replace "class" by "group." Whether one had human rights depended on whether one's group was deemed to be under-privileged or oppressed (and that by itself was an arbitrary determination). Like new stars being formed all the time, new categories of victims were continually extruded by the Canadian psyche. Epitomized—albeit unknowingly—by the Human Rights Star featured in our Epilogue? Thus a critic, responding to Abella's philosophy, asked almost plaintively: "Are the rights of the victims and non-victims really any different? Should the basic conception of fairness involved in *women*'s access to jobs vary from the one involved in *men*'s access?"

If Ms Abella was convoluted, no such confusion was evident in the way the philosophy of Canada's Templeton Prize winner, Charles Taylor, was characterized. Some of his admirers attributed to Taylor a view that persons—individuals—derived their very identities from the groups to which they belonged, and that it was "essential to human *identity* that ones community be recognized both politically and socially." (Emphasis added.) This would certainly be in line with Abella's initial premise that membership and recognition of a group were essential elements in endow-ing an individual with an identity (besides, in her view, entitling him to specific human rights). One also inferred from these views that human identity was a function of *process;* a process of recognition. So, whether I had an identity depended on what other people thought of me and my group! Speaking for myself, I had always thought that my identity was very much a function of my character, my beliefs, my history, and above all, the character and history of my forefathers. Think too of the profound meaning of the identity of a committed Christian. What, if anything, was the identity of the Founder of the Christian faith, if it was not his Sonship of the Father? Would Ms Abella, albeit a Jewess, have rather seen his identity as a function of his membership of yet another group, namely, the Holy Trinity?

On the other hand, one must hasten to recognize that a reading of Taylor's monumental *Sources of the Self: The Making of the Modern Identity* showed a much more nuanced approach than some people thought, and we shall have to return to Taylor when, in the context of multiculturalism, we take a closer look at the source and essence of human identity. Yet, if Abella's vision had a distinct Marxist ring to it, one also learned that "the political has long been a central focus of activity for Taylor" and that his political instincts were markedly socialist. Unlike Prime Minister Trudeau and his acolytes—who abandoned the socialist NDP (New Democratic Party) with its poor election prospects, in order to rather use the Liberal Party as their operational base and vehicle—Taylor stuck with the NDP and in fact lost to Trudeau in the 1965 General Election in a Montreal riding. Another commonality between Abella and Taylor was the derogatory way she alluded to American individualism and Taylor's distinctly backhanded statement that "born-again Christians in the United States cannot help being somewhat influenced by expressive individualism."

How interesting, incidentally, was the fact that just like Trudeau's tactic of separating himself from a minority socialist party—and advising other socialist activists to do the same—and instead allying himself with an established national political party in order to have a practical chance of achieving radicalist objectives, so would Barack Obama's mentor, Saul Alinsky, confess in an interview, when he said: "Pragmatically, the only hope for genuine minority progress is to seek out allies within the majority *and to organize that majority itself* as part of a national movement for change." (Emphasis added.)

These very issues—issues of identity, intertwined with multiculturalism, human rights, and group rights (already so rampant in Canada)— would soon be front and centre not only in the United States but also in the European Community (and most acutely, in Britain, France and the Netherlands).[9] Although not far behind were countries like Sweden where a man committed mass murder to draw attention to the multiculturalist loss of the Swedish identity. (And naturally the Swedish establishment was most anxious to have him certified as insane, as the South Africans had done with Dr Verwoerd's assassin.) In Europe the problem was mostly associated with the Islamic incursions, growing more acute by the day, and not least of all on account of the high Muslim birth rates. Americans had their own problems with a large and fast growing Hispanic diaspora.

The South African ideological father of apartheid would have been delighted if he could have known that in 1992, in the Canadian province of Ontario, the (socialist) government asked all government board, agency and commission members to complete a survey obliging respondents to state whether they were a "First Nation person, Black, East Asian, South Asian, Southeast Asian, West Asian, Arab, white or other." Helpfully the survey guide advised: "If you were born in Canada, but are of Egyptian descent, you would select West Asian and Arab. If you are of European descent, but were born or brought up in the Middle East, you would select white." In 2008, in the capital city of Ottawa, one also saw how finely differentiated a group-based segmentation could become when the city's police force launched a program targeting "visible minority, aboriginal, female, gay, lesbian and transgendered recruits" respectively.

In South Africa the classifications never went beyond the four main racial groups, and within the black community, there was recognition of

---

9    In March 2015 The London Telegraph lamented that "Britain is indebted to the former equalities head for highlighting the mess in which multiculturalism has left us all." While back in Canada, in the same month, and in the same context, a major newspaper in the province of Quebec headlined, "Quebec's new identity battlefield."

a relatively limited number of differentiated tribal affiliations, and there were certain differences among their respective legal customs, so that, when I studied law, I also had to study so-called Native Law (discovering, to my astonishment, strong resemblances among the principles of Native Law and ancient Roman Law)! But tribal distinctions, of course, had nothing to do with race. Compared with these fine Ontarian distinctions, we never saw anything like that in the land of apartheid!

When societies start to disintegrate the process may be slow, but it could also be swift and shocking. One might claim that apartheid was a consciously disintegrationist tool, and that a similarly disintegrative group-based multiculturalism had also become a hallmark of the 'Canadian condition', but that in the United States the country was drifting into a problem it could have foreseen but had neither desired nor planned. There, matters were complicated by the fact that the Hispanic debacle also involved questions about the upholding of the rule of law in the face of illegal conduct on a quite massive scale.

Another big difference was that whereas in the United States 'cultural rights' were mostly asserted and exercised in the *private* domain, in Canada they were an integral part—indeed one of the underpinnings— of *public* policy. And (one should add) an active and potent political vote-gathering tool. In Gene Veith's words: "In the United States, (an) official tolerance allowed for a true cultural pluralism....making it a matter of private ties rather than public identity. Rights and privileges were given to individuals, not cultures." Whereas in Canada not only was a Canadian *Multiculturalism Act* proclaimed (along with a *Canadian Human Rights Act*) but an entire Multiculturalism and Citizenship Department followed in its wake. So much so that in 1988 an Australian advisory council observed that "the term 'multiculturalism' is a Canadian creation. Canadians are to enter the 21$^{st}$ century as the world's best prepared country, enjoying an in important advantage over her friends and competitors..."

The judicial foundation for these 'advances' in social engineering had already been laid by the Canadian Supreme Court in the 1986 *Oakes* case, when it was called upon to decide on the meaning of the values and principles of a "free and democratic society," a new criterion introduced into the country's Charter of Rights and Freedoms. Among the applicable values and principles (the court concluded) was "respect for culture and group identity," now constitutionally entrenched!

In 1992 two Canadian commentators enthused that the *Multiculturalism Act* was the world's first, and the creation of the afore-said government department "should add even more lustre to Canada's already solid credentials... Only the foolhardy or the blind dare to under-estimate its potential for *reshaping* our collective self-image." (Emphasis added.) The country's transformational objectives, one was given to understand, "relied on the creation of commissions, codes, and tribunals." Multiculturalism (groupism) was constitutionalized, said the author, in the full knowledge that "a constitution provides a blueprint for society in that it encodes dominant values and aspirations by establishing the rules by which the social order is governed." That the project was political was readily admitted by its Canadian apologists: "The political party in power views multiculturalism as critical for re-election… The politicization of ethnicity... has brought about a new multicultural order..."

By 2008 an editorial in the newspaper serving the capital city would boast:

> "As Canadians, it is revealing to see ourselves as others do. We look at racial and religious tensions in Europe—the burning cars, the crazed imams, the ghettos—and never really fear that such is our future too. Multiculturalism is already part of the fabric here, so much so that many Canadians don't really see it anymore... the truth is that this diversity looks good on us."

In the same year (and ever since then) even a supposedly Conservative government was not averse to treading the same path in the hope that the multi-ethnic voters of the cities would bolster its political fortunes. It made a deliberate decision to compete on the ethnic front with the main opposition party, which was boasting that, at election time, no fewer than one hundred of its members in parliament were actively cultivating the votes of distinct ethnic groups "on a daily basis." These groups, it was explained, always voted *en bloc*. A newspaper heading reported the matter as a "No-holds-barred fight for ethnic vote." Concurrently, at the provincial level, the government of Ontario began to experiment more purposefully, not only with Afro-centric education (as was already happening in the United States) but Afro-centric public schools.

A notable difference between the South African and Canadian versions of groupism was that the former was never unanimously supported by the white electorate (far from it) nor was it held out as a model for the rest of the world, and least of all was it earmarked for export to other countries. Not so in Canada. When the Canadian Parliament passed the *Multiculturalism Act not a single member voted against it.* Nor, incredibly, was a single voice raised against it in the preceding parliamentary committee hearings (at least according to an Ottawa newspaper). This meant, said the Multiculturalism Minister, "that Canada is in essence a microcosm of the world... The passage of this bill will send a signal to every corner of the globe..."

Would the Canadian experience—especially with the country's penchant for setting itself up as a model for the rest of the world—serve as an object lesson for Europeans and Americans alike? Was Canada proof of what might happen if these manifestations became not only socially and politically endemic but self-sustaining and self–perpetuating, as the American writer Jonathan Rauch predicted? This issue, I surmised, could yet be at the very core of the self-definitional problem in western societies. One only had to consider the degree to which some freedom-minded citizens of Quebec started to fret over new mandatory school curricula designed to ensure the "reasonable accommodation" of particular groups, notably Muslims and practising homosexuals. Reminiscent of the Obama administration's new health insurance mandates affecting Catholic institutions, Catholic schools in Quebec were not exempted either (whether public or private). In 2012 there were reports of Catholic parents in

Montreal driving their children a considerable distance across the border, every day, to attend school in upstate New York.

Would it thus not behoove Europeans and Americans to take note of the early warnings uttered, over the years, by their own prophets, and to revisit the arguments underpinning those prescient misgivings? In Britain, of course, Enoch Powell was crucified on account of his own utterances of so many years ago. A few voices were raised in Canada, but it was in the United States—as I would gradually discover—that the most incisive and insightful writing on the problem of multiculturalism and groupism was to be found.

Already, by the year 1994, Jonathan Rauch proclaimed that "Groups are us." He said that post-War political theorists of pluralism thought that "more groups equals more representation equals better democracy" but they had miscalculated in assuming that "the group-forming process was self-balancing and stable, as opposed to self-feeding and unstable... As more groups make more demands, and as even more hungry groups form to compete with all the other groups, the process begins to feed on itself and pick up momentum." Rauch called it a condition of "hyperpluralism." Another American voice was Gene E. Veith's commentary in *Postmodern Times*. Postmodern existentialism, unlike its predecessor, he said, taught that meaning is not created by the individual but by "*a social group and its language.*" (His emphasis.) Personal identity had become a social construct. The segmentation taking place in society was more than just a form or a sign of diversity. "People are finding their identities, not so much in themselves, nor in their families, nor in their communities or nation, but in the group that they belong to." (Not even in their ancestors?) When the segmentation appears in the political sphere, "it destroys a common ground for argument or persuasion." And when, lacking a "common philosophy and a common language", interest groups can no longer persuade one another or forge compromises. Instead "they can only exert power over each other. One wins, the other loses, and the battles are often ugly and ruthless." With the groups at one another's throats, a new form of class warfare erupts. Those who once demanded integrated schools, clamour instead for "African immersion schools." (Or Hispanic, for that matter? Or, already in parts of Europe, Muslim schools?)

These problems had been foreseen as early as in 1960 by the American political scientist, Sheldon S. Wolin, in his *Politics and Vision*. Even then Wolin had already noted the emergence of "'a group theory of politics'... In the words of one of the most influential of the group theorists, 'When the groups are adequately stated, everything is stated.'" "The chopping-up of political man," Wolin added, "is but part of a broader process which has been at work in political and social theory" (and we ourselves might justly add, not just in theory, but in Canadian and incipient American practice). This, Wolin argued, was a socially and politically disintegrative process. Groupists demanded specific functions from the state, and those functions in turn, said Wolin, were the "complement to a determinate number of human needs." And hence (as we might well note) the related emphasis on group-related and group-based human rights. There ensued, according to Wolin, "a picture of society as a series of tight little islands." He concluded his book with the following warning, in the form of a question: "Is it rather that the contemporary challenge is to recognize that totalitarianism has shown that societies react sharply to the disintegration wrought by the fetish of groupism; that they will resort to even the most extreme methods to re-assert the political in an age of fragmentation? If this should be the case, the task of non-totalitarian societies is to temper the excesses of pluralism."

Likewise did Allan Bloom, in his *Closing of the American Mind*, toll the same bell when he wrote: "...the blessing given the whole notion of cultural diversity in the United States by the culture movement has contributed to the intensification and legitimization of group politics, along with a corresponding decay of belief that the individual rights enunciated in the Declaration of Independence are anything more than dated rhetoric." And so did Michael Novak of the American Enterprise Institute (with whom I had the privilege of sharing the platform at a public symposium on the proper limits to the power of the state). "To secure human rights in the original sense," Novak wrote, "required government to protect and respect the private realm; to secure the new human rights will require government to intervene in the private realm and eventually to destroy it." He warned of developments that "may well dissolve the national sense of the common good by breeding interest groups attached to their own claims to goods, in a zero-sum competition for power and influence over state decision-making." Judging by the record of Canada's numerous human rights tribunals, both federal and provincial, this prospect would soon come to fruition just on the other side of 'the world's longest undefended border.'

Of course the Canadian example was of groupism with a friendly face, at least towards human rights claimants, but rarely if ever benevolent with respect to defendants' interests, for not only were Canada's numerous human rights tribunals not subject to the age-old and tried justice-promoting rules of evidence and procedure. On top of that, while the state covered complainants' expenses (however unjustified the complaint), defendants had to bear their own (even if they were acquitted), and many would be financially ruined in the process.

A salutary reminder of the dark side of groupism came from the historian Paul Johnson in his *Modern Times*, where he referred to the terror of the Leninist regime. "Within a few months of seizing power," said Johnson, "Lenin had abandoned the notion of individual guilt, and with it the whole Judaeo-Christian ethic of personal responsibility... First came condemned categories... Following quickly, however, came entire occupational groups... Quite quickly the condemned group decree-laws extended to whole classes and the notion of killing people collectively rather than individually was seized upon by the Cheka professionals with enthusiasm." The notorious Dzerzhinski himself said: "The first question we ask is: to what class does he belong... This is the essence of the Red Terror." For some defendants in Canadian human rights prosecutions (Christians especially) that feeling became all too familiar. Compare too the dark face of South African groupism-in-action. Nor does anyone have to be reminded of the nature of groupism-in-action in the Germany of the 1930s and early 1940s. One could well ask why—in principle, and especially in light of the broader consequences for the socio-political structures—should groupism with a friendly face be any less problematical than groupism with an evil face, if there should be an implication that you can have any system you like as long as it is groupist?

This may therefore be the opportune moment to jump to Gene E. Veith's treatise on the groupist face of *Modern Fascism*, the title of his 1993 book. "We must know," Veith said, "what fascism is so that we can recognize it when we see it." In the fascist mind—and reminiscent of our earlier reference to the philosopher Charles Taylor—he noted, "the individual had no autonomy *and only achieved the status of a human being as a member of a community.*" (Emphasis added.) The mass rallies and parades and their appurtenances were all "mechanisms for creating group identity." Veith conceded that contemporary multiculturalism was "very different from the fascist model of superior cultures lording it over inferior ones," as it was during my years in South Africa. On the other hand, he contended, the modern manifestation "values pluralism and diversity, *but it is a diversity not of individuals but of groups.*" (Emphasis added.)

Turning back to the 'Canadian condition,' why should one then have to be surprised that with just about every claimant to discrimination of one sort or another in litigation arising under the Canadian Charter of Rights and Freedoms or the Canadian regime of human rights tribunals, the claim proceeded on the basis of his or her membership of one or other group; never in the complainant's individual capacity. In vain did Harry Underwood (a Toronto lawyer who attended the same symposium I shared with Michael Novak) protest that "surely the whole point of the Charter is that rights appertain to us as individuals, and not as members of a group." A rare exception to group-based human rights complaints occurred in Ottawa in March of 2012 when a woman who had previously worked for a human rights tribunal launched her own complaint action against the local municipality, claiming—under her own particular circumstances—as a basic human right her right to park her car on the street in front of her house.

Not at all clear was whether the resulting Canadian jurisprudence would also lead to a belief that discrimination against a single member of a group or a class, constituted discrimination against every other member of that group or class. Almost like a class action in reverse. But would that not be a logical conclusion when Ms Abella and others insisted that human rights were group rights? It should surely, and especially, apply if groups were looked upon as *solidaristic*, not merely associative. What's sauce for the goose, is sauce for the gander. This was more or less the difference between a German *gemeinschaft* and a *gezellschaft*. *Gemeinschaften* were corporatist, *gezellschaften* (on the other hand) associations of otherwise distinct and independent entities. If discrimination against one member of a group entailed an offence against all members of that group, those people would have to be regarded as the equivalent of human clones. At the very least it would be a reflection of the meaning of the typically fascist acclamation of "organic societies;" societies as organisms. Speaking at a convocation in Nova Scotia in 1992, Prime Minister Trudeau even elevated that ideal to the international level, when he called for "a true society of nations... in the sense of a really organic society." What realism! Even the founders of the League of Nations, the (British) Commonwealth, and the United Nations would have been amazed. Not to mention the contradiction between such a dream world and the trappings of Canadian multiculturalism! So there may well be merit in the claim made by the French political philosopher Jean-Luc Nancy in his *Gravity of Thought* that "the horizon of twentieth century totalitarianism" involves an understanding of community "as a totality in which all voices or expressions are equated or like-minded." Clones indeed! Cloning was not just a biogenetic enterprise. Solidarity plus!

Even if the Canadian jurisprudence and the associated political processes and actors stopped short of the proposition that "discrimination against one is discrimination against all," whenever an individual claimed that he suffered discrimination merely on account of his membership of a group, his vindication by Canadian tribunals would certainly serve to reinforce the sentiments (and *ressentiments*) of his own group. Their sense of officially recognized victimhood would be greatly bolstered. Was that what Jonathan Rauch meant when he warned that in the United States the group-forming process was beginning to feed on itself, when "hyperpluralism" became self-reinforcing? Would this problem not be endlessly exacerbated by the ability of politicians to use sophisticated research and computer-driven com-munication technologies to pinpoint and segment ever-smaller *interest groups* among the electorates, each tailoring his message to pander not only to the interests of those groups but also their grievances, real or imagined? And how well are those techniques not suited to a politics of groupism! It would not be the first time in history that the mere availability of a technology made its use imperative.

In 2012 the Canadian Public Policy Forum issued an indictment of the country's Conservative government. By this time the party commanded a majority in parliament. The report described the party's groupist tactics as a "consumer model of politics," having "transformed the consumer model into a science of electoral success. Micro-policies such as tax credits for minor league hockey are carefully tested in advance and then marketed with the secure knowledge that they will win approval among distinct slices of the public. Such initiatives are peddled as part of a direct transaction: particular policies earn specific votes. Hence the analogy to consumerism." A documentary film, *The Century of the Self*, attributed President Clinton's second-term win in 1996 to the same kind of tactic. This worked much better than a "Big Idea" politics, the advocacy of a greater good for the polity as a whole. Sheldon S. Wolin would have immediately recognized such an abuse of the political process. Barack Obama was a past master at the business of pinpointing, down to targeting and communicating with small groups of people gathered in one another's homes. But then he also had the advantage that black people voted for him *en bloc*.

Almost comic was the way political leaders sitting or speaking in the Canadian Parliament—aware that they were constantly in the eye of the television cameras—would ensure that immediately behind them would be sitting one or more members of the House who were either black, attractively female, or preferably, wearing a turban. And if he or she was visibly identifiable as such, why not also a member of a homosexually-oriented interest group? A transvestite?

There were broader implications. When Canadian defenders of the country's groupist orientation inveighed against American individualism (or such remnant that would survive that country's own increasingly groupist manifestations) one might well remember the insightfulness of Sheldon S. Wolin's assertion that with respect to the origins of *le groupisme*, one of its attractions was that when an individual submitted to a communal judgment, as a member of a group, "he avoided dependence on another individual." This could be traced back to Durkheim's thesis that one could be a moral person not in one's own right, but by virtue of a "collective conscience." More particularly, identification with a group, observed Wolin, enabled the individual "to be free from any personal authority or power." In other words, groupism was also escapist; an escape from responsibility.

Was this the same ethos driving radical feminism (along with the diminution of or even disrespect for fatherhood), and their energetic exploitation of the Canadian Charter of Rights and Freedoms? The one thing the modern liberated woman cherished above all else, was to be completely "free to choose" *even within the framework of a marriage*. And nothing was more anathema than to be dependent on a man as the head of a traditional family, however responsible and caring he might be. No, you would much rather surrender yourself to the authority of the whole, of the group, and let the group endow you with an identity. Already, in the province of Quebec, a married woman was no longer allowed to identify herself, legally, by her husband's name. Fritjof Capra, the New Age physicist, underlined how even group therapy had not been developed by psychotherapists "but grew out of the women's movement (and was then) practiced in political consciousness-raising groups. The purpose of these groups is to integrate the personal and the political by clarifying the political context of personal experiences." Integrating the personal and the political was yet another facet of a solidaristic groupism.

According to an archetypal and very active Canadian change agent, Canadians were proud that they "have reacted derisively to the (American) melting pot metaphor, preferring to view this method for managing diversity as less enlightened than their own… Held against the insensitive melting pot of our southerly neighbours, our mosaic invites a certain smugness." Naturally, because the problem with the American melting pot was precisely that it embodied, or sought to embody, Wolin's ideal of a political society where politics was concerned with the pursuit of the common good. Instead, Canadians (and not forgetting Madam Justice Rosalie Abella) preferred the *separatist* small 'melting pots' of their seemingly open-ended list of solidaristic groups, where each member's identity was both submerged in and derived from its own separate and distinct collectivity, and where each group then became a claimant on what remained of the common good, and a participant in—in fact in a playing out of—Garrett Hardin's *Tragedy of the Commons.* Ever so perceptively (albeit in a slightly different context) Wolin observed how, as a result, "the sum of group functions is then subtracted from the totality of socially necessary functions, and the precious little that remains is allowed to be the province of the (common) political order." Less and less of the public square remained.

Would I have been so exercised by North American groupism if I had not grown up in the land of apartheid, a land of Group Areas Acts and occupational reservations for particular groups, as had happened in Nazi Germany? From several points of view having to do with the source and ground of personal identity, are modern groupisms of the North American kind any worse than groupisms focused on race? We're a long way away from the Christian conviction that beyond being a function of memory and tradition (John Paul II) identity is a function of the dignity and uniqueness inherent in every man and woman created in the image of God. And the concomitant rights and freedoms preceded any and every Charter wrought by human hand. Pope Benedict rightly observed how modern man, with no time for faith, worshipped "facts." He worshipped facts because they are *facta*; things that he has made himself, his own handiwork. Including his Charters of Rights and Freedoms.

*Except... except, was it not all a lie?* Underpinning Canadian multiculturalism was a "doctrine... that all cultural systems be approached (and assessed) *as if* (*not* my emphasis) they are equally good and valid," wrote two ardent Canadian defenders of the system. "Ideally," they asserted, "no cultural lifestyle is regarded as superior to another." No better welcome mat for, among others, the expectations and demands of fundamentalist

Islamists in our midst! And it just so happened that those two little words, "as if," would be popping up in several other contexts. What they signalled was the mind-set of purveyors of magical transformative operations, whose success depended on deliberately confusing reality with the dream world.

Recall that Sheldon S. Wolin noticed, with respect to 'group think,' how some of its exponents distinguished between 'functional' and 'dysfunctional' individuals in their midst. The problem was that "like the non-conforming person, the individual fact is wayward, eccentric, unclassifiable..." And no society was quicker than the Canadian to insist on fitting people into boxes, a tendency the country's official multiculturalism only served to exaggerate. Here was another echo of the sources of Canadian anti-Americanism, whether realized or subliminal. Group-centric societies, especially where people are quite content to rely on the state for their entitlements—and even for the recognition of their groups, and through their groups, of themselves—could be expected to be antagonistic to any society where there was still a strong ethos of individualism and self-reliance. No wonder that under the Canadian Charter of Rights and Freedoms groups were not only guaranteed equality before and equal access to the law, but equal entitlements to the "benefit of the law." This novel provision was a late addition to the Constitution at the behest of feminist groups. In other words, no longer was it just a matter of procedural, but also of substantive rights (entitlements). Earlier we mentioned how, in the new Constitution, those strange and undefined "principles of fundamental justice" came to be substituted for an age-old reliance on the principles of natural justice. A group-based politics was the ideal vehicle for securing the associated "benefits."

Here, Michael Novak was also careful to examine the pitfalls when people insisted on confusing 'goods' with rights. "The Constitution," he observed, "guarantees my precious rights—to speak and publish, to travel, to worship—but it does not recognize that the exercise of those rights be publicly funded." Moreover, serious problems arise when people begin to think of "works of justice in terms of 'rights.' "It is not necessary, said Novak, to employ the language of rights in order to assure the works of justice." When the Canadian polity, almost literally, swooned in the face of Prime Minister Trudeau's touting of the "Just Society," this was precisely the problem, namely, a hopeless confusion of the "language of rights" and the "works of justice."

*Then there was the small matter of liberty.* The classic notion of rights served to impose limits on government, said Novak—in line with his previously quoted statement—"whereas the new rights tremendously increase the power of the state." And especially if the state (as in Canada) was constitutionally bound to deliver the "equal benefit of the law for all." One application of the new dispensation was the Supreme Court's reminder to Parliament that medical care was a basic human right. History would show what mutations of the Canadian virus, which had originally blown across the Atlantic (even against the prevailing winds!) from revolutionary France, would yet drift further south on the northerly winds. As for Canada itself, even more interesting was a confluence of such influences with a fascination for the Maoist cultural revolutionary model in the land of the cadres, the subject of a following chapter.

But to get back to Charles Taylor and the nature of identity. Earlier we distinguished the question of identity from the (judicial and governmental) incidences of the politics of groupism, but it has been noteworthy how often the same question has cropped up in both discourse and literature. Naturally, if identity was a function of one's membership of a group, then those two elements would be indissolubly linked. If, in addition, those elements were *fused* (one with the other), then one would immediately begin to recognize a familiar aspect of fascist thought. Person and group would be seen as a single 'organic' unity. The recurrent claim that "the personal is political, and the political personal" had the same implication.

That there was an acute and continuing concern among Canadians about their identity, or rather lack thereof, was revealed once again by the conclusion reached by a photographer, no less! He was the one who was reported in February 2012 as having said, after his nation-wide survey, that "there is no rhyme or reason to the culture here." If the country itself was celebrated for its 'nowhereness' and transformationists were repeatedly counting on the country, the society, and particularly the youth, as offering a convenient *tabula rasa* (of which several instances are cited at various points in this narrative) then clearly identity (*including its absence*) would be a major preoccupation, and that would quite naturally extend into the groupist domain.

Not surprisingly (as by this time we know so well) these preoccupations were closely linked with multiculturalism, both in theory and in practice. Indeed, the same phenomenon reared its head in the 2008 American presidential election, where a fierce debate was waged in newspapers such as the *New York Times* on the degree to which an "identity politics" was rearing its head. There the nature and potential seriousness of the issue was clearly demonstrated. Between the two final contenders on the Democratic side, one candidate's merits were conflated with her womanhood, as if her membership of that particular group was a defining factor. The other candidate's membership of the Afro-American community seemed to be equally uppermost in the popular imagination in judging what ought to have been a question of his personal—his individual—abilities and qualifications for the highest office in the land. When just about every black elector would be voting for him, was it not because he was black? Except that the candidate himself, given his unusual antecedents, appeared to be unsure of just who or what he was. In the same way the runner-up in the contest for the Republican nomination was seen primarily as a member of yet another group, in this case the Evangelicals. Here too, identity and group affiliation appeared to merge. And that was remarkable in a society whose sense of individualism (or what remained of it) was so often the subject of Canadian anti-individualist fear and loathing, so much so that even a Charles Taylor was not immune from it.

A different version of groupism emerged as one of the central electioneering planks of the incumbent president in 2012. In his campaign for fairness in taxation he was pitting the haves against the have-nots to the point that his opponents accused him of starting class warfare for the first time in the history of the United States. In fact, three distinct and separate groups were bandied about: the super-wealthy, the middle (income) class, and the poor. No longer would Americans see themselves as individuals spread along a classless and seamless spectrum stretching from the very poor to the very rich. Or rather, finding themselves on a ladder offering opportunities for climbing, but also opportunities for falling. Groupism had embraced yet another dimension. Here the high rates of unemployment (and under-employment) and the fact that many Americans had started to live in despair, was the kind of opportunity Obama's mentor, Saul Alinsky, would have relished, given what he had said: "The despair is there; now it's up to us to go in and rub raw the sores of discontent..."

As for Europe, there was reason to wonder whether the British too had not already reached a point of no return in the flowering of their own group-based multiculturalist politics. Already in October 2007 Chief Rabbi Jonathan Sacks was reported to have remarked that "British society had become the arena of competing ethnic, religious, gender and racial groups claiming victimhood and asserting that each one's special pain, oppression, humiliation merited first special rights and then special treatment..." Matters came to a head when none other than the Archbishop of Canterbury found himself in deep water on account of remarks on the desirability (perhaps even the necessity, he implied) of a limited recognition of Islamic Sharia law and practices. Except that there was hope that the European Court of Human Rights had seen the light when, in the *Refah Partisi* case, it rejected a claim that a "plurality of legal systems" should be recognized and respected. That proposal, ruled the Court, "would introduce into all legal relationships *a distinction between individuals* grounded on religion, would categorize everyone according to his religious beliefs and would allow him rights and freedoms *not as an individual* but according to his allegiance to a religious movement." The Court added that "such a system would undeniably infringe the principle of non-discrimination *between individuals*... which is one of the fundamental principles of democracy." (Emphases added.)

Here I could advance a simple debating point based on my own life story. If my identity derived from my membership of a group, I would now have to lay claim to at least six different identities, having spent substantial slices of my life in no fewer than six quite distinct cultural milieux on three continents. Not to mention a working life divided among at least five very different and distinct professions or disciplines. So whence my identity?

On this score we must return to Charles Taylor's *Sources of the Self*. His allusion to human identity as a function of the recognition, by others, of "one's community both politically and socially" is a lot less persuasive than when he approaches the question from a much broader perspective. In the first instance Taylor observes that "people may see their identity as defined partly by some moral or spiritual commitment, say as a Catholic, or an anarchist... To know who you are is to be oriented in moral space, a space in which questions arise about what is good or bad, what is worth doing and what not, what has meaning and importance for you and what is trivial and secondary." Of course, much depends not only on the size but also the quality of that moral space! Consider Pope Benedict's allusion to "the wide-open spaces of truth that is common to all."

Again speaking for myself, apart from my memories and antecedents, I would see my identity more in the light of my personhood, and my personhood in the light of having been created—and uniquely created—in the image of God, and possessed of unique endowments. Especially in the context of the Catholic 'theology of the body,' I would regard myself as a unique and distinct and integrated combination of body, mind, soul, and spirit. This does not mean that Taylor is wrong when he adds that "the full definition of someone's identity... involves not only his stand on moral and spiritual matters" but is also "in reference to a defining community." But it cannot possibly mean that one's membership of a community is the decisive element, if only because many people, in the course of their lives, will have belonged to different (and in some cases many) and distinct groups or collectivities. And speaking of theology, consider too the supreme importance in Scripture of the meaning and meaningfulness of names and naming. In 2011 Pope Benedict urged Catholic parents "to stop giving their newborn kids 'celebrity' names." "Every baptized child," he said, "acquires the character of the son of God, beginning with their Christian name..." He was not even referring to a modern tendency for parents to invent wholly fanciful, artificial, euphonious, and meaningless names for their offspring; names without any connection to the history of the family, let alone any other tradition or even living person. An atomistic society may not only exist in space, but also in time!

Taylor goes on to qualify his allusions to a person's "orientation to the good" when he argues that "this sense of the good has to be woven into my understanding of my life as an unfolding story." To make sense of ourselves we have to "grasp our lives in a *narrative*." (His emphasis.) "In order to have a sense of who we are, we have to have a notion of how we have become, and of where we are going." He reiterates his argument by stating that for me to know "my place relative to the good, requires a narrative understanding of my life, a sense of what I have become which can only be given in a story." Now something that should be abundantly clear to any reasonable mind is that *no two people's stories are ever the same.* What can be more discriminating in and by itself than a groupist doctrine of human rights which does not recognize the differences, and often crucial differences—the differential merits or demerits—among the individuals associated with a particular group?[10] I would, of course, argue that Taylor's stress on narrative is not the whole story either. My identity is not simply a product of the *processes* with which my life has been associated, or to which I have been exposed. If I believed that, I would be in the same camp as the transformationist shapers and moulders of a New Age, and those theo-logical apostates who would go so far as to see God himself as being in process.

And therefore I was so greatly encouraged by Charles Taylor's concluding observation, namely, that "there is a large element of hope. It is a hope that I see implicit in Judaeo-Christian theism... and in its central promise of a divine affirmation of the human, more total than humans can ever attain unaided."

The groupist definition and celebration of human identity is manifestly false.

---

10    Niall Ferguson recalls that "it was only in the second half of the twentieth century that eugenics and the related concept of 'racial hygiene' were finally discredited with the realization that genetic differences between the races are relatively small, and the variations within races quite large."

# CHAPTER NINE
# THE CHINA SYNDROME

If I was at all interested in socio-cultural transformation and transformationists, how could I possibly ignore or overlook a Canadian-Chinese nexus in my fascination with the wonders of my newly adopted country of residence? And was it all possible that the nexus might even become an axis? Prime Minister Trudeau and several of his entourage have shown a peculiar preoccupation with Communist China, Chairman Mao, and the Chinese Cultural Revolution. The way they expressed it, it was not connected to any economic interest, whether investment- or trade-related. Latterly, of course, western countries have also been increasingly focused on financial and currency-related problems with the Chinese. By contrast, the Canadian preoccupation with China and the Chinese revolution appears to have been almost exclusively political and cultural in nature. Literally and figuratively, a rather pronounced 'orientation!' If a world transformationist Trudeau had his field of vision filled with images of Communist China, so, one day, would a world transformationist successor of his, Barack Obama, have his field of vision filled with images of the Muslim world.

Canadian Prime Minister Mackenzie King's 'spiritual' interest in Adolf Hitler—and tangentially, his concern for the sensitivities of Joseph Stalin—were a great deal less sophisticated in comparison with Trudeau's Chinese excursions. We know that in 1949 Trudeau left Shanghai just before the 'liberation' of that city by the forces of Mao Tse-tung. He then hurried back to Canada to take part in the launching of *Cité Libre*, a journal that took credit for its role in fostering the so-called Quiet Revolution in Quebec; Quebec's own cultural revolution. He first came to public notice when he marched in support of that province's notorious Asbestos Strike (capitalized in the hagiography). One biographer has noted that Trudeau "was able to observe at Asbestos what he later described in print as 'a turning point in the entire religious, political, social and economic history of the Province of Quebec.'"

And that's why (thinking of the Asbestos Strike) I'm intrigued by the historical parallelisms with the origins of Germany's National Socialist regime in a "regenerated workers' movement"—linked with the peasant insur-rections on the west coast of Schleswig-Holstein (so well described in the German author Hans Fallada's novel—and the fact that the NSDAP (the Nazi Party) was not only rooted in the National Socialist German Workers' Party but that the NSDAP also established its first major regional newspaper at that time. And so—thinking of *Cité Libre*— what a coincidence too that the Hitlerite version of Engels's *Peasant War in Germany*, written by one Ernst von Salomon, should have been titled *Der Stadt*. There had been various strikes at the time, including the Berlin metalworkers' and transport workers' strike, but the most notable was an uprising that prompted the author of *Der Stadt* to describe the strikers as "the shock troops of a new reality... aiming at a radical transformation of the German situation." A harbinger of *Cité Libre*? A different *Tale of Two Cities*?

---

As an aside, what was it, one may ask, about the world of labour and labour relations that should have been so vital at the very beginnings of the Trudeau saga; in the works of Karl Marx; in the founding of the Nazi movement; and even in Chairman Mao's worker-related activities of 1922 (when he organized a strike in Changsha, supported the workers' movement in Anyan, and then served as head of a workers' club)? So too was the definitive formulation of systematic apartheid at a conference in South Africa built on a concern not only over the education of poor whites, but mainly their displacement by black labour. And so, looking forward to the end of this story, why (one might even ask), should the organizers of a monumental temple dedicated to Human Rights—erected in the Canadian city of Winnipeg—have been so conscient that not only did Winnipeg have "a rich history of human rights struggles" but that the museum's celebration of labour rights would be linked to "the Winnipeg General Strike of 1919?" Is life one fearful symmetry after another? Is it only required that there be an informed observer?

Christians do or ought to look upon work, and working, in a quite different light. I never really thought about these connections during or even after years of activity as an unpaid consultant and speaker (and contributor to their journal), in the affairs of the only overtly Christian labour union in North America and the associated Work Research Foundation. This remarkable organization, headquartered near Toronto, was particularly effective in representing workers in the construction trades and nursing homes across Canada, and was able to boast that rarely, if ever, did they have to resort to strikes. Having fought for a long time to gain accreditation, the Christian Labour Association of Canada (CLAC) was the *bête noire* of the organized labour movement, for whom antagonistic labour relations and the strike weapon were virtually definitional. Even when CLAC's members were engaged in the potentially dangerous work of laying and welding oil and gas pipelines, mysterious acts of sabotage were not unknown. So much for freedom of association in the land of the Charter!

––––––––––

In the revolutionary universe it was not only cities that were so prominent. There was also the attraction of Chairman Mao's reliance on the peasantry of the Countryside (often capitalized), reminiscent again of the peasant insurrections of Schleswig-Holstein. When Professor Ivan Head, Trudeau's principal foreign policy adviser, was given control of Canada's International Development Research Foundation (IDRC) with its distinct Third World-oriented transformational mandate, he too showed an acute awareness of the need to cultivate the people of the "countryside." In Maoist doctrine the countryside was seen as the base for an assault on the privileged capitalist bourgeoisies of the cities. One of the Third World directors on the IDRC board by the name of Rex Nettleford, hailing from Jamaica, had some remarkable things to say along the same lines. At times

Nettleford's utterances and figures of speech were very much like those of Saul Alinsky.

The more challenging aspect of the revolutionary doctrine of the countryside was that Chairman Mao was not just thinking literally of the Chinese countryside and Chinese cities. In his mind and the minds of the Ivan Heads of Canada and the Jorge Castanedas of Mexico (Jorge Castaneda y Alvarez de la Rosa was that country's Foreign Secretary from 1979 to 1982, and succeeded by his son, Jorge Castaneda Gutman, in the same position, between 2000 and 2003) and their like- minded counterparts in a few other western domains, the metaphor of the countryside was extended to encompass all of the Third World countries of the 'South' in their relations with the privileged and oppressive 'cities' of the 'North.' Here was a classic example of what I've called a politics of contrived oscillation, where domestic and international agendas could be used not only to complement but to reinforce one another.

Yet the Canadian change agents could not care less about the domestic vicissitudes of the Chinese people, just as, years later, few Canadian politicians could care about the persecution and sufferings of China's Falun Gong. What really interested them was the international potential of the metaphor. Canada already brandished its own North-South Institute (given a new lease of life in 2015), with Professor Head's IDRC going out of its way to bolster the two "Brandt Reports" of 1980 (the first titled *North-South: A Programme for Survival*). They were the handiwork of an international commission chaired by the socialist German Chancellor. (It was a member of Brandt's personal staff who leaked to the Russians the precise routes of NATO's fuel supply lines across Western Europe and whether this had anything to do with Herr Brandt's *Drang nach Osten*— the urge to look east—nobody would ever know.) The IDRC promptly issued its own report, *Beyond the Brandt Commission,* looking "to the kind of follow-up action needed *at national and international levels* to accelerate the transition during the 1980s toward a more equitable world order." (Emphasis added.) In a foreword to a book titled *Third World Ideology and Western Reality*, Jean-François Revel was quite blunt: "The objective of the Third World ideology is to accuse and, if possible, destroy the developed societies, not to develop the backward societies... This attitude appears transparent in the well-known Brandt Reports..."

Revert then to the apparent link between Canadian and Communist Chinese interests when Professor Head gives a talk to the Society for a Better Understanding of China, at the University of Ottawa, on January 9, 1981. Paraphrased (from my personal notes taken on the occasion) Professor Head underscores "the need for understanding the interconnections between culture and development," saying that the social sciences are most important to IDRC. "On this score (Maoist) China has also been very successful... Canada was approached by China a couple of years ago. So the question is whether Chinese qualities can be used elsewhere, so as to explore their exportability... Canada is the first country to help to take Chinese experts into the Third World. *IDRC is not interested in a transformation based on Western models.*"

But then the speaker is visibly embarrassed by a questioner who thanks him most profusely for having given him (the questioner) employment at IDRC, adding (per my cryptic notes): "the Chinese case is probably unique in human history… best social goals of any large country today... Socio-political revolution the most important. Must see how the Chinese revision of Marxism has done it."

My learning curve in the New Canada has been rising exponentially! I think I can begin to understand why Chairman Mao himself has placed Canada in the "intermediate zone," a phrase he first coined in a speech to the Supreme Soviet in Moscow on November 6, 1957. American imperialism, the Chairman contended, "interferes in the internal affairs of all nations, particularly in the various nations of the intermediate zone situated between the American and socialist camps." 1964 was the year when the official Chinese political media first began to use the term Third World as representing "the countryside of the world, while Europe and North America were its cities." This was part—we learned in 1976—of Mao's "great strategic concept." And, fully consonant with a Canadian interest in a mutually reinforcing oscillation between domestic and foreign escapades, Mao held that "if the traditional Chinese image of world order was an extension of the Confucian moral order" (something of which he disapproved strongly) "so was the Maoist image of world order an extension of revolutionary order and justice at home."

These declarations and developments have been well documented by others and do not need to be belaboured any further, but to me, most significant is the way the Canadian leaderships have continued to align themselves with the thought processes of the Chinese Cultural Revolution. Not long into the third millennium the renewed Chinese incursions into the countries of Africa and Latin America may well have shown that 'geo-strategically' the tiger had not changed its spots. Here was part of the background against which all too many Canadians consistently saw themselves as 'Third World' victims of western imperialist forces, notably American, or, at the very least, as a country well-placed to be in solidarity with the oppressed.

As we've already seen, in this respect there was a constant reminder of the importance of Canada's role not only in the (formerly British) Commonwealth, but in the organizations of the *francophonie* as well. Countless was the number of times Canadian spokesmen would claim that Canada, unlike the "imperialist" powers, was "trusted." As for the "countryside" of the South besieging the "cities" of the North, the one Canadian journalist who was the most active and effective path breaker in the popular press for Trudeau's accession to power, actually wrote an article illustrated by a drawing of a United States of America squeezed as in a vise between Canada and Mexico. This vision began to look realistic when the energy crisis of the early 1970s armed the Canadians and the Mexicans with considerable self-perceived political and economic leverage, leading directly, in Canada, to the formation of a state-owned Petro-Canada International whose mandate was a great deal more political than economic, as it was meant to spread Canadian influence in solidarity with the Third World. But whether in the countryside or in the cities, it was still necessary to find ways of energizing the masses. In this respect the Chinese Cultural Revolutionary rhetoric proved well-nigh irresistible. Americans had to wait until 2008 for their own energizer to burst upon the scene.

In 1961 Trudeau and his friend Jacques Hébert (subsequently elevated to the Canadian Senate) wrote *Two Innocents in Red China,* a highly ambivalently written account of a journey through the Middle Kingdom, which may or may not have taken in international trade union meetings held in both Moscow and Beijing. The story was as ambiguously couched as a set of guidelines Trudeau was writing, at about the same time, on how, tactically, the cause of socialism could be advanced across Canada. In the midst of great festivities on China's newly proclaimed national day, Trudeau met the Chinese prime minister Chou En-lai as well as the old Chairman himself: "It is a stirring moment: these greybeards... embody today the triumph of an idea, an idea that has turned the whole world upside down and profoundly changed the course of human history... Mao Tse-tung, one of the great men of the century, has a powerful head, an unlined face, and a look of wisdom tinged with melancholy." (Not all that different from Prime Minister Mackenzie King's description of Herr Adolf, at least in tone.)

In January 1984 Trudeau hosts a visit by Chinese premier Zhao Ziyang, who is given the honour of addressing a joint session of the Houses of Parliament in Ottawa, and where Trudeau boasts that Canada has been the first country to extend diplomatic recognition to China. Recalling yet another visit of his to that country in 1973, he expresses his "life-long fascination with your philosophers, artists, strategists and historians," and how he has had the opportunity not only to once again meet Chairman Mao but "to discuss politics with Chou En-Lai far into the night..." He was heartened, he says, by Chairman Mao's "understanding... and sympathy for Canada's foreign policy."

In fact the 1973 visit to China happened to culminate in the celebration of Trudeau's own birthday, on October 18, and (curiously) he would be back in China on other birthdays in the future. On October 19, 1973, back in Ottawa, Trudeau reported to the Canadian House of Commons, noting that "Chairman Mao Tse-tung extended to me the courtesy of a long conversation. Premier Chou En-lai met with me for many hours of formal discussions over the course of several days and chatted with me at even greater length in informal circumstances on a number of occasions."

What could have been the subject of such extensive conversations? That was not explained. Trudeau added that "it has not been the vastness of the Pacific that has acted as a barrier between Canada and China. The gulf has been found all too often in the minds of those who are unwilling to recognize the magnitude of one of the most significant revolutions in the history of the world..." In a chapter contributed to a book titled *Social Purpose for Canada*, published in 1961, Trudeau had cited "the experience of that superb strategist, Mao Tse-tung" as a backdrop to his own, apparently parallel, ideas for his own countrymen.

After his brief resignation from politics in the summer of 1979 (a stressful time for him), Trudeau took off for Tibet and was spotted in transit at the Beijing airport by an alert Canadian reporter. In his book *The Chinese: Portrait of a People* the Canadian journalist John Fraser too recalled that Trudeau "was on his way to Tibet shortly after the Canadian voters had rejected him as prime minister." Whether he had gone to consult his close associate Maurice Strong's Tibetan Buddhist guru of the Black Hat Sect is not known, except that he must have been dispirited, and then sufficiently inspired—judging by his spectacular political come-back early in the next year—to be seized with an absolute determination to give Canadians their culturally transformative Charter of Rights and Freedoms. In April 1986 Trudeau was once again back in China where he met with the new leader Deng Xiaoping and again with premier Zhao Ziyang, recalling that two years before, in 1984, he had brought his world peace crusade to Beijing. His final meeting with Deng, he said, was "mainly a friendly conversation about old times."

An ardent supporter of the Chinese Cultural Revolution was a Professor Paul T.K. Lin, based in Montreal, who wrote passionately of "the conscious and direct action of many working, creating human beings, transforming society and nature" and how "future cultural revolutions (no doubt on a progressively higher level of sophistication in theory and practice) will very likely be necessary." By October 1987 the same Professor Lin had become the Rector of Macao's University of East Asia, and was then able to confer an honorary doctorate on one Pierre Elliott Trudeau. Professor Lin, it was reported, had returned to Canada from

China in 1964 "to take up China's cause as professor of Asian Studies" at a Montreal university (most likely the same university where Trudeau was teaching). Speculated Canada's *Globe and Mail* that as "a Chinese nationalist and worker in China for 15 years, many Canadians, diplomats especially, wonder where his loyalties are and shy away from him. His sympathy for the Beijing Government left him open to charges that he was too tolerant of its excesses..."

Wallerstein and associates too—who (as we've seen) were among the people so taken with the Canadian experiment—were already fixated on the Chinese model. But Trudeau was ahead of them. The legacy seemed to endure because well into the next millennium the official web site of the Canadian embassy in Beijing carried a reminder that "throughout his life, Mr Trudeau maintained a strong interest in China." "In 1949," reported the embassy, "he travelled through China in the tumultuous months before the establishment of the People's Republic. Mr Trudeau returned to China again in 1959 with his colleague Jacques Hébert, a visit chronicled in their 1961 book *Two Innocents in Red China*." In October 2005 we learned that "a Chinese-language version of *Two Innocents in Red China*, a book written by Pierre Trudeau and Jacques Hébert some 45 years ago, is now on the shelves in China. Hébert, 82, and the late Prime Minister's son Alexandre (Sacha) Trudeau were in Shanghai this week to help launch the book." "This book," Hébert told a news conference, "looked to China with open eyes, with innocence, (and) made it easy for more people to give a chance to China." Hébert and Trudeau's son were back in China in April 2006 to make a commemorative film on the occasion of an important Maoist anniversary. And Trudeau himself and his two sons had made a similar pilgrimage in 1990, except that, to the puzzlement of Alexandre, who spoke "about my father's attitude towards China," Trudeau "did not want to judge the Chinese for Tiananmen Square." In 2007 Alexandre and Hébert updated *Two Innocents in Red China* for re-publication in Canada. Meanwhile the other son made a successful move to enter the world of Canadian politics. He delivered a notable speech at a leadership convention of the Liberal Party (although Alexandre could not be present on that occasion since he was away in Cuba to take part in and record an important anniversary of the regime of Fidel Castro). Not long after his speechifying debut he, like his father before him, became the leader of the Liberal Party ("Canada's natural governing party") and an aspiring future prime minister. He was heard to refer wistfully to the apparent ability of the Chinese Communist leadership to get things done, in contrast to the way Canadians were hampered by their slow democratic decision processes.

Given the grandiose visions of a transformed world situation, one should not only ask, in Charles E. Lindblom's words, just *who* were these "Maoist energizers of the masses" who would put "ordinary citizens through extraordinarily tense experiences from time to time", but also *how* would they go about it? One way was foreshadowed by Senator Jacques Hébert in 1980. In that year, in an extraordinary testimony before a Canadian parliamentary committee, Hébert waxed lyrically in his wish to see replicated in Canada, the transformative spectacle of "the millions of jugglers, singers, acrobats, onlookers and dancers," he witnessed in Beijing. He proposed "a great brainstorm... But it has to be global. If it is not global, and if it is just one fraction of our society that is involved, nothing will happen. It has to be total, like in a global war; everybody is involved in some way or the other; it is total. If it is not total, it will fail." Totalism forsooth! Thus he suggested that the main Canadian official holiday, Canada Day, be changed to the "People of the World Day," and that Canada be transformed into a "vast construction site... where the means for ensuring the harmonious development of the whole earth could be tried out." This required an "information blitz such as has never been seen in the world [except, perhaps, in Mao's China!] ...and one day our citizens will be grateful for their political leaders for having involved them in a great and noble adventure... the Great Collective Project."

One does not have to be reminded of how spectacular public performances also served to energize the masses in Nazi Germany. "'Bread and circuses' is an ancient and well-tried formula for social control," observed David Harvey. "But spectacle can also be an essential aspect of revolutionary movement (see, for example, Ozouf's 1988 study of festivals as a means to express revolutionary will in the French Revolution). Did not

Lenin, after all, refer to revolution as 'the festival of the people?' The spectacle has always been a potent political weapon."

We shall still have to attend to the similarities, in other respects, in the thinking and pronouncements of a Mao Tse-tung and a Trudeau, and especially their thoughts on (revolutionary) strategies and tactics.

And when Trudeau pronounced on a "country in search of a purpose," were he and Senator Hébert not singing from the same song sheet? Trudeau heaped fulsome praise on a coffee table book written by a friend of his, Harold Town, titled *Canada With Love*, in an introduction provided by Trudeau himself. The same Town had illustrated the campaign brochure accompanying Trudeau's successful bid for power at the 1968 leadership convention of the Liberal Party. Wrote Town: "We are wanderers in the largest uninhabited country in the world, refusing to weld ourselves into a specific people who bear a banner of race or mission... we stand on the threshold of identity..."

The following question then arises: If the Canadian polity lacked a common identity, what could that identity have been, or what could it have been rooted in? One possibility (and apparently the only one on offer, other than a commonly shared and negative anti-Americanism) was explored in a book by one Janet Ajenstat, titled *The Canadian Founding: John Locke and Parliament*. "Canadians have no shared sense of history (and) there is no consensus about cultural identity," she wrote. Canada's founding fathers "rejected the idea of a national cultural identity." Instead, they established an institution—Parliament—to serve as the cynosure and lynchpin of a collective cohesiveness. "They thought that Parliament would define the nation... that is, it would give them what we now call an 'identity.'" Faint hope. Things did not work out that way. We know that thanks to the indefatigable labours of Canada's new founding father and creator of a new constitution, with a Charter of Rights and Freedoms as its centerpiece, Trudeau succeeded in kicking out the one prop the preceding argument was able to propose, namely, a sovereign parliament. The *central structural and operational function* of the Charter was to deprive parliament of its sovereignty (and also deprive it of one of its main *raisons d'être*, namely, the ability to protect the weak and the defenceless in the case of the unborn, as I argued in support of the pro-life cause in the constitutional debates). Now, the country was wide open and vulnerable not only to the machinations of its political change agents but also to the whims of an unelected judiciary, for one thing, and to the transformative processes of not only the Charter but a system of arbitrary human rights tribunals, not to mention all of the other transformative devices—whether legislative, regulatory, administrative, fiscal, financial, or propagandistic—that were gradually brought to bear.

As for working on the youth of the country—yet another preoccupation of Senator Hébert—Supreme Court Justice Rosalie Abella had also written a piece for a Canadian Royal Commission, titled *Equality in Employment*, where she (I believe, not having verified it myself) referred to children as "the young of the state." And so it seemed that the Canadian experiment was in a direct line of a long tradition focused on the minds of the youth. Lenin was the first person to point the way, if ever so brutally. Reputedly—in a pamphlet titled *Communist Rules for Revolution* (discovered in 1919 in a raid conducted in Dusseldorf)—Lenin wrote to the effect that "the future of any nation lies with its youth. So corrupt them. Since religion teaches moral virtue, erode the churches and divert the young from religion. Make them interested in themselves... Get them addicted to privileges and rights." These words, in the quoted form, were allegedly elaborated in a set of ten rules taught at the Lenin School of Political Warfare in Moscow.

In the Canada of 2012, Christian parents were to contend with provincial governments, with Ontario leading the way, that were determined to force upon all schools a curriculum designed to normalize active homosexualism in the minds of the young. More and more parents had to make considerable sacrifices by taking recourse to home-schooling their children, while continuing to have to pay taxes in support of public schools.

Nothing as crude as Lenin's prescription will, of course, fall from the lips of the contemporary idealistic transformationist, however radical. Far from it. When Trudeau's mentor, F.R. Scott, addressed a meeting of the Young People's Socialist League in 1931 he explained that "you cannot grow a socialist tree in unprepared soil." Because of "their growing numbers and the superior justice of their ideas," he said, the new enlightened youth would "gradually and surely attain control of the organs of the state and use them for the benefit of the masses." While Hitler and Marshal Pétain (see below) had their own youth organizations and Chairman Mao his Red Guard—one day to be followed by the young militant Islamic terrorists born and bred in the very heart of European societies—H.G. Wells (warmly embraced by New Agers) advocated a much more peaceable "Open Conspiracy" in which "young men and young women may be collected into groups arranged upon lines not unlike those of the Bohemian Sokols or the Italian Fasci."

The very first issue of *Cité Libre*—founded by Trudeau and his colleagues in 1950—was dedicated to the memory of one Emmanuel Mounier. Mounier moved among strange friends in Nazi-occupied France, where he was associated with an extraordinary project of the Vichy regime. A system of youth camps was established where (astonishingly) "soon 90,000 boys were passing through... every eight months." A biographer of Mounier described this movement against a background in which "Nazi 'French expert' Otto Abetz and his entourage seemed to envisage the possibility of transforming Belgian and French youth within a new social and economic order." Marshal Pétain was said to have had "sophisticated social engineers in his immediate entourage." One notable graduate of those camps was none other than Jacques Delors, a "founding father" of the European Union who, at the time, was a member of a theatrical touring group engaged in entertaining German soldiers in different places. It was one of Mounier's acolytes, Jacques Hébert, who told a Canadian parliamentary committee in October 1980 that two organizations, Canada World Youth and another called Katimavik, were comprised of "young people between 17 and 21. *So they are still at that stage very pure...*" He also wrote in a book of his that "only young people are still free, still generous, *still pure.*" (Emphases added.) Already, in Katimavik, he said, "young Canadians have lived through an extraordinary experiment..." On the side of Canada World Youth (equally successful), by being exposed to conditions in the Third World, he claimed, young people were learning "that there was another way to live" and it would also give them "a new and more realistic perception of their own country." "Back home, these young Canadians no longer want to live the way they lived before..."

All or mostly to the good? Perhaps. My interest lay not so much in the particular objects and substance of these transformative aspirations as in the anatomy of the phenomenon (so to speak): in the way the transformationist's mind worked; and in the methods and techniques to which it was attracted, offering, as they seemed to do, such a variety of potential applications. Here, with respect to the youth, the intent was that somehow the participants in the youth programs would be trans-formed by their (induced) experiences. To what end was not exactly clear, almost as if transformation was its own end. When we come to examine the theory and practice of functionalism and its variants or extensions, the nature of this way of thinking will be clarified. Whatever the purpose, evidently it was so vital that when a Conservative government threatened to pull the financial plug from Katimavik the senator went on a hunger strike, *until death he said*, lying on a cot in the foyer of the Canadian Senate. Imagine the scene! Would something like that ever happen in the Rotunda of the American Capitol? Eventually a face-saving formula was found to save his life (if one took him at his word, as his friends appeared to do). Lying on his cot, Hébert received visitors, a whole procession of admirers and political colleagues, Trudeau included. And when he finally bowed out of Katimavik, his place was taken by one of Trudeau's sons; the one who would follow in his father's steps. Those sons Trudeau had taken to the Soviet Union in 1985, as he told *The Toronto Star*, "to see this country, about which so many prejudices are held in the West and which is the object of so much propaganda and counter-propaganda" and he had done it, he said, *"while they are still young and impressionable."* (Emphasis added.) An astonishing admission, if one thought about it.

Perhaps the last word on the subject of youth as the object of trans-formative schemes should be left to the ubiquitous Willis Harman, who wrote: "...children are born *tabula rasa*, perceiving the world without any prior filtering system or conceptual framework." That condition, of course, offered opportunities. Well into the 21<sup>st</sup> century Canadian children would, according to plan, be taken in droves (20,000 per annum was the stated minimum) from all over Canada through a new Museum for Human Rights in the city of Winnipeg, at government expense, there to be impressed by the wonders wrought through the agency of a Charter of Rights and Freedoms; a system of human rights tribunals; and the helpful ministrations of a transformative judiciary.

In October 1981 a new government agency bursts upon the scene, as if from nowhere, called a Futures Secretariat. Its stated purpose is to help "24 million Canadians to become aware of and involved in decisions about the future direction of their society," given their "fear of economic collapse; dread of nuclear war; solidarity of common experiences and problems; worries about ethnic assimilation; helplessness when the kids are learning Telidon; frustration over jobs" and with the concomitant need to "involve every Canadian in the search for a just, participatory and sustainable society" and to "translate personal into global understanding" involving "an ongoing critical evaluation of our own goals and assumptions," and relying on "the interaction of thought with action..." One learns that "emphasis should be placed on participation, which generates emotion as well as reflection." Also helpful will be a reliance on the arts, since "one of its longstanding roles has been to challenge some of our most deeply rooted assumptions, not just about social patterns, but equally our sense of time and space and reality," thereby "giving an 'in' to people's motivation which is unique."

Fruitful soil for working on people's minds? After all, just about a year before—in an interview conducted on December 17, 1980 and released on December 28, 1980—Prime Minister Trudeau announced that "I think that the Canada of the twenty-first century is being born... I think I'm taking Canada through a period now of intense questioning of its identity, its political identity, and I'm asking Canadians to make these basic choices..." Two months later he reiterated that "Canadians are being put to the test, the contest is fierce and the prize is nothing less than the future of the country." He was, he said, "taking Canada through its adolescence." Canadians were being taken on a roller-coaster ride.

Back to China once again with Charles E. Lindblom's analysis of the use of "intense and pervasive education" in that country, where it was necessary to deploy "all the ordinary methods of communication." Lindblom remarked on how, in Maoist China, "ordinary citizens (were) put through extraordinarily intense experiences from time to time." For sure, the state-owned and controlled Canadian Broadcasting Corporation was already a powerful culturally and ideologically conditioning agent, so much so that when we switched on the early morning commentaries (sometimes by a man who could have been a Lord Haw-Haw, the Englishman who made those propagandistic broadcasts from wartime Germany) it was accompanied by a silent prayer: "Lord, give us this day our daily poison pill."

As for the emotional outpourings of the Futures Secretariat, we saw similar language coming from Senator Hébert in that memorable appearance of his before a parliamentary committee, when he too diagnosed people's "feeling of helplessness... And so to try to get rid of the anguish, each one of us tries to think about something else..." Right now, he said, "people are desperate because they do not know what to do."

*Mirabile dictu*, was community organizer Barack Obama's mentor in Chicago, Saul Alinsky, not similarly inspired? We've already noted how, in 2010, a contributor to *The New English Review* recounted that "In order to agitate for 'change,' Alinsky and his adherents required the population to be on edge: 'rubbed raw.'" Said Alinsky in an interview: "The despair is there; now it's up to us to go in and rub raw the sores of discontent, galvanize them for radical social change..."

*So, undoubtedly, a psychological element was at work.* Few tools are as effective as the socio-politico-cultural transformationist's deployment of psychology. My first exposure to that insight had been the expertise of South Africa's father of systematic apartheid. Here too, all of a sudden, passing through the psychology gate—and as we shall see—there opens up before one's eyes a broad vista of possibilities and applications. No longer are we just looking at the idolization of process and processes (as in the Alinsky-Obama case), but beginning to take a look at *the critical question of how such processes can be effectively harnessed.*

For the moment, by way of just one example, let us merely take a glimpse at the thoughts of a psychologist highly acclaimed in New Age circles; a man by the name of Karl E. Weick of Cornell University. His book, *The Social Psychology of Organizing* (including community organizing??) contains, in a nutshell, some of the main elements in the unfolding saga of trans-formationist manipulation. For one thing, Weick introduces a particular angle to the means-ends dichotomy, in that respect finding himself right in the middle of not only Chairman Mao's but also Vladimir Lenin's quintessential approaches to political organization and cultural change. At the same time Weick lands solidly in Professor Willis Harman's boat. Harman, we recall, relied on the harnessing, by individuals and especially groups of people, of visualization techniques to make miraculous things happen. Recall too that Harman himself was actively engaged in the field of humanistic psychology.

Considering the states of mind displayed by Canada's Futures Secretariat and by such as Hébert and other would-be exploiters of acute anxieties, we shall attend to the psychological element in the make-up of Voegelin's political Gnostic, as it becomes progressively clearer that the age-old Gnostic heresy—more than anything else—lay at the root of the events and experiences covered in this story. If so much can be encompassed under the rubric of psychology—or at least by dint of psychology—then psychology may as well be the starting point for the more analytical phase of our story.

And we shall not forget that the Gnostic element behind these various manifestations was not confined to the Canadian scene; was in fact as old as Christianity itself (if not older); has never failed and will never fail to rear its head again and again in different places and at different times; and that, for these reasons, one would hope that the Canadian experience might also hold useful and timely lessons for others.

The Gnostic spirit in art:
"As a good realist, I have to reinvent the world."

Alex Colville

# PART THREE

# CHAPTER TEN
# FROM MIND GAMES TO
# THE GNOSTIC MIND

**Psychology:**
1. The science that deals with mental processes and behaviour
2. The emotional and behavioral characteristics of an individual, a group, or an activity
3. The subtle tactical action or argument used to manipulate or influence another

In Chapter Six we've already touched on the possible usefulness of Canada's blankness to the socio-cultural and political change agent. Indeed, Senator Jacques Hébert reminds us that in the Canadian transformational laboratory there existed two kinds of *tabula rasa*. The first pertained to the country as a whole, and by extension, to the Canadian popular psyche. The second was personal, and in this instance attributed particularly to, and in fact aimed at the youth, as we have seen.

Thus, to begin to better understand the Gnostic mind, let us briefly reiterate a couple of themes that have already emerged in the context of the foregoing chapter. They relate to Senator Hébert's thoughts on how it was necessary to "not only to invent original ways of establishing a New International Economic Order but to discover a new art of living and, who knows, a new project of society for Canada." On how, if Canadians in particular were sufficiently exposed to the new ways of thinking "they will never be the same again." On how "In today's circumstances the simple fact of being *a country without a history* constitutes a powerful advantage, and gives us perhaps the right, and certainly the duty, to involve ourselves to the hilt in contemporary history, playing a major role in it and emerging once and for all from our insignificance. As Paolo Freire said, 'It's a question of little by little taking History into our own hands, so that we can make it, not suffer it.'" (Emphasis added.) In other words, a transformationist's paradise!

Edmund Burke had something to say on this subject in his *Reflections on the Revolution in France*, where he wrote: "I cannot conceive how any man can have brought himself to that pitch of presumption, to consider his country as nothing but *carte blanche*, upon which he may scribble whatever he pleases."[11]

Should it be a mystery then that in a progressively humanistic world, where man has become the measure of all things, psychology has ruled supreme? And that a Paul C. Vitz should have written a book titled *Psychology as Religion: The Cult of Self-worship*? Quite early on, both the philosopher-political scientist Eric Voegelin and Karl Popper ("one of the greatest philosophers of science of the 20th century") put the finger on a psychological element. Popper sought to come to grips with the appeal of totalitarian ideas, and "near the center of (his) explanation" was a "socio-psychological concept which he calls 'the strain of civilization.'" Voegelin, for his part, soon decided that "we must move our inquiry to the psychological level" and to "the psychic gain the (Gnostic) receives from the construction of his image and the psychic needs the masses of his followers satisfy through it." His interest originated in "the Austrian events of the time" in the same way the Canadian experience awakened my interest in finding clues to strange behaviours.

My own father had an earned doctorate in psychology. In the land of apartheid, psychology and sociology were the weapons of a man by the name of Hendrik French Verwoerd, who was one of my father's teachers. Psychology was an important arrow, probably the strongest arrow, in

---

11    Blank sheets can be useful. In his *Audacity of Hope*, Barack Obama wrote that "I serve as a blank screen on which people of vastly different political stripes project their own views." Except that people were not out to transform him. Like the Canadian change agents, he was out to transform them.

the quiver of a Willis Harman, whom we've already met in the course of his excursions into the New Canada. Not only was Harman described as "one of the founders of humanistic psychology," he was also a pillar of the American Association for Humanistic Psychology. We have, as well, by way of example, touched on the thoughts of Karl E. Weick. Weick was particularly beholden to the ideas of a New Age guru by the name of Gregory Bateson, one of whose works was *Steps to an Ecology of Mind: Collected Essays in Anthropology, Psychiatry, Evolution and Epistemology*. His ideas will warrant our attention on account of the influence he wielded.

Also mentioned was Joseph Chilton Pearce's *Crack in the Cosmic Egg*. Here he invokes the very anguished sentiments we've encountered in the emotional outpourings of a Jacques Hébert and a Canadian Futures Secretariat:

> Here in this crack, alternatives abound - but only for that lone reader, driven, perhaps, to hate a world of instant death, shifting enemy symbols, perpetually stimulated fears and hatreds, economic servitude, psycho-logical enslavement, and general absence of joy; a world where alter-natives polar-ize into equally abhorrent either-ors... where the only under-ground railway is run by an opposition leading back into the common circles of despair.

Pearce confessed that he himself had "searched for that explosive translation that would marginally halt the grinding forces of war, ease our ideological hatreds, and abate our wholesale battenings on our brothers' blood. I longed to find some clever cosmic sign, signaling abroad the way for mass exodus from a Naked Ape despair, and leading to that ecstasy of being fully human."

Not only was an Alinsky so aware of (an exploitable) despair. The despair engendered by visions of war and bloodshed expressed the most dearly held sentiments in the breast of Professor Ivan Head, and of even greater interest to us, marked the works of a man by the name of David Mitrany (whom we have already met in Chapter Six). Mitrany was one of the fathers (perhaps the main one) of a doctrine known as *functionalism;* to be examined later. Among his published books was *Marx Against the Peasants.* And—in line with Chairman Mao's reliance on the recognition of the countries of the "intermediate zone" —was it not interesting that the same Mitrany also wrote an article titled "Evolution of the Middle Zone?" His own pacifist pre-occupations were clearly shown by a book, *A Working Peace System: An Argument for the Functional Development of International Organization.*

A common denominator in these few examples is the way the agonizing protagonists of transformation move from the *personal* experiential plane to the plane of the collectivity. This was precisely the thrust of Willis Harman's teaching sessions for senior Canadian public servants as well as of the advice tendered by the leading light in Canada's Futures Secretariat when he insisted upon the need to "translate personal experience into global understanding," and observed how participation "generates emotion as well as reflection." As for the underlying sentiments, shades of Jean-Jacques Rousseau's conviction that unhappiness was the very basis of community and that "to communicate is to commiserate?" Of the German lyric poet Holderlin's loneliness and schizophrenia? Of the English poet Coleridge's dark anxiety? Of the German philosopher Heidegger's angst? Was it because his psyche was torn to pieces that Nietzsche wrote "The Joyful Wisdom"? How often have some of Canada's leading transformationists—so distressed, as they have been, by the human condition and its oppressive structures—favoured the words 'joy' and 'joyous.'

A similar degree of pessimism distinguished the environmentalist movement, so that when one examined the discourse of a Maurice Strong or an Al Gore or a superb communicator like the Canadian environmentalist, David Suzuki, typically recurrent words would be 'problems,' 'shortages,' 'fears,' 'suffered,' 'difficulties,' 'conflicts,' 'turbulence,' 'uncertainty,' 'hazards,' and 'contro-versy'; not unlike Professor Willis Harman's 'alienation,' 'goallessness,' 'emptiness,' and 'conflicts.' In his *Patriot Game: National Dreams and Political Realities* the financial journalist Peter Brimelow (who was mentioned in Chapter Six) speculated that with regard to the behaviours of certain Canadian public leaderships "personal psychology may well be a better explanation than political philosophy." Brooding on the same phenomenon on the American political scene, Brimelow recalled that "the conservative American columnist Joseph Sobran invented the useful word 'alienism' to describe it..." Not unrelated either were the Search Conferences organized for the officers of the Canadian International Development Agency. *Searching* was the name of Professor Ivan Head's IDRC house journal. For what were these people searching? (Bearing in mind the undeniable elements of the occult in Willis Harman's bag of tricks, one thought of another 'searching' exercise, reflected in the name of the Quest Society founded in Britain in 1909 as an offshoot of the Theosophical Society and where the poet Ezra Pound, with his own well-known interests in the occult, lectured in 1914.) One of the greatest influences on a Prime Minister Trudeau was the Canadian poet F.R. Scott, who remarked to a family friend that "he was pessimistic, as all good Canadians I believe must be."

By all accounts, was Canada ripe for experimentation? And not just on account of a congenital emptiness. The Canadian psyche had developed an active negativity—beyond a negativity towards the Americans—so aptly described by Margaret Atwood (albeit neither she nor her own writings exactly a paragon of cheerfulness). Her survey of earlier Canadian literature found that the most prevalent symbol was the coffin. As well, the eponymous Canadian hero was not someone who was successful, but someone who managed to escape disaster; not someone who made it, but who managed to make it back. This active negativity was echoed by the content of radio broadcasts, especially on the state-owned broadcasting system, broadcasts dwelling incessantly on pathologies or deprivations or disasters or sufferings of one kind or another, both personal and collective. There was even a complaint from a bus commuter in Ottawa that so much of the advertising inside the buses was of the same ilk, placed there by or on behalf of organizations in the business of alleviating a variety of ills. We would hear from a friend of ours—at that time Canada's top salesman of supercomputers—that he had strict instructions from his employers not to look at a Canadian newspaper or television program or listen to a radio commentary on the morning of an important sales call because his state of mind, and therefore his effectiveness, would have been subliminally affected. The only really positive element in the Canadian *weltanschauung* and the principal means of differentiating themselves from 'those Americans,' was the Canadian public health system, but by the end of the century that prop too had collapsed when the Canadian system had sunk quite low on the international totem pole, with scores of thousands suffering pain waiting for years for things like hip replacements, and hundreds upon hundreds dying prematurely and unnecessarily on account of criminally long waiting times for medical treatment, overcrowded emergency wards and a lack of equipment. In early 2011 an Ontarian orthopaedic surgeon who specialized in foot and ankle surgery announced that patients had to wait for 3 or 4 years if they wanted to see him in particular, and would then have to wait for another 3 or 4 years for an operation. At the same time it was reported that scores of newly qualified surgeons were unemployed because the over-extended public health system was unable to accommodate either them or their services.

Thus, for me it became important to try to divine the possible source or sources of the thought processes of certain prominent Canadian change agents occupying positions of power and influence, and especially over the course of the 1960s, the 1970s and the 1980s. Those were critical times with respect to the country's domestic and international activities, and more important, its very self-definition. (In the narcissistic words of a Canadian Royal Commission Report: "Our evolving understanding of our own identity affects, at every turn, the policy decisions about our future course of action.") Only belatedly (as explained before) would I discover Eric Voegelin's insights: he who enabled me to finally recognize and begin to understand the phenomenon of political Gnosticism at work and the peculiar problems it brought in its wake. Voegelin had seen it all! That led me to other (albeit not political) accounts of the origins and characteristics of the Gnostic spirit at the hand of authors like Hans Jonas and Elaine Pagels.

*And there, as proverbially clear as daylight, was additional confirmation that the peculiar psyches of the most active of the Canadian transformationists could not but be of Gnostic provenance.*

Perhaps more than any other, an understanding of the psychological elements in and behind Gnosticism was important, when we know (as we've already remarked) that Gnostic manifestations have been endemic at least since the dawn of Christianity, showing up at different times, in different places, and in different guises; as they will continue to do. They could well be symptoms of a fundamental and enduring tension in the human psyche.

This, if anything has distinguished the Gnostic psyche. From the very beginning, it has been a sense of despair, lostness and alienation and—one might add—the very antithesis to Christian hope. James Hitchcock, the historian, thought he had found the key to understanding Gnosticism because it had first flourished in late antiquity at a time when the world was thoroughly unsettled, so that "Gnosticism was a response to the anxiety and rootlessness which this situation generated... Gnosticism taught people simultaneously to despair over the universe and to imagine infinite possibilities open to them in the universe of the imagination instead." As well, the Gnostic psyche has been characterized by a spirit of rebelliousness, coupled with a marked degree of intolerance. Of course, almost by definition—and equally important—is the Gnostic approach to epistemology (the branch of philosophy concerned with the nature and incidences of knowledge), because the Gnostic thinks that he has the *gnosis,* the knowledge.

These elements are presented in the rest of this narrative. For the moment, let us note that the Gnostic affliction appeared to be primarily psychological—let alone spiritual—in nature, something Voegelin recognized when he equated the condition with Hegel's alienated spirit and "Heidegger's flungness (*Geworfenheit*, often translated as 'thrown-ness') of human existence." Voegelin was interested in how "both the modern and the ancient Gnostics respond to the condition of 'flungness' in the alien world."

One falls too easily into litanies of woe and dire prognostications focused on a particular personality who has managed to capture the popular imagination at a particular time, when it is far more important to try to come to grips with a *typology*, and especially if it's a *recurrent* typology. The actors come and go, but in the Gnostic domain—and just as human nature never changes—the underlying patterns of behaviour have transcended both time and space. Thus one can observe that typically the Gnostic, including the political Gnostic, confuses reality with the dream, such as in the oratorical outpourings of a Barack Obama in Berlin and elsewhere. Quite problematical is the Gnostic who manages to turn that condition into a political tool, often foisting on an unsuspecting public impossible goals. Such as Trudeau's touting of a powerful slogan he employed in his early electioneering escapades, namely, promises of a "Just Society."

And here, nothing could be more illustrative than Willis Harman's magical exercises. Voegelin himself refers to "magic operations in the dream world." He also says: "The identification of dream and reality as a matter of principle has practical results which may appear strange but can hardly be considered surprising." More subtle in this respect—but I suspect to have been of the same genre—were the utopian visions foreshadowed in Trudeau's 1964 manifesto, although put forward, as they were, under the title of *An Appeal for Realism in Politics*. That here too there was a psychological factor is shown by Voegelin's puzzlement by *what kinds of people* would indulge in such exercises, when he observes that "the attitude toward reality remains energetic and active, but neither reality nor action in reality can be brought into focus; the vision is blurred by the Gnostic dream. *The result is a very complex pneumopathological state of mind...*" (Emphasis added).

When one considers the lives of several supreme champions of the transformation of 'man and his world,' the complexity deepens in light of the ambivalence of the Gnostic attitude toward the body, shown, for example, by odd combinations of asceticism with a distinctly libertine approach to sexual matters, of which Trudeau was probably a classic example. Strange that Trudeau, from various accounts, appeared to have been a libertine in his relations with women, but would happily smoke marijuana in the company of his young wife, and yet would not touch tobacco or a glass of wine, let alone hard liquor. Voegelin's initial preoccupation had been with the Nazi phenomenon. It was noteworthy (according to a contemporary account) that Adolf Hitler was "...an ascetic, a celibate and a vegetarian and he neither smoked nor drank... Hitler's associates know that in respect to women Hitler is far from the ascetic he and the Propaganda Bureau would like to have the German public believe. None of them with the possible exception of Hoffman and Schaub [his personal adjutant], know the nature of his sexual activities. This has led to a great deal of conjecture in Party circles. There are some who believe that his sex life is perfectly normal but restricted. Others, that he is immune from such temptations and that nothing happens when he is alone with girls. Still others believe that he is homosexual."

Gilles Grondin—a Catholic acquaintance of Trudeau's at a time when he, in his early days, had worked in Ottawa for a short time—told me that he sometimes visited Trudeau in his apartment across the river and was struck by just how sparse and ascetic (Grondin's words) was the virtual absence of furnishings and appointments, and that notwithstanding his family wealth.

As for Mao Tse-tung, one observer thought that "Foucault would presume-ably have assigned Mao's theory of ascetic self-discipline, in terms of its bodily practice, to a pre-modern historical formation." And as for Lenin, from a review of a book titled *The Unknown Lenin: From the Secret Archive,* we learn that "there was a strong ascetic streak in Lenin. By suppressing his own sentiments, by denying himself the pleasures of life, he tried to harden himself as a revolutionary and make himself insensitive to others' suffering. Lenin did not smoke or drink, he could not tolerate flowers in the room, and apart from his brief affair with Inessa Armand... he did not have a weakness for beautiful women." One may well wonder what could be deduced from the desperate—and classic—Gnostic cry: "Who has taken me from my father's home and thrown me into this stinking body?"

Equally striking would be how the utopian visions of a Trudeau or an Obama foreshadowed one world, a dream world of universalisms, and so we've already read with interest Voegelin's observation, worthy of being

215

quoted here once again: "*With radical immanentization the dream world has blended into the real world terminologically; the obsession of replacing the world of reality by the transfigured dream world has become the obsession of the one world in which the dreamers adopt the vocabulary of reality, while changing its meaning as if the dream were reality.*" (Emphasis added.)[12] This observation by Voegelin will be even more pertinent when we come to address the subject of the immanent versus the transcendent.

The really interesting and significant development in the history of Gnosticism is that while originally the Gnostic had been desperate to escape from an evil world which was so imperfect, so unjust, that it could only have been the handiwork of an impostor God. But the dawn of *political* Gnosticism marked a crucial about-turn in the Gnostic agenda, when the Gnostic became a man-and-world transformative activist. *He had decided to reverse course, so to speak. Instead of trying to escape from the world, he would turn back in and upon it, fully determined to remake it and so correct God's handiwork for him.*

And yet the (political) Gnostic has remained confused and torn. Working to remake 'man and his world,' he's still capable of resorting to classic gnostic escapist language. Here is one other instance to support my belief that Barack Obama may have been infected with a Gnostic spirit, when, near the end of his Nobel Prize acceptance speech, he cried out: "So let us reach for the world that ought to be; that spark of the divine that still stirs within each of our souls." Because, as we read elsewhere: "For the Gnostics, the divine spark in man is entrapped in an evil realm of shadows, which is a close parallel to the Kabbalist's *Sitra Achra* (the 'Other Side'). This spark, in the guise of individual men, is unaware of its true origins, but nevertheless possesses an unconscious desire to return to its divine home." Some people wondered if Obama himself was sure of his own true origins, and he was most likely not aware of the extent to which he had absorbed and internalized a Gnostic New Age *zeitgeist*.

---

12    Even experts have had difficulty in following Voegelin's thoughts because they are so densely expressed; I've had to re-read his *New Science of Politics* time and again, ending up with just about every sentence underlined!

They were, of course, not alone in this quest. Many a Christian church has inverted the priorities of the Gospels, so aptly criticized by Kenneth Hamilton in *Earthly Good,* the last book he wrote before he died. Even in the Catholic Church, and for related reasons, none other than Pope Benedict had reservations about the signature document produced by Vatican II, the Pastoral Constitution on the Church in the Modern World, *Gaudium et Spes* (Joy and Hope).

And yet we should not give or gain the impression that the 'man and his world' transformationist impetus only came with the charismatic and dream-filled political leaderships of Trudeaus and Obamas and their acolytes. Based on a remote lodge on Cortes Island, north of Vancouver, is the meeting place of the Social Change Institute. Its purpose is to gather "seasoned and emerging leaders with thinkers and trainers from the change-making world." In November 2010 a Canadian national newspaper reported that "the Social Change Institute is a magnet for professionals. Professional activists. Professional environmentalists. And, yes, professional business people and politicians." The centre, we learn, "has been transformed into the virtual headquarters of a powerfully sophisticated and coordinated network of people who are mobilizing millions of dollars 'towards systemic social change focused in one region.'" The plan is to establish a model that could be exported to other regions. "If the world could not be changed in Vancouver... we have a real problem on our hands," confides the leader. Substantial financial support has come from Canadian but mostly American organizations and some well-known foundations, and from people like Carol Newell, "heiress to the U.S. Rubbermaid fortune." Now for the dream. Out of touch with reality, one of the spokespeople informed the *Huffington Post* of "a 500 year vision for the planet, incremented into sequential 50-year strategies." Recalling the tactics of a Saul Alinsky—described elsewhere in this book—here too we are told that once a cause has been identified, the various groups being mobilized are "involved in political agitation and keeping things off balance as much as possible."

But there was still a question of *how* to implement such grandiosities. That became the main focus of my interest in the activities of the

*Cobblestones*

Canadian political Gnostics and a few of their foreign counterparts of the late 20<sup>th</sup> and early 21<sup>st</sup> centuries. Understanding the psychology was important, but only insofar as it was a door opening on to a much wider landscape with the most amazing contours.

# CHAPTER ELEVEN
# MEANS AND METHODS

"It is not enough to set tasks, we must also solve the problem of the methods for carrying them out. If our task is to cross a river, we cannot cross it without a bridge or boat. Unless the bridge or boat problem is solved, it is idle to speak of crossing the river. Unless the problem of method is solved, talk about the task is useless."

Mao Tse-tung (1934)

"Goals have no more reality than the means that are devised to reach them... Indeed, the experience of that superb strategist, Mao Tse-tung, might lead us to conclude that in a vast and heterogeneous country, the possibility of establishing socialist strongholds in certain regions is the very best thing."

P.E. Trudeau (1961)

"The means-and-ends moralists... should search themselves as to their real political position... The most unethical of all means is the non-use of any means."

Saul Alinsky (1971)

Already mentioned was that other great exponent of the primacy of means and method, especially in the form of organization: Vladimir Lenin, as attested, among others, by Leszek Kolakowski, the Polish philosopher and historian of ideas. Georg Lukacs, the Hungarian Marxist philosopher and literary critic, remarked that "Lenin was one of the few great men who succeeded in much, in all the most essential things, and precisely in practice... due to the absolute priority he was prepared to give to practice."

He called Lenin a *"theoretician of practice"*, just as one of Trudeau's major preoccupations was with "techniques of government." (Emphasis added.)

In his diagnosis and treatment of the rise of political Gnosticism Eric Voegelin did not (at least to my knowledge) attend to a concomitant and conscious shift, beyond 'mere' *praxis*, to a *gnosis* specifically of method, of technique. Such knowledge would be essential if there was any hope that 'man and his world' could be efficiently and effectively transformed. Here was therefore a rarely recognized subject of political science! After all, is there not a science behind every technology and technique? And could it be otherwise in the socio-political domain? Yet Voegelin at least recognized that whereas "ancient Gnosticism strongly tended toward apoliticism," there developed instead an interest in "drawing on the power of such knowledge for the transformation of the present world." The operative question we would have to ask is: How would this be done?

We have also noticed, though *en passant*, how Karl Weick equated means with ends, even contending that meaning resided in the means itself. As I learned at a conference held in Niagara-on-the-Lake on the subject of "applying science to global development, where the only just model is a universal model," none other than Albert Einstein was said to have complained that "the modern world is all about the perfection of means and the confusion of ends." Voegelin saw the same problem in an immanentizing world, a world no longer beholden to anything transcendental to or beyond itself; a world where, effectively, meaning was confined to the means, and as Karl Weick contended as well. (Immanence and transcendence are the subjects of Chapter Fourteen following.)

But before we proceed to other examples of the same train of thought, two problems should be brought to the fore. The first (already hinted at) is philosophical, perhaps even moral. What if the focus on the means becomes so dominant *that ends or goals cease to count*, at least for the time being, until the desired transformations have developed a sufficient momentum? What happens when one can no longer distinguish between cause and effect? What happens if the value of an action is confined to itself? Is the world not already self-referential enough? Do we not have enough narcissism to contend with?

Now assume that the transformationist cannot afford to let it be known that he has *no* supervening goals. But then, and alternatively, what happens if—in his portfolio of transformational instruments—means and ends are so *fused* with one another, that the distinction disappears altogether? And thus, would there then not also be an epistemological problem? Because the means-ends dichotomy has at least served the essential purpose of providing a measure of objectivity in human thought, discourse, conduct, and decision making, because the end or the goal, however derived, at least provides or represents some sort of standard. In our brief look at the role of psychology there was mention of one Gregory Bateson. Bateson approvingly cited the view "that we have to find the value of a planned act implicit in and simultaneous with the act itself, not separate from it in the sense that the act would derive its value from reference to a future end or goal." Thus, are we not putting our finger here on a most fundamental problem? One develops a feeling that when humans were to act in this way, their behaviours would not be much different from the conditioned responses of lower members of the animal kingdom.

Though in a different form, this very issue also surfaced in the (already noted) comparative analysis of *Asian and Western Organization* by the Asian Institute of Management. The discussion was about rationality in the conduct of human affairs. The point was made that rationality embraced an element of *objectivity*. In organizations "this means establishing ends and ordering the means to those ends... Objectivity as an ideal flows naturally from this perspective of means and ends..." The study mentioned the problems that arise when people are guided by abstractions, such as the value of mere "participation" in decision making by a group. Participation—it was argued—is "a means, not an end, and when treated as an end, it can become more repressive than the unadorned authoritarianism it is supposed to replace." In his treatment of modern fascism Gene Veith too touched on the problem where meaning is created through nothing more than the exercise of a collective will. *When the means is uppermost, when the means replaces ends, the will prevails and reason disappears.*

At this point let us briefly remind ourselves again of the teachings of Barack Obama's mentor, Saul Alinsky, on the subject of means and ends, because Alinsky was more explicit than others in his dismissal of "morals and ethics as nothing but impediments to political success." If you're only interested in the struggle, and the pursuit of power, as in the case of Alinsky and his acolytes, why bother with *any* external, let alone superior, reference point? Why recognize *any* authority? Do we not also discern an element of Islamist ideology, when we see a critique such as the following: "Alinsky, like the Koran, Sira, and Hadith, represents morality turned upside down or abandoned entirely in favor of cold pragmatism."[13]

Such is the world of the will to power, whether Alinsky's "People Power" or the elements of the "Power Analysis" diagrammed on a blackboard by a left-handed Obama. This will happen in any society where leaderships derive their satisfaction from the mere act of manipulating others and where 'change' becomes both tool and goal, "as part of a national movement for change" (in Alinsky's own words). Transformation for the sake of transforming action. Change for the sake of changingness. One might even see it as the organizational equivalent, at the collective level, of narcissism at the personal level, because Karl Weick argues that in organizations the members first concentrate on themselves, and that "common ends follow rather than precede common means." "People don't have to agree on goals to act collectively." That their contribution is needed "is secondary to the fact that the contribution is made. Partners in a collective structure share space, time, and energy, but they need not share visions, aspirations, or intentions. That sharing comes much later, if it ever comes at all."

A means-oriented regime is where the instrumentalist state of mind comes into full flower. Examples are legion. Spending those trying months observing at first hand, and having to live with, the implementation of Dr Hendrik French Verwoerd's plans for the apartheid state, I had my

---

13    Recognized as the most notable among Islamic gnostic sects are the Sufis and the Yezidi.

first taste of the way a political transformationist would concentrate on the *operationalization* of his ideas. For Lenin, organization was purely an instrument. Even democracy was a tool, not a state of affairs. A Canadian politician talked of "applying the religions of the world." The Chinese learned how to *exploit* capitalism. Yet another Canadian politician talked of "exploiting the arts for transformation." Willis Harman advocated the utility of constant repetition.

Radical feminists in particular depended heavily on *method,* and it did not matter in what class of activity. In fact, hardly any domain of public interest was untouched. Take, for example, *A Feminist Review of Criminal Law* commissioned by the Canadian Ministry of Supply and Services in 1985. On the very first page we learn that "it is important to stress the centrality of feminist *practice*." (Emphasis added.) There is the familiar claim (and "the basic value underlying the review") that "women live in a patriarchal world, subject to male domination and control." "In other words," the report continued, "how can the *criminal law be used as a weapon against patriarchy* and be reduced as a weapon of patriarchy?" (*Their* emphasis!) In the course of more than 200 pages the report lists and spells out in great detail "the major aspects of *feminist method*." (Emphasis added.) Here is also a good example of the use of yet another potent transformative tool, namely, the new Canadian Charter of Rights and Freedoms. Even more revealing was a comprehensive study, also published in 1985, and financed by the Women's Program in the department of the Canadian Secretary of State. Note, again, the first sentence: "The relationship between theory and practice is never very simple." "The report," one learns, "is informed by feminist theory and methodology, and it is prompted by experience and involvement in feminist politics." Theory. Methodology. Practice. Experience. Participation.

Take another instance. It relates to the international treaty generally known as the Law of the Sea, and we recall Elisabeth Mann Borgese's role in the development of that most important addition to international law. When she held out the prospect of a "self-managed society" —where there was "in fact no top and no bottom" (typical Gnostic parlance) and no hierarchy of any kind, but only a "process that feeds back on itself"

—her dreams were not just academic. Here was a good example of the importance of the means and the method to people who aim to turn the world upside down and inside out. In an article in the *American Journal of International Law*, a British commentator, discussing the Law of the Sea negotiations, described "developments in technique" that, for the first time, introduced international treaty-making to a novel way of reaching agreement. The new technique was "a major international experiment in decision making by consensus." No longer would votes be taken! At work was a strange new principle, namely, "that delegates have a right to agree as well as a right to disagree." Everyone is familiar with a right to disagree, but I had never heard of a "right to agree." Think upon it! Another learned journal called the Law of the Sea negotiations "the most impressive law-making spectacle in history." An entire chapter of the journal was devoted to a discussion of "Majority Rule and Consensus Technique in Law-Making Diplomacy." The previous method of decision-making by majority vote was laid at the door of the "American democratic tradition" which, by implication, was backward. What must henceforth count is Jean-Jacques Rousseau's *volonté générale*. Quite brazenly the article admitted that "consensus is not a legal concept of decision-making; it is a political maxim." These were the kinds of measures deemed necessary to be able to engineer a vaunted New World Order. And, of course, if consensus becomes god, disagreement and divisiveness (and undermining people's "right to agree") become Original Sin, and then one is well on ones way to a fascist nirvana. I was surprised—and made it known to him—when, in 2010, a Catholic archbishop expressed regret about a political initiative in Ottawa involving abortion (or it could have been same-sex 'marriage') which, he said, was "divisive."

But perhaps the height of instrumentalism could be seen in a proposition in the *Canadian Yearbook of International Law* that even the pursuit of *peace* was not an objective in its own right, but merely a means to "transform the existing system into a rational system of world order." As we well know, peace can be abused. A Christian might be excused for thinking of verse 25 in chapter 8 of the *Book of Daniel*: "...and he shall magnify himself in his heart, and by peace shall destroy many."

Like a misguided pursuit of peace, environmentalism can be a weapon too; a means to ends that may have little to do with the physical welfare of the planet. One of the most thought-provoking essays I have read came from Mary Douglas, Professor of Anthropology in the University of London, where she dealt with environmentalism long before the star of Vice-President Al Gore shot across the firmament. This was in 1970 and I've kept it ever since. Her thesis was that almost from the dawn of organized humanity the quintessential enemies of society were seen and defined as *polluters* of one kind or another. Exploiting fears and charges of pollution (defined in different ways), she said, was a universal method of exercising control over others. Douglas predicted that the ecology movement "will succeed in changing the idea of nature", just as the abolitionists "succeeded in revolutionizing the image of man." To this end, she said, *time* was one of the final arbiters of control, because of a "kind of time-bomb. Time is running out." In her study of how the Lele tribe in Africa dealt with the "enemy as polluter... time-tabling was used as a weapon of control... Time, money, God, and nature, usually in that order, are universal trump cards plunked down to win an argument." In sum, she said, "I have spoken of pollution ideas which are used by people as controls on themselves and on each other. In this light they seem to be weapons or instruments." The polluting enemy had to be rooted out. In the wake of ideological environmentalism—Douglas observed rather cryptically—would come "the day when everyone can see exactly what is on the end of everyone's fork; on that day there is no pollution and no purity and nothing edible or inedible, credible or incredible, because the classifications of social life are gone. There is no more meaning."

More pertinent to an overriding interest in the supremacy of process and processes and the related organizational theories, is the fact that—as in other domains—the environmentalist tussles of the first decade of the 21$^{st}$ century did not really turn on any realistic, achievable, goals, but depended almost entirely on a reliance on process; in other words, the means. Here too, crucially, the (political) meaning was in the means, and in little else, except for religious and quasi-religious affirmations of an unbounded love for Gaia.

One might want to speculate how Mary Douglas would have reacted to a Barack Obama's emphatic and repeated invocations of the phrase: "This is the moment when..." Was *he* too using time as a weapon? She too would have been struck by the very last word, emphasized and capitalized Obama's Nobel Prize acceptance speech. *Earth*. And what might she have said when, in March 2015, the former head of the Intergovernmental Panel on Climate Change (and co-winner of the Nobel Peace Prize with Al Gore) confessed: "For me, the protection of Planet Earth... is more than a mission. It is my religion and my *dharma*"? Thus does an ideology become a stand-alone religion.

———

First and foremost among the principal devices in the transformationist's tool kit—and mentioned briefly before—is the theory and practice of *functionalism*. "The functional approach, "says Paul A. Tharp, Jr, "begins with the concept of human society as a system of behavior." This brings us right back to the world of applied psychology. So let's try to put together a composite picture of a technique which, essentially, consists of *induced learning by induced doing*. Of *both* of those elements, Trudeau's ramming through of his culturally transformative and constitutionalized Charter of Rights and Freedoms may yet be recognized as the supreme example.

Functionalism, in brief, employs "the power of creative manifestation." Which is actually a good, succinct, definition if it is also tied to the experiential factor. Seen from another angle, it ties in with "process as everything." It can also be related to *praxis,* which is "action informed by theoretical considerations." The ubiquitous Willis Harman was closer to the mark when he talked of "forced functions" and "forcing functions." For one thing, functionalist operations are highly calculated, and indeed, Mitrany himself noted how calculated Vladimir Lenin had been. Another clue lies in it being described as "strategic gradualism" just as the Law of the Sea process was cited as an example of "creeping legislation." The exponents of functionalism have been pictured as "practical dreamers." We shall yet be looking at cybernetics (meriting a separate chapter) as a transformative tool, but we've put functionalism at the head of the list inasmuch as it has been credited with moving "beyond cybernetics."

Having already learned something about the ideas of Karl Weick, one notes with interest that in Weick another crosswalk appears, namely, between functionalism and "organizational dynamics and patterns." Yet another overtone is distinctly Marxist, in that functionalism relates to a transforming process that can alter experience. In Marxist doctrine man is reshaped by entering into relationships. Such a process, as Harman hinted, *was also capable of being forced.* On the Maoist side, one has learned that "correct ideas come from social practice." Functionalists are not only interested in whether things work, but how they can be made to work. Elisabeth Mann Borgese described the "working society" as a "learning society."

Ideally the learning experience must be on both the personal and the political planes, and preferably mutually self-reinforcing. But one problem with a Gnostic "learning society" (which may also be its Achilles heel) is connected with the epistemological insights of the philosophers Michael Polanyi and Alasdair MacIntyre. They argued persuasively—and many people would say decisively—that knowledge cannot be acquired except within the framework and against a background of a *tradition* of one sort or another. All knowledge, they maintained, was tradition-dependent. If this was true, Gnostics—they who are so self-convincedly in the know—could most certainly not acquire knowledge from the contents of their *futuristic* exercises and their futuristic dreams (or even their current practices), since those are the very antithesis of tradition. On the other hand, they might counter that their gnosis was based on a long tradition of Gnostic thought, or (as I might add) a tradition of rebelliousness. But on the latter point one detects yet another weakness in the Gnostic armour, because Polanyi and MacIntyre contended that within the framework of a tradition the acquirer of knowledge would, in addition, have to be submitting to *authority* of one kind or another. Which, of course, rebels cannot do. Would it not be funny if the very high priests of *gnosis* were to founder on a theory of *knowledge*!

———

Catholics in particular know, or should know, everything about the importance of *tradition* in the religious domain. Not so well known are T.S. Eliot's thoughts on how indispensable tradition is even in the world of the *poet*. He wrote that "we shall often find that not only the best, but the most individual parts of his work may be those in which the dead poets, his ancestors, assert their immortality most vigorously." Therefore, Eliot maintained, a poet needed "the historical sense, which we many call nearly indispensable to anyone who would continue to be a poet beyond his twenty-fifth year, and the historical sense involves a perception, not only of the pastness of the past, but of its presence; the historical sense compels a man to write not merely with his own generation in his bones, but with a feeling that the whole literature of Europe from Homer and within it the whole literature of his own country has a simultaneous existence and composes a simultaneous order."

Here I have to confess that so much of what I've written is underpinned and inspired by an image in my mind of the lives and the work of my forebears—Huguenot and Dutch and South African—generation after generation. It is as if they're looking down from their imagined (and some of them real) portraits on the wall of the library in my home. Is it therefore a wonder that quite belatedly in my life (and despite my Calvinist roots) I should have been so attracted to an institution whose teachings have been so dominated by the works of those early Fathers of the Church? I think too of the connection with that little book written by John Paul II titled *Memory and Identity*. Without memory, no tradition. And without either, no identity...

Should one then wonder when Barack Obama's mentor, Saul Alinsky, says about history that it cannot be known. In his words: "Who is to know where mythology leaves off and history begins - or which is which..." This caused a commentator to say that "without a knowable historical record there can be no learning from past events, and no trust in previous knowledge." One may therefore well ask about Obama's apparent rootlessness and lack of clear identity, so that he could describe himself as a blank page on which people could write their own aspirations.

Anyway, we can see why functionalist processes are described as "seeing by experiencing." Or as Mr X (of our earlier acquaintance) would say: "We must actually do." Referring to fire walking, our overwrought author of *Cosmic Egg* fame (also mentioned before) intoned that "once the notion that it could really be done was implanted in experience, it became a part of our reality potential." (Obama's "*Yes We Can*" 2008 campaign rally cry?) Purely psychological in nature is the contention of our distressed author that "we act ourselves into ways of believing and believe ourselves into ways of acting."

So, in short, functionalism applies the age-old and hallowed principle and practice of "learning by doing", *except that—we may as well repeat—in the hands of the political transformationist those learning experiences are induced.* In Goethe's *Faust* the deed came first, then the knowledge. In yet another of his books, *Foundational Theory of Politics* (1975) David Mitrany defined it well. He was obsessed with the deployment of functionalism in the service of world peace, and thought that world peace could only be achieved if a "man can be weaned away from his loyalty to the nation state by the experience of fruitful international cooperation." Referring to *national* governments, he argued that "one important pillar of their authority—the loyalty of citizens—would have been weakened in the development at the popular level of a *social-psychological* community which stressed 'co-operative' goals". (Emphasis added.) In other words, a contrived conditioning process. Naturally, once such a technique was properly refined, it could be exploited for other socio-political and culture-transformative purposes. And this may well have been what Barack Obama had in mind with his repeated mantra of "Change." Not just ordinary changes, but changed *processes*. Elsewhere we mention how Saul Alinsky's son attributed Obama's electoral success in 2008 to the methods Obama had learned in Alinsky's Chicago; methods, he said, that could be replicated on a larger scale.

Consider then the unbounded enthusiasm for functionalism on the part of Pierre Elliott Trudeau. He quoted Lord Acton on the harmful effects of "nationality" that "will be marked with material as well as moral ruin, *in order that a new invention may prevail over the works of God and the interests of mankind."* "This new invention," said Trudeau, *"may well be functionalism in politics..."* (Emphases added.) Stronger language can hardly be imagined. The very first issue of *Cité Libre*, of June 1950, launched (as we have already noted) by Trudeau and his colleagues soon after the former returned from the fall of Nanjing and Shanghai, was not only dedicated to the memory of Emmanuel Mounier, but devoted to the subject of functionalism. There, in an article titled *"Politique fonctionnel"* Trudeau wrote: *"The time has come to borrow from the architect the style that is called functional, to scrap the thousand prejudices that clutter up the present and to start building for the new man. Let us throw down the totem poles and violate the taboos, or better yet let us consider them as non-existent. Let us be coldly intelligent."* (Emphasis added once again.) Chairman Mao could not have said it better. Nor Alinsky.

In Canada, at least, the political transformationists believed that the best way to kick-start a functional learning process in any sphere was simply to go ahead and introduce a law or a government measure or a program of action (however controversial) by acting with "boldness and audacity." Memories of Danton's French Revolutionary slogan: *"Il faut de l'audace, encore de l'audace, toujours de l'audace."* This way of going about things could not have been better shown than by the veritable *blitzkrieg* of Trudeau's pursuit of a Canadian Charter of Rights and Freedoms. Skeptics were told that they should hold their noses.

In Britain, as we've seen, Prime Minister Thatcher was greatly upset by the way the Charter package had been sneaked into the 'patriation' of the Canadian constitution. Revert then to our earlier references to the way Canadians were being tested, and the rest of the *rodomontade* of the time. One was reminded of the *Futurists' Manifesto* associated with the rise of European fascism, proclaiming that "we want to sing the love of danger, the habit of energy and rashness. The essential elements of our poetry will be courage, audacity, and revolt." Willis Harman's sessions in Ottawa consisted of "Action Learning." The new Gnosticism was described as "a superior knowledge of an active character." As to revolt, did not the slogans of the French Revolution represent "a program to be carried out directly in actual practice"?

The French Declaration of the Rights of Man is an eerie reminder of how Canada's own Charter of Rights and Freedoms was designed—one has to suspect, by this time, and with good reason—to serve as a tool for inducing functionalist societal learning processes, and very successfully, as it turned out. So much so that to begin to recite examples would be beyond the scope of this book. In any case, they've been well-documented elsewhere. Suffice it to quote just one sentence from a Canadian Royal Commission Report, in reference to the same Charter. "It will involve governments at both levels in micro-social engineering as they seek to readjust the status order produced by history: in the public sector, in education, and probably, by contract compliance, in the private sector." This latter function would be bolstered by the introduction of a countrywide system of human rights tribunals (at both federal and provincial levels) with extraordinary powers to enforce suitable behaviours on the part of ordinary citizens. And these kangaroo courts—veritable people's courts, mostly staffed by legal amateurs—were neither constrained nor restrained by the safeguards built into the age-old judicial rules of evidence and procedure. The "forcing function" was augmented by public subsidies for any citizen (group, in effect) who felt aggrieved and sought to use the Charter to challenge any law or regulation of their choice. To that end the government created and funded a Court Challenges Program. (In the course of a general election campaign in 2011, and after the government of the day put an end to the program, the leader of the official opposition vowed that he would reinstate it.) In tandem with this program was the creation of a Women's Legal Education and Action Fund, with the same objectives. In the case of the human rights tribunals the dice was loaded against defendants, because, as we noted earlier, while the state paid for the litigation expenses of complainants, defendants had to bear their own costs. Force-feeding the transformational process was the order of the day.

On the international front Mitrany's hopes for functionalism were focused on pacifist causes, but one Allan Ezra Gotlieb—a right-hand man to Prime Minister Trudeau in several government departments, and especially active in the domain of foreign affairs, including a stint as the Canadian ambassador in Washington—advocated unilateralism (simply forcing other countries' hands) "as a way of pushing the development of international law." The fact that Gotlieb also presided over the formulation of Canada's new (and certainly transformative) immigration and refugee policies—I was in a meeting where this was discussed, with him in the chair—conjures up something said by Paul Tharp, a professor of political science at the University of Oklahoma. For Tharp, *migration* was itself a *technique* "…in shifting loyalties and attitudes at the level of the mass public… Increased daily personal interactions of private citizens may result in the destruction of parochial loyalties." Was it not Mitrany who saw functionalism as a tool to get rid of national loyalties? Might one even dare to confess to a sniff of subversion? And perhaps a step beyond Trudeau's musing that the day might come when Canada would no longer exist?

––––––––––

It was not my purpose to chronicle the history of Canada's functionalist 'successes' but simply to try to understand what the techniques comprised (or purported to achieve), and most important, what mentality was behind—or associated with—their deployment. If functionalism was practised on groups of people, even on an entire nation, and even internationally in treaty-making settings, the technique itself was by no means secret knowledge. What might well be the secret element could be knowledge that the technique was deliberately employed, without people being aware of it. If the means and the method was the uppermost priority of the political Gnostic, what an irony that my very first job in the Canadian government—in a regional economic development department—was that of an Organization and Methods Officer!

When all was said and done, and even as functionalism was a behaviour-modifying tool capable of being applied to a wide spectrum of required learning situations and experiences—and even as functionalism was a manifestation of the primacy of the means—a yet more pervasive attribute distinguished it, in tandem with some of the other transformative devices. Functionalism was also tied up with *systems,* and its deployment one instance of the workings of what I came to recognize as the *systems mind,* the subject of the next chapter.

"Multiculturalism and 'affirmative action' are allies in the assault on the institution of American identity."

Roger Kimball
'Institutionalizing our demise:
America vs. multiculturalism'

# CHAPTER TWELVE
# SYSTEMS, THE SYSTEMS
# MIND, AND TOTALISM

**System, n.**
1. Any organized assembly of resources and procedures united and regulated by interaction or interdependence to accomplish a set of specific functions
2. A collection of personnel, equipment, and methods organized to accomplish a set of specific functions
3. Systems thinking is a social approach using systems theories to create desired outcomes, or change

In her comment (so many years ahead of events) on the anthropological origins of aggressive environmentalism, Mary Douglas also remarked on how "ecologists have perceived system. In fact, their whole science consists in assuming system." She found that "the most odious pollutions are those which threaten a system at its intellectual base." In other words, a close link existed between systems thinking and exercises in social control. Ought one then to be surprised to learn that apart from his activities in the field of psychology, no less than Willis Harman was also a systems analyst? He taught systems analysis at Stanford University in California, where he "…began attempting to apply the methods of systems analysis to issues of social policy - a largely untried and somewhat daring field at that time." In *Angels of Light?* Lawrence Osborn noted that "a disproportionately high percentage of Neo-Pagans and New Agers have found employment in areas such as systems analysis."

Nor should one wonder why systems thinking ran hand in hand with functionalism, given Paul Tharp's definition, namely, that "the functional approach begins with the concept of human society as a system of behavior." As well, Ervin Laszlo—one of the most prolific high priests of the systems-for-world-transformation cult, publishing out of New York, and to an extent that one had to wonder who was financing the enterprise—was aware that "within systems analysis, some scholars have focused upon a 'functional' approach." In his analysis of *Mitrany's Functionalist World Order*, Justin Cooper (president of Redeemer University College in Ontario) discerned that functionalism was "akin to piecemeal social engineering, gradual system-building or growing systemness..." Not only in this respect, but in others, I shall discover yet more linkages and inter-relationships among the change agent's manipulatory tools.

Voegelin, certainly, had seen the *Gnostic* elements in the world of the systems mind when he referred to "the obscuring of reality through systems (*scotosis*) and the prohibition against the asking of the Question as a principle of the systems..." He thought he had seen idea patterns at work that involved a "closed 'system' the internal logic of which was tyrannically used to displace human experience and the exploration of reality." No wonder that a Willis Harman—a systems man to the core—so excelled in conjuring up and deploying dream worlds! Though he never referred to the 'systems mind' as such, Voegelin would have realized that it *had* to be Gnostic because, *to exercise control over reality, the Gnostic must construct a system*. Systems building, in Voegelinian thought, was a Gnostic form of reasoning. Like models in general, systems were an *abstraction* from both nature and man.

---

Americans might ask what Barack Obama might have had in mind with his controversial health care system, but did his opponents realize (except perhaps instinctively) that there could well have been more than met the eye? As a measure of government intrusiveness it was virtually unprecedented in American history; at least at the federal level. Individuals would be compelled to buy things they did not want and might not even need. Catholic institutions (among others) would have been mandated to go diametrically against their religious principles and convictions by having to provide their employees with insurance covering contraceptive devices, morning-after abortion-inducing pills, and sterilizations. In the governing legislation the Secretary of Health was empowered to avail herself of no fewer than 700 provisions containing the word "shall"; 200 provisions underpinned by the word "may"; and 139 by the word "determines." Once Americans submitted to and started to accept such a system, a successful introduction would have satisfied just about every element of a transformative political and cultural functionalism at work. Almost by definition such all-inclusive systems are incompatible with notions of freedom. "Obamacare"—as it was called—was also a classic example of the Gnostic systems-minded belief in measures that were not only "global in scope, and universal in application" (in Trudeau's words, as in his Mansion House speech in London, also mentioned below). And Americans would have been put through a remarkable functionalist transformative and conditioning 'learning process.'

Here I'm only referring to impacts on the American way of life. A universal public health care system supported by the general revenues of governments would not be essentially different from social security or a general system of taxation affecting all taxpayers, and therefore not aimed at particular individuals. In other words, it operated in the public sphere. Obamacare, on the other hand, was designed to force behaviour on individuals, and mostly in the private sector. That, unlike in the Canadian system, some people could opt out, merely underscored the fact that the scheme was targetted at the individual level. In New Age parlance: "One by one by one." In other words, there are two quite distinct types of applied universalism.

———————

If *scotosis* is defined as a deliberate "deformation of truth by obscuring reality", what better example could be found—as we have seen—than in the imposition of a new voting system, namely, an essentially falsely contrived *consensus* in international treaty-making processes in the place of the truthful reflection of reality by the taking of actual votes? Not only can the transformationist's system not tolerate contradictions; it can apparently not tolerate even the *appearance* of contradictions. As Voegelin made clear, it cannot even permit the Question. There was the night, in a country of the south, so many years ago, when a man was dragged off a platform and brutally assaulted because he was not allowed to ask the Question. He not only offended a system but, in Mary Douglas's words, was threatening its intellectual base. Systems do not brook questions, let alone dissent. By definition, within interconnected systems proper, necessity rules. Once such a system was put in place, it would then ask of people, in Prime Minister Trudeau's own words, to have "the will to be commanded by necessity, to embrace obligation." A "will to be commanded" makes me think of a *happily* compliant slave.

And there would have to be obedience because—again by definition—all the components were interconnected and therefore interdependent. Thus, in a colloquium delivered in Vancouver on December 8, 1980, Professor Ivan Head talked of a "desperate need" to ensure that "no single component in the social system leads to the failure of others." In what was touted as possibly the most important speech of a lifetime, on the subject of a transformed world order, Trudeau told an audience at the Mansion House in London, England, on March 13, 1975, of the primary imperative to recognize "the interconnection of all phenomena." Or, in Chairman Mao's version—as recounted by Professor John Gurley of Stanford University— "...the cadres must pay attention to the fact that everything depends on everything else." More loftily expressed was the Catholic priest Teilhard de Chardin's formulation, namely, "that since everything in the world follows the road to unification, the spiritual success of the universe is bound up with the correct functioning of every zone of that universe..." As the physicist and systems theorist Fritjof Capra (much acclaimed in New Age circles) stressed, the internal interconnectednesses also had a requirement of "overall self-consistency."

Just to be again reminded that the systems mind continued to be alive and well in the political domain, the American columnist George Will noted that Barack Obama "has consistently argued, in effect, that the health-care system is like a Calder mobile - touch it here and things will jiggle here, there and everywhere. Because everything is connected to everything else, merely piecemeal change is impossible."

We have already touched on totalism in a previous chapter, but not specifically in a systems-related context. The totalism of the systems-based world transformative vision was not confined to the internal connectedness and harmonious functioning of *all* of the parts, but extended as well to its overall scope and universality. Indeed, as in the Mansion House speech, transformationist initiatives coming out of the *high priesthood* of Canadian political Gnosticism went hand in hand, as we have noted more than once, with demands that whatever was contemplated or proposed had to be "global in scope, and universal in application." When Willis Harman spoke in Ottawa under the wing of Canada's Undersecretary for Foreign Affairs, he insisted that the desired change had to be "in total terms", because there had to be a change in "the whole world system - not just a partial solution." "We need a whole system change - everything, and since it is a social change it must be evolutionary." Thus a Senator Jacques Hébert too stressed that in his Maoist-inspired vision of a new society, the transformation had to be "total." In fact, the ill-fated Club of Rome—with its dire prognostications of a world running out of resources—had sprung out of a discussion of "A Framework for Initiating System-wide Planning of World Scope." Preparatory work on a "world problematique" had been undertaken by the International Institute of Applied Systems Analysis in Vienna. Since Maurice Strong too clamoured for a "better world system" one began to wonder where the environmental movement would be heading; and again through and by dint of a vaunted "necessity?"

Yet who could have suspected, or at least expected, that my reference to a high priesthood was not just a figure of speech? How could it have been otherwise if political Gnosticism had become a religion in its own right? Where systems-based totalism reared its head on the environmental front there would be less of a puzzle. After all, was Gaia not a goddess, and had *Time Magazine* not, in November 1989, commended her for getting the cadres to "focus on entire systems?" Had *Time* not joined the congregation of Gaia worshippers because "she integrates living things and inanimate forces into a unified system, allowing both science and religion *to look at life as something more than a mere accident?*" (Emphasis added.) This went well beyond the normal domain of ethics, when one considered Erich Jantsch's assertion in *The Self-Organizing Universe* that "ethics refers to the dynamics of systems" and when he reminded his readers that C. West Churchman (a pioneer in operations research) too insisted upon the "ethics of whole systems."

In his life's *magnum opus* a Canadian professor of theology (and prolific author), Kenneth Hamilton, dealt (definitively, indeed devastatingly, in my view) with the systematic theology of a notoriously liberal fellow theologian, Paul Tillich. In *The System and the Gospel*, published in 1963, Hamilton wrote, if rather impishly: "This theology is not *also* systematic, for it is *thinking in a system*. And the difference between systematic thinking and thinking in a system is as wide as the difference between arguing heatedly and arguing in the heat." Tillich taught that "the smallest problem, if taken seriously and radically, drove me to all other problems and to the anticipation of a whole in which they could find their solution." "Every part of a theological system, says Tillich, is dependent on every other part" but, says Hamilton, "no theology can be merely - or mainly - a logically consistent whole." Referring to the existential philosophy of Soren Kierkegaard, Hamilton said that for Kierkegaard it was a "matter of whether system shall have authority over faith, or whether faith must assert its authority in spite of system."

And so, in the systems-dominated and dominating temple, ethics soon yielded to religion because religion itself (*religare* = to connect) was appropriated by the systems god. Thus, Jay Forrester (an expert in systems dynamics) even painted a "systems dynamics picture of the nature and role of religion." One learned that "religious beliefs interact with other decision-making influences in a social system and are part of the total policy structure that may produce either good or evil." And that's why Forrester presented a study to the National Council of Churches titled *Churches at the Transition between Growth and World Equilibrium.* God himself was being harnessed. Or was He replaced? In the same vein one

Ralph Burhoe (who won the Templeton Prize in 1980) was convinced that "the world ecosystem created man..." and that man lives "by grace of a system for transcending himself." Interpreting Hegel, a Frenchman by the name of Brice Parain argued that "*any* system which is indeed a *system*, which culminates in a synthesis, is fundamentally religious, and that the synthesis, being absolute, is in reality a metaphor for God."

For former Vice-President Al Gore, recipient of the Nobel Peace Prize for 2007, "the climate crisis is not a political issue, it is a moral and spiritual challenge to all of humanity." He added that "it is also our greatest opportunity to lift global consciousness to a higher level." In other words, the climate crisis could also be seen in a functionalist light. It could well be a catalyst for transforming global consciousness into a religion. So was aggressive environmentalism merely a tail wagging a much bigger dog? Having already witnessed 'psychology as a religion', why should such a development strike one as extraordinary? Nor should one be tempted to fall for Mr Gore's downplaying of politics because, in the unfolding Voegelinian universe, politics itself had become a religion, and this was because transcendence had been "pulled into history and identified with political enterprises so that, as Camus remarked, 'politics became religion.'"

When politics morphs into religion, we may also want to recall Pope Benedict's reservations about the Encyclical *Gaudium et Spes*. In a controversial analysis of "The Social and Political Thought of Benedict XVI" Thomas R. Rourke commented on Benedict's concern about the neglect of "the necessary distinction between progress conceived politically, economically and scientifically... and the advancement of the kingdom of heaven," *when a true "politics is not the working out of the divine plan, that it is essentially limited and anti-utopian, and this for its own good."* (Emphasis added.) Kenneth Hamilton was on the same wavelength in his very last book, *Heaven on Earth*.

Mention of Mr Al Gore reminds one once again that no field has lent itself more to the ministrations of the systems mind, than the battlefield of environmentalism. Especially when coupled with Barack Obama's passionate preaching of his gospel of fundamental "Change." Quite early on I told the story of our soulful visit to an island near Ottawa, my first exposure to what I later recognized as an exercise in political Gnosticism. And in Chapter Ten the reader was transported to yet another island, Cortes Island on the Georgia Strait, nearly a hundred miles to the north of Vancouver. Not covered in the previous account was how the leadership in the Social Change Institute aimed to "apply a whole-systems approach to change." There as well, one discovered that systems, change, and agitation were the operative watchwords.

---

The fact is that the systems mind encompassed not only politics, not only religion, and not only environmentalism, but psychology as well. (Does one have to wonder why, in this narrative as well, everything seems to be connected with everything else, and why some of the same elements raise their heads in so many different contexts?) Was psychology not, after all, one of the gates through which we had come on to this entire spectacle? And how useful therefore that at the very University of North Carolina at Chapel Hill I should not only have discovered David Mitrany but also the psychologist Robert Jay Lifton, M.D. That was where Lifton's book *Thought Reform and the Psychology of Totalism*—first published in 1961— was reprinted. One of Lifton's findings was that "the totalist milieu maintains an aura of sacredness around its basic dogma, holding it out as an ultimate moral vision for the ordering of human existence. This sacredness is evident in the prohibition (whether or not explicit) against the questioning of basic assumptions..." All very familiar! Who would want to bet that the day might not come when the questioning of the basic assumptions supporting Mr Gore's crusade would not only be sacrilegious but punishable? Lifton's work was *A Study of 'Brainwashing' in China.* An echo of Professor Harman's auto-suggestive conditioning exercises?

Now that I have been so exposed, here in Canada, to the totalist ramifications of the systems mind, I have to ask myself what totalism really means. However threatening to freedom, it is something more than totalitarianism as normally defined, which, by general agreement, is usually confined to the regime of an all-embracing and oppressive state apparatus.

Normally one would think of totalism as something embracing a whole, a totality, a collectivity if you will. Indeed, tyranny can be diffused over a collectivity (and it often is) but when tyranny strikes an *individual* it takes on a very different meaning… for that individual. That's when it behooves us to sit up whenever we come across expressions like "one by one by one."

On the prosecuting side—namely, of the agents and perpetrators, or would-be perpetrators—who was it who observed that in countries where certain ideologies become ever so powerful and pervasive, *a point may be reached where every man thinks of himself as the state* and behaves accordingly? For all we know, the Stasi informers in East Germany thought of themselves in the same way. This is the anthropologist Mary Douglas's world where everybody knows what is on the end of everybody else's fork. When those Canadians who were already transformed sang their national anthem, pledging that "We stand on guard for thee," did each of them too think of himself as the state?

Here I'm reminded of New Age jargon which, in reference to the collectivity, typically invokes the abovementioned mantra of "one by one by one." Marilyn Ferguson, of *Aquarian Conspiracy* fame, made that clear when she referred to the meaning of the "old slogan: *Power to the People. One by one by one.*" The solidaristic nature of the new society beckoning 'man and his world' seeks a peculiar oneness. One cannot overstress the need to understand the nuance, and to remind ourselves that in the shaping business oneness means not just the whole, but *everyone*. Nobody is excluded. That is the real meaning of "one and all." In 1983 the Canadian *Canada One* yacht competition adopted as its advertising slogan: *One for All, and All for One.* The point of the foregoing is how Ferguson linked the mantra of "one by one by one" *to an exercise of power.*

Let us now turn to the receiving end, pertaining to the people who are the *objects* of the mantra. There, for sure, nobody is excluded. Often it comes in innocuous terms, as on the political hustings, with words like "every" being bandied about, as in: "We shall not rest until *every* child in America..." Hillary Clinton and her husband used to talk like that. "*No* child left behind"? Imagine.

The very same phenomenon could be found among the numerous transformationist admirers of the Canadian experiment: the aforementioned Wallersteins and Richard Falks and Willis Harmans and Johan Galtungs. By way of an additional example, there was an Indian by the name of Rajni Kothari, author of a book titled *Footsteps into the Future: Diagnosis of the Present World and a Design for an Alternative*. The book was part of a *Preferred Worlds for the 1990s* series sponsored by the Institute for World Order in New York. Among the countries Kothari listed where a new globalism could strike a local root were "progressive" Yugoslavia and Canada. Canada, said Kothari, was itself "going through a deep sense of being dominated by its giant neighbor", the United States. "It will be necessary," he stated, "for radicals of the New Left variety to meet the crisis in their own countries before undertaking worldwide missions. If they succeed in shaking the dominant value systems and institutional arrangements within these societies... they will have simultaneously contributed quite significantly to the removal of patterns of dominance and injustice in the world as a whole." But the relevant point with respect to the foregoing discussion was Kothari's insistence that the model for the new world would have to be a model "*from which no one is excluded.*" (Emphasis added.)

Most of us find it hard to escape the tendency—in fact the need—to put labels on things. One of those labels for collective forms of totalism— and especially if they are also authoritarian—has been the term *fascism*. And indeed, Eric Voegelin's interest was precipitated by the Nazi-related events in Austria. In one of his books, *The Authoritarian State*, published in 1936, Voegelin said that "it was my first attempt to penetrate the role of ideologies, left and right, in the contemporary situation and to understand an authoritarian state..." In that book he dealt, for the first time, with "the theoretical problems related to the words *total* and *authoritarian*." In his *New Science of Politics* he mentioned that students would often ask him to define fascism, or socialism, "but he would explain that movements of that type were part of reality (and) that only concepts could be defined but not reality." In other words, one could *observe* such things, but it might be difficult to *tell*. And undoubtedly quite a few of the manifestations described so far in this book had a great deal in common with fascism. Such as when oneness became a religion; when there was talk of the people of the world being or becoming a single community or "a really organic society"; as well as talk of "the international community acting with a single will", as Canadians learned from their Secretary of State for Foreign Affairs when he spoke in Ottawa to the Canadian Human Rights Foundation on March 27, 1981. Not to mention Obama's invocations in Berlin, calling for virtually all barriers and boundaries to be erased, and not just overcome.

Undoubtedly the object of Voegelin's inquiry—to the extent that it could be labelled as fascist—was of the collective kind. But when we also consider the applications of totalism when they involve individuals—either as "prosecutors" or at the receiving end—does the fascist label still hold? Apparently it does when totalism embraces both a totality and the mantra of "one by one by one." The French writer and social commentator Bernard-Henry Lévy must have had the latter aspect in mind when he talked about the "bottom-up totalitarianism" of the fascist. As when every individual in such a society thought of himself as the state. And indeed the Canadian writer William Gairdner did draw a distinction between "macro-fascism" and a fascism of the individual, which he called "micro-fascism." What the two had in common, he said, was a determination "to bend nature and human nature to the will." But when all is said and done, in the end fascism remains a *merging* force, as in Jean-Jacques Rousseau's "complete absorption of all individual wills into a single national, or General Will."

The problem is that the fascist label has not only been greatly overused (and abused). Typically (as we've noticed) it has been associated with authoritarian collectivities. This is why we need another term to better describe and understand the full breadth of the phenomena we've been grappling with in this narrative. And the reason for this is that the *merging* element in fascism has much wider applications in the world of the transformationist. Recall, for example, how we've already taken account of the problems associated with efforts to fuse means with ends. And thus, for my own purposes, I've coined the term *fusionism* as the closest approximation to reflect the essence of this aspect of the transformationist syndrome. What I think we've witnessed so far, is that *the political Gnostic was—and still is—in the business of fusing and short-circuiting just about everything in sight.* This was much more than the mere pursuit of 'equality,' that increasingly pervasive (and ever so handy) *shibboleth* of a modern age. Not for him any Voegelinian articulation. The political Gnostic fused political morality with strategy and tactics (following Trotsky and indeed Alinsky); the mind of humanity with the universal oneness; ecology with planetary humanism; the past with the future (as noted in Karl Popper's *Conjectures*); the material with the spiritual; and most potently, the immanent with the transcendent, as Harvard law professor Laurence Tribe (he who represented Al Gore in a presidential vote counting dispute) saw it. Tribe said that under certain circumstances "what must be sought is a synthesis of immanence with transcendence... such a synthesis requires... evolving processes of interaction and change." "Such a synthesis, it should be clear," he added, "must eventually cut across the received categories of 'nature' and 'culture,' for implicit in that classic dichotomy is a denial of any possible union between the immanent and the transcendent." No room whatsoever for traditional Christianity in such a world. Imagine, fusing the immanent with the transcendent, where God was not just present *in* the world; He became *of* the world, and the world *of* him. The two became indistinguish-able.

Therefore—and one might say understandably—in political Gnosticism fusion was a *religious* thing. According to Richard John Neuhaus (of the journal *First Things*) not even contemporary "mainstream" academic theology had escaped the fusionist syndrome. Thus, said Neuhaus, "the conflation of the human and the divine, the transcendent and the immanent, the supernatural and the natural" was even rampant in "both Roman Catholic and Protestant" circles. "In the end," he concluded, "anthropology and theology converge." *Religious* has fusion been from the beginning, in fact amounting to the most egregious *confusion*.

At this point it would have been remiss of me to have failed to invoke that most incisive commentary by Cardinal Ratzinger, in *Truth and Tolerance*, on what he called "the Mosaic distinction", in contrast to the call "that we must go back to 'Egypt.'" "By the 'Mosaic distinction,'" he said, "I mean the introduction of a distinction between true and false in the realm of religion." The "call to go back to Egypt" represented a demand that that most basic distinction be done away with. "As the 'source of all religions,' Egypt stood for the 'ultimate convergence of reason and revelation, or nature and scripture.'" "Egypt" meant that "the distinction between true and false can be removed from religion if the distinction between God and cosmos disappears, if the divine and the 'world' are once more seen as an undivided whole."

Fact is, said Ratzinger, "the distinction between true and false in religion is indissolubly linked with the distinction between God and the world. The return to Egypt is the return to the gods, inasmuch as it rejects a God who stands over against the world but regards the gods merely as symbolical forms of expression for nature, which is divine." Imagine a more egregious development than a fusion of the true and the false! But then we're already living in a world of entertainment (and even manipulated photography) beholden to the falsity of "virtual realities."

Of the very same genre was the following Gnostic attribution to Jesus, quoted by Elaine Pagels in *The Gnostic Gospels*: "When you make the two one, and when you make the inside like the outside and the outside like the inside, and the above like the below, and when you make the male and female one and the same... then you will enter [the Kingdom]."

The American Catholic philosopher and historian Thomas Molnar too, in his treatment of *The Gnostic Tradition and Renaissance Occultism*, cited the "fundamental monism... underlying ancient Gnosticism and occultism of the first three centuries A.D." Given our interest in means and method, noteworthy as well was Molnar's reference to the "important part played by *techniques* used by the ancients (as well as modern 'New Agers') to escape from this present world into an 'inner world' of ones own, or else to master it through attempted *fusion* or self-identification with God - the pantheist 'One.'" (Emphases added.) Molnar then proposed a most useful template, reflecting several of the elements we've already encountered in this narrative:

First, said Molnar, there was the motto "'As above, so below,' which allows the magician to change the substance of the world/reality." Then there was the notion of the "coincidence of opposites", followed closely by "the notion of original man as the 'androgyne' in whom male and female are fused." In addition—reminding us of the symbolism of the geodesic globe dominating Canada's euphoric Expo 67—Molnar drew attention to "the symbol of the Sphere, denoting the fused totality of all things... as well as Nothingness."

All of this adds up to the conclusion that fusion is salvational.

Here two arresting images or metaphors come to mind. One of them is the portrayal of the Egyptian god Osiris as a serpent swallowing its own tail. (How coincidental then that Professor Ivan Head's IDRC named two of its "developmental" programs, Isis and Osiris respectively; they were seen as "tools of liberation.") When he criticized a writer by the name of Assmann, I was struck by the fact that Cardinal Ratzinger too alluded specifically to "a great example of his (meaning Assmann's) universalistic concept of divinity... Isis, as she was understood and invoked in the 'Graeco-Egyptian' cult of Isis." (Ratzinger also cited Assmann's view that the concomitant process of assimilation developed into a "general technique of culture." Technique of culture! A future Pope seemed to be well aware of the deployment of techniques of cultural transformation.)

The other image that comes to mind—especially with its religious overtones—is Teilhard de Chardin's Omega, which culminates in a single ("fused"?) static and transcendent point, "...reminiscent of Dante's vision of the great, glowing heavenly rose at the end of *The Divine Comedy...*

Time progresses toward this point, species by species, until, with the ecstatic apotheosis of humanity, all individual minds coalesce into a unified planetary consciousness, a mental singularity that is the final ethereal counterpart of the physical singularity from which the Big Bang erupted at the beginning of time."

A more fanciful formulation than de Chardin's is hard to imagine. But in the end, as I have hinted before, was the joke not on me? Throughout my teenage years in South Africa my hero was Field Marshal Jan Christiaan Smuts. His picture was the only such that adorned the wall of my room throughout my university years. He also happened to be the father of the philosophy of Holism; and that had been as close to Teilhardism as anything else I would encounter in later life. As well, Smuts was a passionate believer in international solidarity, whether in the form of the (formerly British) Commonwealth of Nations, or the United Nations itself. Should laughter be reserved for the gods? In any event, such was the profusion of cobblestones lining the way on an eventful journey.

---

So often—and in so many contexts—has the name of Jan Smuts cropped up in the course of my story, that you can imagine my interest when, in 2010, Gregory Garland—an insightful researcher at the American Foreign Service Research Institute in Washington, D.C.—wrote an article titled "The Strange Disappearance of Jan Christian (*sic!*) Smuts and What It Can Teach Americans." He wondered why, historiographically, a towering figure like Smuts ("perhaps the most effective internationalist ever") should have been forgotten so soon, and then went on to draw a comparison with the story of the American J. William Fulbright, when Fulbright, unlike Smuts, was "secularly canonized." Among the remarkable parallelisms in their careers, was the fact that Smuts and Fulbright shared a certain ambivalence in their attitudes to the political rights of black people. "Let us open the book on Smuts again," Garland concluded, "not just to know the man better, but to know ourselves; our own blind spots in the never-ending struggle to steer our own American narrative away from deceptive pieties and nearer to an untidy truth." What I found equally interesting was that an *American* should have written such a perceptive account of the legacy of Jan Smuts, just like the fact that the books of a South African theologian named Andrew Murray— whose legacy played such a role in the spiritual lives of my own parents—were still being published in the United States (even in electronic form) but not in South Africa. So perhaps it says something that I have not entrusted The de Vos-de Villiers Collection of documents to a South African institution, but rather to the archives of the Pitts Theology Library in Atlanta, Georgia.

———

Fusionism has had multiple applications, but none more crucial than when the transformationist sets out to fuse the transcendent with the immanent, as Laurence Tribe had done. Why? Because it impinges directly on the Christian faith. That will be the subject of a later chapter.

# CHAPTER THIRTEEN
# CYBERNETICS

"*Cybernetics* comes from the Greek word *kybernetes* which means *steersman*. It reduces behavior to two essential ingredients, information and feedback, and claims that all processes can be understood as amplifications and complexifications of both."

Jeremy Rifkin

"In the world of tomorrow, the expression 'banana republic' will not refer to independent fruit-growing nations but to countries where formal independence has been given priority over the cybernetic revolution."

P.E. Trudeau

"Thus the Maoist view is that economic policies succeed when they change both the objective conditions and 'man' himself, and that 'man' is changed by his own attempts to change the world."

John G. Gurley

"I think that cybernetics is the biggest bite out of the fruit of the Tree of Knowledge that mankind has taken in the last 2000 years."

Gregory Bateson

When, finally, the Gnostic vision turned back toward creation, and the Gnostic spirit morphed into political Gnosticism, bent on transforming both 'man and his world,' it simply had to embrace science and technology, albeit of the soft kind. What counted most, thenceforth, was the *gnosis* of the means and the method. And no method, no technology, would be more powerful, more promising, and become more pervasive than the art and craft of *cybernetics*; and even more so in the age of the computer. Already in the domain of "work and power" (part of the subtitle of Shoshana Zuboff's book *In the Age of the Smart Machine*) a veritable revolution was in the making. It had to be so if the introduction talked about "Transformation in the Age of the Smart Machine," and large sections of the book were devoted to "Authority: The Spiritual Dimension of Power," and "Technique: the Material Dimension of Power." The tool maketh man.

Since Canada became a self-appointed transformational laboratory—initially inspired by a euphoric Expo 67 dedicated to the glories of *Man and his World*—the country could well serve as a focal point of any study of the use, or at least the advocacy, of cybernetic techniques for sociocultural and political purposes. Seemingly the possible applications of cybernetics were without limit.

There are two kinds. The traditional kind is a function known as *negative feedback*: self-regulating control devices designed to prevent machines and systems from running out of control, or even just to ensure that they stay on an even keel. They range from simple thermostats to regulators on steam generating boilers, to elaborate devices designed to bring various kinds of systems back into a state of equilibrium, or even to shut them down (for example, in a malfunctioning nuclear power plant). In other words, negative feedback is mainly used as a safety device. Given a relatively free press, it even helps to keep politicians relatively honest!

*Positive feedback* devices or processes are quite different. They act as amplifiers. In them, elements and events feed back upon themselves, thereby amplifying their effect in a potentially limitless series of cumulative repetitions. Those exponential growth curves appearing in stock prices and even speculative housing bubbles are classic examples of positive feedback mechanisms in action. In short, they exploit the power of self-referentialism. In the social milieux, most often they involve the actions of the self-interested but collectively thoughtless participation of large numbers of people. The formation of unruly mobs is a typical and increasingly familiar example of such a process at work. Lately, of course, greatly aided and abetted by the proliferation of the so-called social media, and especially among young people. In most cases the process becomes self-defeating, and time and again the exponential curves collapse of their own accord; under their own weight, so to speak. Such is a rule of nature, a rule well-known to epidemiologists. But before they collapse a great deal of damage may have been done.

Positive feedback mechanisms can be beneficial. Thus, they have been credited with the transplanting of farming methods to the soil-rich valleys of the Nile, the Tigris, the Euphrates, the Indus and the Huang-ho, which "resulted in a hundredfold increase in harvests, making possible a 'social surplus' that unprecedentally increased population numbers and densities, and freed many persons to work in occupations and localities removed from the fields."

But when positive feedback systems (hereafter simply called cybernetics) are applied in ways reflected by the title of Norbert Wiener's book *The Human Use of Human Beings: Cybernetics and Society,* serious questions have arisen, and particularly when this has happened in the hands of the man-and-world-transformative political Gnostic.

The possible range of such applications can be astonishing. *Psychology* was the first of the transformative tools (already explored in Chapter Ten). In psychology, self-preoccupation is the primary element and without this element of self-preoccupation no positive cybernetic process is possible. One could say that almost by definition, the practice of psychology is the epitome of self-referentialism in action. Willis Harman was the eponymous exponent of what he called "psycho-cybernetics," exploited so bizarrely (and not only in the Canadian laboratory) in various administrations of his *Course in Miracles.* In those instances generous use was made of self-reinforcing auto-suggestive repetitions, also called "auto-catalysis." One notes, in passing, Sherry Turkle's account of how "major sectors of the artificial intelligence community have given new life to the self-analytic method, and in doing so have developed a somewhat para-doxical identity as the cybernetic descendants of Freud."

We successively moved into the field of *functionalism*, where" learn-ing by doing," based on induced learning experiences, also constituted the very essence of the cybernetic art. Professor Laurence Tribe too had something like that in mind when he pronounced on the uses of "'means-ends fluidity' with its 'feedback' effects upon the chooser's ends." This process is especially prominent in group-based or organizational settings. Sheldon S. Wolin was struck by Lenin's use of organization "as the action medium best suited to a mass age," and ever since then organization has been a prime target for transformative operations. Hence Prime Minister Trudeau's pronounced interest in "techniques of government." For him, from Leninist organization to "cybernetic planning" (his own term) was only a short leap. The lead article in a 1978 issue of the *International Journal*, titled "The impact of Prime Minister Trudeau on foreign policy" noted that "Trudeau's interest in the mechanisms of planning and rational decision-making stems from his total commitment to the principle of rationality in all forms of human behaviour. He thus approaches cyber-netics more from the perspective of a rational humanist than from the professional orientation of the technocrat." Echoes here of Trudeau's call, "Let us be coldly intelligent?" One of his favourite maxims was *"La raison avant la passion."* Previously, the only person, in my experience, whose approach to human affairs and transforming a society had shown such attributes, was Dr Hendrik French Verwoerd, the ideological father of (systemic and systematic) apartheid. The thing about cybernetics is that, once put into motion, it is an impersonal, mechanistic device or process and therefore perfectly suits the needs of a cold, calculating mind. The one outstanding feature of Dr Verwoerd's philosophy (not to mention actions), was its utterly cold and relentless logic. The same mechanistic coldness, I believe, marked the political transformationist's frequent use of the word "inevitable." Of this I could quote many examples, but it would be tedious.

That there were crosswalks between cybernetics and the workings of the *systems mind* was, of course, self-evident. Laszlo's General Systems

Theory was quite clear in this respect when he wrote that "a system is a complex of interacting elements; or a system is the sum of the parts of an entity and their interrelations. These interrelations are characterized by feedback or a circular causality. Hence the entity is a cybernetic system."

Applied cybernetics was also in the business of manipulating *time.* Recall Karl Weick's idea that one could bring about a desired future by writing about it in the past tense? In the course of one of the Canadian Broadcasting Corporation's *Ideas* programs, aired in 1985, one of the participants, a Robert Rosen, referred to certain "material systems which are organisms... which pull the future into the present and allow the organism to modify its present behaviour on the basis of a predicted future." Here we have a cybernetic process operating not only in but also upon time. It is also an illustration (mentioned earlier) of a magical deployment of the notion of "*as if.*" You write about the future as if it has already transpired. As in a blink of an eye, you make the unreal, real.

So far we've discovered some of the impacts of cybernetics, or at least a belief in cybernetics, in the *political* domain. And some proponents of its use in politics were quite open in their advocacy, so that a book on *Policy and Action* recognized that "the cybernetic approach has been taken up by political scientists interested in exploring models of political communication and control." No mention of the political activists! Since the Canadian prime minister was so clearly open to the promises of cybernetic manipulation it was almost inevitable that someone like the Englishman Stafford Beer, the founder of *Management Cybernetics*, was a welcome visitor to the prime ministerial offices in Ottawa. He was also doing much work for the socialist Allende administration in Chile, overseen by a Chilean finance minister who said that he had always been interested in "the application of cybernetic concepts in the socialist project." In Canada, Stafford Beer was preparing cybernetic learning teams, "one team for every province, one in Ottawa." In Chile, however (and in his own words), he favoured *simulated* conditions in a control room, "instead of experimenting on the poor old nation and discovering ten years later that your policy was wrong."

No such scruples in Canada! Stafford Beer must have known that in the Canadian case there was no such concern for a "poor old nation" among the political Gnostic transformationists who were happy to treat their country as one large experimental socio-cultural laboratory. (So that we might as well remind ourselves that we've already alluded, if only metaphorically, to the fact that Ottawa was the only capital city in the world boasting a large Experimental Farm—partly an Animal Farm—in its very centre.) What if the Canadian Charter of Rights and Freedoms had first been tested under controlled laboratory conditions, say in one province? The same could also have been asked with respect to Canada's experiments in official multiculturalism, or the country's immigration and refugee policies, since we recall that even "migration" had been fingered as a functionalist technique (and a particularly apposite candidate for Norbert Wiener's cybernetic "human use of human beings"). Both of those Canadian experiments, naturally, would have virtually irreversible impacts on the society.

Potentially more telling though was the capacity of cybernetically induced 'oscillations' to cause disturbances or disequilibria in a given system, whether physical or socio-cultural or political. (Barack Obama's mentor, Saul Alinsky, with "his desire for endless agitation," seemed to be on the same wavelength.) So this was where I became interested in a possible link with chaos theory, because here was one of the greatest opportunities beckoning the transformationist political Gnostic.[14]

Considering the way people have mistakenly tried to see a nexus between Einstein's Theory of Relativity and the general incidence of relativism in non-physical domains—such as ethics or morality or whatever—little deterred the transformationist from trying to translate applications of chaos theory in the world of physics, to the domains of

---

14    Chaos theory can be generally defined as the study of forever-changing complex systems. Discovered by a meteorologist in 1960, chaos theory contends that complex and unpredictable results will occur in systems that are sensitive to small changes in their initial conditions. The most common example of this, known as the 'Butterfly Effect,' states that the flapping of a butterfly's wings in China could cause tiny atmospheric changes which over a period of time could affect weather patterns in New York.

politics and culture, especially with an eye on the power of positive feed-back. Trudeau's enthusiasm for cybernetics ought to have raised a warning flag or two, even before his accession to power. In a way Saul Alinsky, if he had known about chaos theory, would have recognized his instinc-tive exploitation of it because he was always looking for the small button that could be pressed to create disorder in a complex system. One such application was quite funny, actually. As the story goes, Alinsky had been unable to squeeze benefits for a poor neighbourhood in Chicago out of the legendary Mayor Daly. It took just one telephone call from Alinsky to get the mayor to capitulate. O'Hare International Airport—the world's busiest at the time—was the apple of the mayor's eye, his pride and joy. Alinsky told him that unless he was amenable, Alinsky's supporters would occupy every toilet at the airport on the busiest night of the week, lock the doors and just sit there. Naturally the 'butterfly effect' would have seen spectacular consequences.

In Chapter Six we encountered a Nobel Prize-winning chemist-phys-icist, one Ilya Prigogine. Why, I asked myself, were socio-cultural-polit-ical change agents so interested in him, as they were in people like the theoretical physicist David Bohm (author of *Wholeness and the Implicate Order*)? The Science Council of Canada (where Bohm spoke) was quick to take note of the "current work in non-equilibrium thermodynamics, evolutionary biology, cybernetics and systems science theory (and) the crucial bifurcation epochs in human history where new biological species and human societies have evolved from the old." And why not, in our age, the evolution of the New Man in the Just Society? The very fact that Prigogine's book, *Order out of Chaos,* should have been published out of Boulder, Colorado (a New Age mecca) by a company bearing the name of Shambhala, attested to the attractiveness of Prigogine's work to the new change agents.

Prigogine (like Bohm himself) took part in an episode of the Canadian Broadcasting Corporation's *Ideas* program when the overall topic was *Religion and the New Science.* Here the New Age overtones were unmis-takable. One of the other participants in the program alluded to James Lovelock's *Gaia: A New Look at Life on Earth.* Like Willis Harman, he referred to hermetic philosophies and the associated practice of alchemy. It was on this occasion that Prigogine himself explained the principles of chaos theory. It was, he said, about the way a system could be pushed into a state of disequilibrium, "because far from equilibrium, you can have completely new situations." "Bifurcation" was "the point when one solution becomes a different solution." Note, not a new solution, but a *transformed* solution. Transform-ation is not reformation! (Just as a revolt—as Jacques Ellul observed—is not a revolution. The French Revolution itself was misnamed.) "We can," Prigogine continued, "hope to achieve great results even with small causes, and that is I think something which will slowly penetrate *and is penetrating already slowly into other fields of human activity, in ecology, and economics, and other fields.*" (Emphasis added.)

After all, as a commentator on Voegelin observed, "the Gnostic vision of the world as a place of total chaos which would itself be transformed into a world of perfected, durable order by divine or human intervention" was quite an old phenomenon. Gnostic symbols of reality resulted in a "steady acceleration in the intensity of the revolt against God and man in the attempt to realize one or another of the Gnostic dream worlds that have become the new versions of reality."

Gnosticism was not just a heresy of the Christian era. It had more ancient roots. Watery chaos (with its creative potential) can be found in the cosmologies of the Egyptians and Phoenicians and the Babylonians as well as in the Vedic literature. And if chaos theory involved the science of turbulence, one only had to think of the role of pandemonium in Greek mythology, and the following quotation: "...a pandemonium develops that, revealing the heights and depths of the world, casts him between sublime rapture and unutterable terror. And nature, being suddenly released, shouts out its power and plunges everything into turbulence." Thus, already in the 1950s, Oliver Selfridge—described as a "brilliant young disciple of Norbert Wiener" (of cybernetic fame)—"proposed a machine, Pandemonium, whose name captures his idea of what it might take for intelligent order to emerge."

Was chaos not—come to think of it—an apt description even of the state of mind of our proverbial Gnostic? He who was in such a congenitally pathetic state of flungness, dislocation, and psychic discombobulation, and sur-rounded by such a chaotic (and unjust) world, and so unsure of his own identity? North Americans and British people had already been introduced to Donald Schon's *Loss of the Stable State* (that too was featured by the Canadian broadcasting media), and Kenneth Galbraith's *Age of Discontinuity.* A postmodernist preoccupation with a fractured and fracturing polity (fore-shadowed by Picasso's broken women?) even showed up in architecture; in deconstructionism (a worse case than the world depicted by Yeats); and in the unfolding realities of Canadian multiculturalism... soon to be even more keenly felt in Europe and subsequently and progressively in the United States.

Other examples abounded. There was the high priest of planning Erich Jantsch's commendation of positive feedback "or destabilization and the development of new forms" that dovetailed neatly with Alastair Taylor's invocation of a higher level of cybernetics which could induce "a new level of societal organization" to the point where no mechanism "can prevent the rupturing of the basic systemic framework." New 'societal technics' would help to 'build a new world order.' There was Willis Harman's Association for Humanistic Psychology pontificating that "the very chaos of contemporary existence provides the material for transformation. We will search (out) new myths, and world visions." And there was the Canadian government's Steering Group on Prosperity touting "The Learning Organization" as a catalyst for "Managing Turbulent Times". Opportunity all around!

On October 17, 1995 I looked at a program on a government-owned and operated television channel featuring a certain John O'Manique. Referring to Professor Ivan Head's IDRC's interest in "Gender Foundations in a New World Order" O'Manique said: "In periods of great disequilibrium social systems are capable of great transformation." Elsewhere the same John O'Manique addressed "The Response of the Principal Sectors of Canadian Society to the New International Economic Order." "Fundamental transformation" in the United States, he said, was a prerequisite, and that, he said, would only come about through withdrawal of consent from institutions and the establishment of "networks" in which "each cell has its own leader."

If Americans thought that none of this applied to their own polity, they might be reminded of how one of President Obama's chiefs of staff welcomed "a good crisis" as an opportunity to bring about meaningful change. O'Manique's cells-based prescription for Americans may not have been far off the mark either given Obama's successful pre-election deployment of an extensive internet-based network of grass roots supporters who, as we've observed, were invited to form small cells meeting in their own homes or elsewhere. The system was assiduously maintained after he reached the White House. Had Obama read O'Manique? On February 24, 2012 the *Washington Post* reported: "As if to keep attention trained on Republicans and how they navigate these issues, the Obama campaign helped organize more than 1,000 house parties on Wednesday for women to come together to watch the presidential debate."

This was how the Obama campaign spread the message: "On February 22, women across the country will hold hundreds of house meetings to build relationships in their community and hear from First Lady Michelle Obama via conference call. House meetings are at the core of our strategy to win, and attending an event is a great way to inspire others to take ownership over this campaign in your community. Women are coming together in living rooms to talk about the issues that matter most to them, and why organizing for President Obama in 2012 is so important in this election."

Soon after the Democratic National Convention in Denver, in 2008, Saul Alinsky's son had written: "Barack Obama's training in Chicago by the great community organizers is showing its effectiveness. It is an amazingly powerful format, and the method of my late father always works to get the message out and get the supporters on board." As for O'Manique's reference to a concomitant withdrawal of consent from institutions, Obama's re-election campaign in 2012 also happened to coincide with a widespread public mood of dissatisfaction with the governmental apparatus in Washington; and not just with one or other of the political parties. A political institutional failure (more than even Wall Street) was being held responsible for the lack of meaningful action in the face of a severe economic and budgetary crisis.

As for Canadians, some of Trudeau's antinomian utterances over the years may well have anticipated the development of a most interesting paradigm. In short, transforming 'man and his world' in fundamental ways by harnessing the self-referential power of positive cybernetic feedback mechanisms (in their various forms) became one of the most favoured and most potent devices in the transformationist's already well-equipped tool bag.

We may conclude, and sum up, with Alastair Taylor's description of *Cybernetics II*, which, according to him, addressed itself to "two types of societal experience: systemic self-organization and development, and systemic transformation." Think back on how the former had such appeal for Elisabeth Mann Borgese. In the environmentalist context the latter component of Cybernetics II was termed "quantization." "Quantization," said Taylor, "occurs when deviation is amplified to the point where no deviation-correcting mechanisms can prevent the rupturing of the basic framework, i.e., when the latter can no longer contain and canalize the energies and thrust which have been generated." Saul Alinsky would have recognized this kind of language. Nor could I help thinking of same-sex 'marriages' as yet another amplifying deviation serving to rupture the framework of humanity's oldest and most basic institution. Systemic transformation indeed!

These insights might yet prove to have been prophetic for the unfolding saga of aggressive environmentalism at the beginning of the 21st century with all of its other transformationist overtones. Aggressive environmentalists were responsible for pushing Barack Obama into his decision to delay, if not kill, a much needed pipeline meant to transport oil from Canada to refineries in the Deep South. But one could readily predict that if environmentalism were to run out of steam, *some other development or threat or instrument would be harnessed to the same ends. As*

Saul Alinsky taught, once you've energized the masses, having endowed them with People Power, they can then be expected to move on from one issue to another. For, whatever the issue in hand, it would still and always be necessary—reminiscent of Lenin's "giving history a push" —to add to the impetus.

Not unlike that of Sisyphus, the Gnostic transformationist's work will never end. His efforts will be persistent, relentless, and indefatigable, because, from the very beginning, the Gnostic has not been working for but against the Created order. The Created order was the handiwork of a transcendent God, who sent his Son to pull 'man and his world' up and into his glory. By contrast, the new Gnostic was intent on pulling him down into his own Creation and assimilating him, even if, in the process, it meant transforming the Godhead himself… the subject of the next chapter.

# CHAPTER FOURTEEN
# IMMANENCE,
# TRANSCENDENCE,
# AND FREEDOM

**Immanentism:** Any of various religious theories postulating that a deity, mind, or spirit is immanent in the world and in the individual.

"The true dividing line in the contemporary crisis,' Voegelin wrote three decades ago, 'does not run between liberals and totalitarians, but between the religious and philosophical transcendentalists on the one side, and the liberal and totalitarian immanentist sectarians on the other.'"

Russell Kirk

"Set your minds on things that are above, not on things that are on earth."

*Epistle to the Colossians* 3: 2

Russell Kirk made his quoted remark in his *Enemies of the Permanent Things.* At the very core of Voegelin's diagnosis of the modern condition was the "immanentization of the Christian *eschaton.*" A belief in salvation beyond world and time had to give way to "a belief in the transfiguration of man and society in *this* world and in *our* time." This was a quintessentially Gnostic development which, according to Voegelin, morphed into an activist and energetic political Gnosticism. It gradually dawned on me that here was the very phenomenon driving the world of public affairs on the experimental farm called Canada. For indeed, Canada seemed (and even touted itself as) a microcosm of a modern world where the spirit of immanentism was fast discarding a heritage of beholdenness to a transcendental view of reality, rooted in Christian belief.

The remarkable thing about the Canadian laboratory was a political Gnosticism that was not academic or theoretical but almost entirely focused on *praxis*. To an extraordinary degree the focus had shifted to the means and the techniques whereby the required transformations could and should be brought about. And so, in this narrative there unfolded an insight into *how immanentism became operational*. Those manifestations of a political Gnosticism-in-action were rooted in that most basic divide in human affairs Russell Kirk identified. One was looking at a very old virus but only in the course of the late 20th century was this virus consciously and deliberately introduced in the political domain, intent on self-salvationally transforming 'man and his world.'

What had to be understood though, to begin with, was that activist—operational—immanentism was not only political, but that (like function-alism) it also needed to be *forced*. Partly, of course, because it was unnatural, working against the Created order. Thus Voegelin contended that political Gnosticism was a direct threat to human freedom. As one commentator put it: "Totalitarianism threatens from without, but the more dangerous enemy is the insidious Gnosticism within the western world which weakens and could paralyze its will to resist." Whatever threats came from without, the totalitarian mind (for lack of a better word) was *internal* to and virtually defined the immanentist spirit-in-action.

Immanence may be taken to denote a God who is present and active in the world and in human affairs, and of that we can have no doubt, unless we are deists. One only has to think of the role of Covenants in the Old Testament. But the problematical immanence we are looking at is not only a form of, or very close to, pantheism—where God is indistinguishable from, and part and parcel of, his own Creation—but may also lie behind the belief system of many a political Gnostic. In the world of the pantheist everything is God, and God is in everything. The world has not only been divinized but spiritualized, or, failing which, must be rendered such. For the political Gnostic, the Creation order must be transformed in the here and now.

Accordingly, before trying to come to grips with the anatomy and the incidence of a world-transformative spirit of immanence, we should have to first clarify its relationship to the spectre of totalitarianism, and—in turn—its own connection to the systems mind. Voegelin (see the quote at the head of this chapter) did make the connection. The totalitarian spectre had energized him in the first place and launched him on his life's work, in search of "an in-depth understanding of totalitarian movements and their intellectual foundations." He saw the associated idea patterns as a "closed 'system' the internal logic of which was tyrannically used to displace human experience and the exploration of reality."

And we have certainly seen what the 'systems mind' represented. I had spent a major part of my formative years and my father virtually gave his life in a confrontation with people whose assault on freedom and human dignity (so interlinked) was part and parcel of a self-contained and logically conceived system. In Canada I came across people in the corridors of power whose transformationist obsessions even gave rise to an *officially funded* stressing of the need for not only a "world fit to live in, but people fit to live with." Attended by thousands was a conference of the World Future Society held in Washington, D.C., in 1980. The proceedings were published under the title of *Through the 80s: Thinking Globally, Acting Locally*, with a foreword generously provided by none other than Edward R. Schreyer, Governor General of Canada, and an introduction by that most ubiquitous Canadian and international change agent, Maurice Strong. Relevant to the present theme was a contribution by one Joseph Martino of the University of Dayton (Ohio) titled "Freedom and the Future of Local Action." He was also the technological forecasting editor of a journal, *The Futurist*. The main chapter of the 1980 publication was headed "Coercion is Needed for Survival." The presenter mentioned that "Garrett Hardin is not the only futurist who believes that coercion, established by majority rule and centrally controlled, is required for survival."

He approvingly quoted Daniel Bell to the effect that 'ours is a world that will require more authority and more regulation.' But more telling was his reference to Robert Heilbroner's assertion that "the passage through the gauntlet ahead may be possible only under governments capable of rallying obedience *far more effectively than would be possible in a democratic setting.*" (Emphasis added.) And equally thought provoking was his citation of three other people, who had written—going well beyond Garrett Hardin's vision—about the need for "the resurrection in modern form of the pre-industrial polity - a polity in which the few govern the many and in which government is no longer of or by the people." The focus here was on the environmentalist agenda, but the statements quoted were in general terms.

In the Canadian laboratory, political correctnesses, bolstered by a Charter of Rights and Freedoms, 'anti-hate' laws, and a whole slew of kangaroo courts acting as human rights tribunals, were putting a chill in the hearts of dissenters. In the latter case (as we've already noted) so much so that the general counsel for Canada's Civil Liberties Association confessed that he never expected that tribunals designed to fight discrimination would become suppressors of both thought and freedom of speech.

We know that Canada was not the only country where *forced* political correctnesses so distorted the life of the polity. The same was happening in the United States, in Great Britain, and more widely, under the auspices of the European Community. In my youth I had run into another and earlier regime where the very Question was *verboten*, not only in the public square but also in academia, only to find the same thing happening in Canada.

So much for the totalitarian element in the mind set of the political immanentist. Let us now turn forthwith to immanentism itself, and not just as a belief system about which more than enough has already been written by philosophers and theologians alike. So vast and so far-reaching have been the tentacles of immanentism-in-action that the best we ourselves could do, by way of a reprise, would be to attempt to present it in the form of a collage. And the same would apply to its opposite: the transcendental. Out of such an ensemble might one be able to derive an overall impression; and one hopes, not only that, but also to achieve comprehension.

If Eric Voegelin was right and one was witnessing the blossoming of an immanentist world spirit—expressed in and carried by an *active* political Gnosticism as its handmaiden—an understanding of its character, its incidences, and its methods of operation, could not but be described as imperative. In fact, it was necessary not only to understand the immanentist phenomenon, but also to understand it in the light of the *other* side of the coin identified by Russell Kirk: the transcendental view of reality. For far too long has public and political discourse been skewered on the increasingly useless, and indeed fatuous, twin forks of the 'left' and the 'right.' If ever there have been two over-used clichés, they are 'left-wing' and 'right-wing.'

As well, for far too long has the eruption of immanentism been discussed in abstract terms—and mostly by academics and theologians—when the real developing problem has been its *operationalization* in the political domain. Voegelin himself was either unable or simply failed to explore—except in limited ways—contemporary applications of his insights, that is to say, beyond the ravages of German National Socialism. He did invoke the Marxist emanations of political Gnosticism, but the *praxis* of a Lenin and especially a Mao Tse-tung seemed to have eluded him.

There was also the literally monumental work of Cornelio Fabro, whose *God in Exile: Modern Atheism* ran to 1,230 pages (in English translation). Fabro's exhaustive (and exhausting!) treatment of immanence versus transcendence had to be seen to be appreciated. He recognized the *activism* of the immanentist virus, which was evident even from the extended subtitle of his work: *A Study of the Internal Dynamic of Modern Atheism*. If anyone wanted to comprehend the origins and essence of immanentism (from a Christian point of view at least), I should think that Fabro's masterpiece would have to be essential reading. Quoting Jacques Maritain—and as his subtitle suggested—Fabro understood how the "modern principle of immanence" had been "absorbed into the dynamic of temporal existence." Or, as we have already seen, how it had settled in *process* itself. And when Fabro, again quoting Maritain, had seen that "all the norms of conscience" became "thoroughly relativized", what else was that other than Professor Laurence Tribe's "means-ends fluidity?" When it came to *fusion*, what more fundamental fusion could there have been than that seen by Fabro in his statement that "the boundary line between creator and creatures has been hopelessly blurred?" Here was in fact the core element of the phenomenon of immanence. A fusion of God and world. Light-years removed from Saint Augustine's City of God and the City of Man. When we think of the driving force of cybernetic positive feedback processes, what better example could it have been of Fabro's insight into the workings of the "various systems" with their "forms of self-actuation?" Auto-genesis (self-creation) was the order of the day. And, of course, we would be seeing increasingly alarming incidences of auto-genesis in the experimentations of biogenetic manipulators, where man was actively engaged in efforts to displace the Creator: in effect to make him redundant.

What then were the roots—the *fons et origo*—of a thoroughly immanentist ethos? An ethos that may even be described as a world spirit? One theory is that it had all started in the ancient Babylonian myth, where the "primeval sweet-water ocean" and the "primeval salt-water ocean" merged, so that "matter and divine spirit (were) united and coexistent, like body and soul." "In sharp contrast to this," wrote Alexander Heidel, author of *The Babylonian Genesis*, "the Book of Genesis speaks of only one divine principle, existing apart from and independently of all cosmic matter." For the Babylonians, matter was eternal. By contrast, "In the Book of Genesis divine spirit and cosmic matter were not coexistent and coeternal. Instead, divine spirit created matter and existed independently of it." So was that where *fusionism* began, in the Babylonian myth? Was that the *fons et origo* of Professor Laurence Tribe's "synthesis of immanence with transcendence," a synthesis which depended on the "evolving processes of interaction and change?" (Or, in the more ancient jargon, simply "flux"). Here, arguably, was the original fountain from which drank an F.R. Scott, mentor of Canada's Prime Minister Trudeau, when he (Scott) "vivified" nature, following a Bergsonian *élan vital*. Were there subliminal links here with both Rosicrucianism and alchemy, "which sort of gave vitality and life to matter" (in David Bohm's words)?

Here, I believe, was the atavistic inspiration for Gregory Bateson's contention that the mind was immanent and with no transcendent connection: where any "complexity of causal circuits and the appropriate energy relations will surely show mental characteristics", and with the mental characteristics being "inherent or immanent in the ensemble as a whole." "If you put God outside," he said, "and set him vis-à-vis his creation and if you have the idea that you are created in his image, you will logically and naturally see yourself as outside and against the things around you." This was quite unacceptable to the transformationist. In other words, choose and associate yourself with the transcendental God and you're against the world! "If I am right," Bateson added, "the whole of our thinking about what we are and what other people are has got to be restructured." Then fast forward to politics, because, contends Bateson, "we should trust no policy decisions which emanate from persons who do not yet have that habit;" the new habit he was advocating. Shades of Canada (and the world) being in dire need of leaderships "fit to live with." If God was not inherent in his own creation, men who think they have been created in his image had better not align themselves with him. In the Batesonian world there was no room for the transcendental. As Bateson explained, "Transcendent mind or deity is imagined to be personal and omniscient, and as receiving information by channels separate from the earthly... Immanent mind has no separate and unearthly channels by which to know or act..." Whereas Saint Paul, intoned Bateson, said that "God is not mocked," what we ought to say is that "the immanent mind is not 'mocked.'" Can one conceive of a greater challenge to the very foundations of the Christian faith?

How fitting that since the Babylonian myth involved the oceans, Gregory Bateson should have been attached to the Oceanic Institute at the East-West Center at the University of Hawaii. Bateson had gone back to his origins! Back into the oceans from where our first ancestors crawled on to the land! So had Elisabeth Mann Borgese, high priestess of the self-managing society, and First Lady of the Oceans, who founded the International Ocean Institute in 1972, with headquarters in Malta and operational centers in 25 countries. And since Bateson took in vain the name of the apostle Paul, and given the apostle's association with the island of Malta—where he and his companions had been driven by hostile seas—what a poignant place with which to link Bateson's observations! Elisabeth Mann Borgese herself, as we observed earlier, eventually found a safe harbour in Canada, courtesy of Pierre Elliott Trudeau. Whether her safe harbour was any better than the Fair Havens where the apostle and his companions sheltered was doubtful (at least in the opinion of this writer)!

Secularists have not been alone in these respects. Starting with the theologian Friedrich Schleiermacher, Protestant liberalism made great strides in its "retranslation" (in Richard John Neuhaus's words) of the supernatural and the transcendent "into the framework of the naturalistic and the immanent." That, said Neuhaus, was part of the general loss of belief in the supernatural and a radical "turn toward humanity." Even a secularist like Walter Lippmann ("I didn't go to church, but then, I'm not a Christian and only go to church for the occasional political meeting")—in commenting on "the good life of this world, but the perfect life of heaven"—was moved to say that "the confusion of the two realms" was "an ultimate disorder. It inhibits the good life in this world. It falsifies the life of the spirit." Sometimes it takes a non-believer to state a truth which has escaped many a believer!

Even more problematic was Teilhard de Chardin's romantic idea that matter was drifting towards spirit. Speaking of matter, Teilhard said: "The virtue of Christ has passed into you." If matter was drifting towards spirit, and vice versa, one was not far away from Feuerbach's thesis that God was a psychological projection of the human consciousness or mind, only then to be projected back to 'man and his world;' a game of mirrors. Thus could be set up a potent oscillation, like the futurist visualization of a desired future, which could then be promptly projected back in order to re- engineer the present. Man as God, and God as man (very difficult to accept whenever one sees a naked male human specimen), *except that now the idea has been translated into an active process.* Cornelio Fabro too detected "this reciprocal immanence of God in man and of man in God," like an "action whereby the mind contemplates itself." Narcissism plus! In broader terms, Fabro saw "a fundamental bent of modern thought" consisting in "a swing from the object to the subject, from the world to the self, from the external to the internal." In fact, the classic Gnostic had gone further with his folding of the outside into the inside, and the folding of the inside to the outside. Or, in Fabro's terms, when "all talk of the transcendental absolute was nothing more than an objectification of those internal processes which the human thinker had discovered in himself."

Like the Sadducees of old, there are those modern theologians who cannot accept the truth of the Resurrection when, indeed, through the Resurrection, the Son of God pulled 'man and his world' into the next. Why this should be such an unpalatable doctrine to churchmen is hard to understand. It might be instructive if the selfsame theologians were asked to pronounce on the words of the Apostle John: "He that cometh from above is above all: he that is of the earth is earthly, and speaketh of the earth: he that cometh from heaven is above all." And again: "And he said unto them, ye are from beneath; I am from above: ye are of this world; I am not of this world."

Somewhat difficult for me to take (as I've already confessed), having so admired Jan Christiaan Smuts, was the distinct Teilhardian bent of his philosophy of Holism. New Agers in particular were pursuing a new spirituality marked by the cultivation of a "holocentric over a theocentric perspective," which began with "a vision of the whole of reality that overcomes the antithesis between divinity and humanity."

At the very least—one would have to protest—there was a big difference between a God 'fused' with creation and his divine *presence* in both world and cosmos. Jan Smuts, Lloyd Morgan, and Samuel Alexander were the three greatest exponents of holistic philosophy. Jan Smuts appeared to be the forerunner, although he did not publish until he was able to make use of a break in his political career in the 1920s. When that happened to Winston Churchill he became a bricklayer instead! Alexander's major work, *Space, Time, and Deity*, was based on his Gifford Lectures of 1916-1918. His fundamental thesis was that God was "in a continual process of becoming via the evolution of the world," and that the whole universe was tending toward deity. The "deity of God remains entirely within the world and he is in no sense outside of it." A stronger expression of immanentism could hardly be conceived.

———————

Coincidences can be strange. I'm in the process of reading the American Walt Whitman's collection of poems, *Leaves of Grass*. My copy is an old edition, published in Boston in 1905. My mother has just arrived, visiting us from South Africa. She could not have had any idea of what I'm doing. The reason I'm reading Whitman is that his humanism was a major influence on Jan Smuts's thinking when he developed his theory of Holism as an undergraduate at the University of Cambridge. I had actually bought my copy of *Holism and Evolution* at Smuts's home, a humble farm house preserved at Irene, outside Pretoria. A humble abode, because it had been a British officers' mess during the Anglo-Boer war, clad in corrugated iron sheets. After his death in 1950, Smuts's ashes were scattered on the nearby *koppie*. My mother says she has brought me something she picked up on the same hillock shortly before she departed for Canada. It's a single leaf of grass, and now, as I write, it still nestles in the front of Whitman's book.

Here is another coincidence. On the day when I'm writing these words my wife and I also attend an illustrated lecture on the life and art of the Dutch painter Vincent van Gogh, presented at the National Gallery of Canada in Ottawa. The lecture is a precursor to a major exhibition of no fewer than forty-five of Vincent van Gogh's works, some of them never seen before in public. Noteworthy, says the lecturer—a most accomplished lady—was how, gradually (and not generally known), the artist started to focus on small things, including leaves of grass...

———————

If true transcendence was unacceptable, there did emerge an alternative, and indeed substitute, in the form of a 'self-transcendence.' *Transcendence became self-referential.* Hegel fought the whole idea of the truly transcendental but his effort amounted to no more than converting a "vertical transcendence," says the philosopher Jean Hyppolite, to a "horizontal transcendence." If the world itself was sacred (à la Rousseau) then, naturally, one could conceive of a horizontal transcendence. The self-transcendence of the New Age was of the same ilk. Vaclav Havel impressed a lot of people when, as the President of the Czech Republic, he spoke in Philadelphia on July 4, 1994, where he received the Liberty Medal. Lauding, inter alia, the Gaia Hypothesis (which he found "so inspiring") Havel proclaimed that the cure for all the world's ills "must be rooted in self-transcendence." But what did he mean by that? Was this the same kind of self-transcendence described in the psychologist Paul Vitz's analysis of the narcissist, namely, of the self building on the self?

Fritjof Capra, the New Age physicist (whom we've already met) waxed eloquently on the power and the merits of "bootstrap theory." Simply put, it meant that you lifted yourself up by your own bootstraps. He even referred to "the bootstrap program." And it had all sorts of applications. "A bootstrap approach," he said, "similar to the one that contemporary physics has developed, may be most fruitful." In fact, he added, the "bootstrap approach is very close to general systems theory." Systems theory again! Bootstrapping could also be used as a psychological tool and a self-healing device, Capra maintained, as, for example, in a form of group therapy (mentioned earlier as well) "which was not developed by psychotherapists but grew out of the women's movement (and) practiced in political consciousness-raising groups." One gathered that this form of self-transcendence was an element in "transpersonal psychology." Distinct overtones here of a self- salvational process. One thing is for sure, and that is that a self-driven transcendence is anything but teleological in character.

And yet self-transcendence is typically presented in an ethical light. A similar whiff came from Arthur Koestler's definition in *The Ghost in the Machine*, where he referred to "the feeling of integrative participation in an experience which transcends the boundaries of the self." One could also see a link between a self-transcending ethics and Cornelio Fabro's description of a "positive" or "constructive" atheism. Normally, atheism is seen as a negative term. Fabro saw "positive" atheism as a "new principle of immanence." Would it be too much of a jump from "positive" atheism to the merits of positive feedback systems? Wheels within wheels.

And what if, instead of denying God, He was simply by-passed (making one think back to how General Douglas MacArthur leap-frogged over the Japanese on their Pacific islands, to their utter frustration, instead of fighting them)? In one of the Canadian *Ideas* programs, referred to earlier, a *priest*, a Father Thomas Berry, suggested that "we put the Bible on the shelf for 20 years and begin to read the scripture of the natural world and enter into the dynamics of the natural world." This was because, he said, "the primary revelation, the primary divine manifestation is the natural world... and to enter into this creativity that's taking place in the natural world or throughout the universe is the primary element in what I would call the religious life." In other words, a positive, but distinctly atheist immanentism. Going further, in the same forum, the claim was then made that a *fusion* of gnosis and science could be seen as a new redemptive process. Self-referentialism was alive and well!

Erich Jantsch—a favourite of New Agers—made it quite clear that ethics simply referred to "the dynamics of systems." At least, unlike Obama's mentor, the means-focused Alinsky, he was not abandoning ethics altogether. Ethics, according to Jantsch, was not subject to revelation, "as is the ethics of religions with a personal god. Rather, it may be experienced directly by way of the dynamics of self-organization and creative process." No, as Capra himself stressed, in the new paradigm of human- and world-centred transformation "there is no goal in it, or purpose", but only process, only activity. I have often wondered whether the pyramid featured on the back of the American one-dollar note, with the all-seeing eye on top, was not a symbol of an earth-based and earth-bound, rising, self-transcendence. Geometrical thinking has its uses! Especially when one also sees the pyramid as an expression of that mysterious *nisus* or energetic thrust so beloved by the holistic New Ager.

*Certainly a self-generated salvational self-transcendence was very much in tune with the process-oriented thinking of our political Gnostic.*

In trying to put together an admittedly complex collage, we have ended up with an overarching vision of reality in which there's neither a transcendence of the Deity; nor a transcendence of standards (a point made by Allan Bloom in *The Closing of the American Mind*, expressing the notion that man is "a value-creating, not a good-discovering being"); nor a transcendence even of purpose (as Gregory Bateson made abundantly clear). Truth to tell, there was not even a transcendence of the past. How apposite then that Charles Taylor (already identified as the winner of the 2007 Templeton Prize for "Progress Towards Research or Discoveries About Spiritual Realities") also published a book titled *A Secular Age,* where he asked: "What does it mean, and how has it happened, that we, as westerners, have shifted from being an 'enchanted' God-centered civilization to being a 'disenchanted' civilization in which belief in a divinely ordered world is no longer a given?" Taylor thought that the acceptance of a scientific epistemology, and indeed, "the moral appeal of science," had much to do with a shift to a "science-based, human-centred perspective," representing an "atheism of 'exclusive humanism.'" In the wake of this shift came, he said, "new forms of malaise (alienation, meaninglessness, secularization, instrumental rationality)..." And concluded that "as a result of the denial of transcendence... we are left with a view of human life which is empty, cannot inspire commitment, offers nothing really worthwhile, cannot answer the craving for goals we can dedicate ourselves to." What a miserable prospect! The alienation and the meaninglessness in the life of the poor Gnostic... The instrumentalist rationality of the functionalist and the cyberneticist…

Voegelin would have understood, inasmuch as the new scientism was itself so intertwined with the modern manifestations of the Gnostic spirit. And was, what Taylor saw as a secularism, not just a facet of the immanentist syndrome? Voegelin had the same problems in mind with respect to the political Gnostic's abandonment of the constitution of being ("made by God") in favour of a world-immanent order of being. In response to these developments, said Taylor, new forms of "spirituality" emerged. But we know that the new spiritualities, mostly grounded in the human self, would have very little in common with the faith of the fathers. And they would undoubtedly still fail to satisfy man's deepest needs.

By now one should have been able to grasp just how fertile a soil was provided for the seed of political Gnosticism, not only to sprout, but to grow so vigorously. Not only was the political Gnostic a rebel engaged in a revolt against transcendence (as Veith pointed out in his anatomy of modern fascism) but in a "positive" mode, the immanentist mode, this rebel was even more energized and potentially more successful. In *Christianity and the World Order* the British theologian Edward Norman divined that politicization in our time was not mere political activity but "the internal transformation of the faith itself, so that it comes to be defined in political values." God had been pulled into the world in more than one sense, *because faith itself was redefined.* There was (or should be), he reiterated, "a clear distinction between the involvement of religion with politics and the reinterpretation of religious values as political values." Lamenting for Christianity, Norman feared that even "its moral idealism has forfeited transcendence." And indeed, Norman too detected the shift from the "negative" to the "positive:" "Christianity was once about human fallibility... Now it is seemingly preoccupied with human capabilities."

Meanwhile, Marxism was not completely outdated because, to the extent that the political Gnostics of the late 20th century were Marxist, they had come to embrace the sophistications of one Antonio Gramsci, an Italian, who was more attuned to the Maoist doctrine that if the cultural superstructure was first transformed, the transformation of the economic superstructure would follow. Thus the leader of a socialist opposition party in Canada pointed to Gramsci as the main influence on his own development. Gramsci too started to play with the meaning of the dichotomy of the immanent and the transcendent. "For Gramsci," said the Catholic writer and apologist Malachi Martin, "they were unavoidably paired and yoked." For the revolution to be successful, the immanent and the transcendent had to be effectively fused. *In this way Christians could be co-opted into the revolutionary process.* But the overall aim remained, namely, "that the residue of Christian transcendentalism in the world had to be replaced with genuinely Marxist (read Maoist) immanentism." Here we were straight back in the world of the transformationist political Gnostic. Here too the emphasis was on *praxis*. Real transcendence had to bite the dust, because a salvational transformation of 'man and his world' was a political project. As we have already discussed, at considerable length, *immanentism had to be operationalized in the socio-cultural and political domain.*

But in the end, was it not about freedom, or rather its antithesis? And thus taking us back to the connection between an immanentist world spirit and an oppressive totalitarianism. No theology of real freedom was as powerfully expressed as by Karl Barth, who was indeed known as the "*Theologian of Freedom.*" Freedom, for Barth, was rooted in man's complete acceptance of the transcendental. To adequately explore the connection would be beyond the scope of this book (as well as beyond the capacity of this writer!) Barth believed that revelation came "perpendicularly from above", rather than that it emerged from human religious consciousness. "God is in heaven, and thou art on earth." God and humanity were not a continuum. And an anthro-pocentric theology was a distortion of Voegelin's order of being.

In 1965, when a thoroughly immanentist political Gnosticism was about to break over the heads of Canadians, Kenneth Hamilton wrote his *Revolt Against Heaven: An Enquiry Into Anti-Supernaturalism.* Fittingly (given what we've already seen) his work was uppermost in the minds of the participants in a special forum held in conjunction with, and on the site of, Canada's euphoric Expo 67, dedicated, as it was, to *Man and his World.* The participants recognized that Hamilton was a "reactionary" voice crying in what was soon to become a Canadian spiritual wilderness, especially in Quebec. He warned that a "revolution in our understanding of modern Christianity will result if we cease to think of God in the heights and learn to think of him in the depths." "The anti-supernatural view", he said, "...requires for its foundation a theology of immanence as distinct from a theology of revelation received by faith." Hamilton, of course, had no idea that very soon the society around him would be suffused with an active political Gnosticism, inspired by an immanentist world spirit, and perhaps to a degree and with a sophistication even an Eric Voegelin might not have been able to imagine. By comparison its immediate Nazi antecedent had been but a crude manifestation.

# CHAPTER FIFTEEN
# HUMANISM AND
# HUMAN RIGHTS

"There are only human rights tribunals; there are no human freedoms tribunals."

Anonymous

The spirit of immanence encompassed and suffused understandings of both Earth and Man. We've noted how the word Earth—capitalized—was the last word in Barack Obama's 2009 Nobel Peace Prize acceptance speech. Environmentalism was its most potent manifestation. While the human rights syndrome became the hallmark of self-worshipping Man. The Dutch philosopher Herman Dooyeweerd would have called them the "leading powers" of the age. Canadians had their Charter of Rights *and* Freedoms, but overwhelmingly talk was about equality and inequalities; groups and group rights; collective rights; identity politics; entitlements; affirmative actions; justice and the Just Society; and the demands of multifarious group-based victims of oppressive structures. If freedom did feature, it was mostly in relation to "freedoms from" rather than "freedoms to." Enterprising people, for the most part, appreciate "freedoms to," while victims, on the other hand, are more beholden to their "freedoms from."

In the name of equality and human rights, the not-yet-born had been wantonly and almost systematically aborted for decades on end and in horrendous numbers, even though in one western country after another (as well as Japan) the growing imbalance between young and old would be playing havoc with the sustainability of taxpayer-funded old age security systems and health services. While the unborn were deprived of a right to live, in the name of equality a right to die marked a growing proliferation of legalized euthanasia and assisted suicide regimes. In the same cause of equality and human rights, marriage was no longer an exclusive relationship between a man and woman.

With such a profusion of slogans floating about, how fitting then that a reproduction of M.C. Escher's 1928 woodcut, *Tower of Babel*, should illustrate a Canadian report titled *Religious freedom, Gay Rights and Human Rights Legislation*. Reading the article, one could not have imagined a greater confusion—and a more chilling message for dissenters—than that shown by a litany of judicial and quasi-judicial decisions and pronouncements by Canadian courts as well as a panoply of human rights tribunals, especially in the light of their impact on the lives and the freedoms of individuals who had transgressed against the ruling ethos of political correctness. So much so, as we have noted earlier, that even Canada's Civil Liberties Association expressed alarm, notwithstanding their earlier vociferous support for the country's human rights syndrome. A regime originally meant to protect the individual against abuses of the power of the state, had itself become an instrument of oppression. And Canada was not alone in that respect.

Tensions and contradictions have always marked important public policy issues, showing up the only too frequent discrepancies between good intentions and bad consequences (known to economists as 'externalities'), and of which there are all too many examples. In South Africa my father observed the birth of systemic and systematic apartheid at a conference whose original purpose and intent had been to come to grips with the education of poor whites and labour market-related concerns, all genuinely held. And how could anyone possibly be against the advancement and protection of human rights? Think too of the endemic tussle between the genuine aspirations of particular groups and the interests of society at large.

Centuries ago the question of human rights prompted a John Locke to formulate his theory of natural rights in his *Two Treatises of Civil*

*Government.* The same sentiments underpinned the jurisprudence of William Blackstone. In his *Commentaries on the Laws of England,* Blackstone talked about the absolute rights of the human person "which are such as appertain and belong to particular men, merely as individuals or single persons." *Human rights and freedoms were not groupist!* Nor did they come from the hands of the state. The same message infused the American Declaration of Independence of July 4, 1776.

Locke must have been influenced, in turn, by his knowledge of the age-old opposition—a veritable tug-of-war—between the collectivist philosophy of a Plato and the Aristotelian insistence "that justice is not, as Plato would have it, the health and harmony of the state, but rather a certain way of treating individuals" because "justice is something that pertains to persons." "This individualism, united with altruism," said Sir Karl Popper, "has become the basis of our western civilization. It is the central doctrine of Christianity ('love your neighbour,' says the Scripture, not 'love your tribe')" (or, as we might now say, group.)

On the subject of altruism, Karl Popper denied most emphatically that collectivism and unselfishness are coterminous (as Canadians were fond of claiming with respect to their "caring and sharing society"). An individualist, he said, was fully capable of being altruistic. In other words, individualism was not inherently selfish. One may indeed ask whether, typically, and by contrast, collectivist charity (a.k.a. social justice) is not highly impersonal. No "I and thou" in those relationships! And who, in those instances, is thy neighbour? When it comes to the enforced extraction of benefits, through taxation, again in the name of equality and human rights, the providers of those benefits are anything but charitable.

But even Karl Popper could not have imagined the extent to which groupisms-in-action would elbow aside notions of personal freedom, to become the driving force and indeed *sine qua non* of the human rights syndrome in the multiculturalist polities of the western world. Whereas Plato and Aristotle would at least have recognized the way Rome succumbed to the disintegrative forces of its own multicultisms and multiculturalisms, thereby threatening to change entire cultures beyond recognition. In the countries of the west the problem was exacerbated by their growing dependency on large-scale immigration of people with a multiplicity of mainly non-western ethnic origins, in an almost futile effort to compensate for their own falling birthrates.

To a great extent the new human rights syndrome was associated with the city, at least metaphorically. Canadians had been sold on the dubious promises and premises of a *Cité Libre*. The racist and tribalist patrimony of the German National Socialists included the journalistic outpourings of *Der Stadt* whereas the compatriots of Plato and Aristotle were citizens of a true city state. Many of the same underlying tensions were common to all three of them. And when Martin Gilbert (the historian and Winston Churchill's official biographer) wrote his 1994 essay on "Jerusalem: A Tale of One City," this was most certainly not the Jerusalem of Saint Paul's Epistle to the Galatians.

In my life too there was a "Tale of One City;" the city of Durban in the South African province of Natal. A city indeed, because its very origin was figuratively 'urban,' inasmuch as it was named after a British governor of the Cape Colony, Sir Benjamin D'Urban. (As an aside, Durban even had its own Paul Revere, a young man by the name of Dick King, who, in May 1842 rode a distance of 600 miles on horseback to Grahamstown in the eastern Cape to warn the British authorities that my Boer forefathers were laying siege to their garrison back in Natal.)

Durban was where my parents were launched on the path of that indivisible trinity of values—the values of freedom, truth, and courage—especially in my father's fight against the influence in the churches of that most secretive of political organizations, the *Broederbond*. Durban was where Sir Henry de Villiers presided over the Convention which culminated in the founding of the Union of South Africa in 1910. We've noted that Durban was where Mohandas Karamshand Gandhi honed his doctrine of passive resistance; more correctly known as *Satyagraha* ("truth and firmness"). What an irony that Gandhi should have been locked in political combat, in the cause of human rights, with a young Attorney General of the Transvaal by the name of Jan Christiaan Smuts, the irony being that Gandhi was inspired by the humanism of a Tolstoy and a Henry David Thoreau, whereas Jan Smuts's theory of Holism was rooted in the humanism of a Walt Whitman. When Gandhi finally returned to India (in 1914) Smuts wrote to a friend: "The saint has left our shores, I hope forever." And yet, when Gandhi departed he gave Smuts a pair of sandals he had made with his own hands. In 1939, on Gandhi's 70th birthday, Smuts returned the sandals to him with a message: "I have worn these sandals for many a summer, even though I may feel that I am not worthy to stand in the shoes of so great a man."

And it was in Durban, in the name of equality and human rights, that the world assembled in August of 2001, in the form of a United Nations Conference Against Racism. Halfway through the proceedings the American delegation walked out in protest in the face of a virulent anti-Semitic and anti-Israel campaign. It could well be claimed that the agenda, and the conference itself, were a continuation of the North-South (post-colonialist) conflict between the peoples of the Third World and the 'cities' of the privileged 'North' (to invoke the Maoist metaphor).

Above all, Durban was an example (a prime example) of how, almost mysteriously, lives and events can intersect, and not always in the form of fearful symmetries, but certainly with strong symbolisms. Unlike the interlinking stories of the British writer W.G. Sebald, as far as I was concerned the story of Durban was very different from "a walking tour through the haunted landscapes of the past." Sebald's melancholic journeys were those of an unregenerate pessimist, a man with the bleakest of bleak outlooks on life. Instead life ought to be, and can be, a source of gratitude, and I had much to be grateful for in the city of my early youth. Although attending the same school in Durban, I might not have met Johan van der Vyver, but for the fact that our respective girl friends were friends of each other. Born in the same year, we could not have been much older than seven or eight. My parents were not pleased when I started to give away some of my most cherished books to my lady love, including an illustrated story of Pinocchio, the liar with the long nose. And now, as I'm writing, the same Johan van der Vyver has become one of the world's leading authorities in the field of Human Rights and International Law.

Moreover—and again by apparent coincidence—he happens to be based at the same university in Atlanta, Georgia, where the archives of the Pitts Theology Library now host the historical records and some family papers comprising The de Vos-de Villiers Collection.

Fact is that I've not seen Johan since 1944. Like my father, his father was caught up in the political turmoil of the war years, only to be interned for the duration of the war by Field Marshal Smuts. And yet he was innocent. For years, Johan thought, mistakenly, that somehow my father was responsible for the calamity that had befallen his family. The internment camp was not far from where my mother's family (members of the de Villiers clan) settled when they moved into the interior from the Cape of Good Hope. Her parents owned three farms; large sheep farms. Sheep farms had to be large because the grazing was so sparse. The main homestead was on a farm named *Helpmekaar* (Help One Another). The farm my mother inherited was *Steunmekaar* (Support One Another). The third farm was *Soekmekaar* (Seek Out One Another.) Not a wonder that my maternal grandfather, Tobias de Villiers, was known as such a good-natured and benevolent representative of the human race. As symbols of human (individualist) altruism in the best tradition of Karl Popper, those farms were surely unsurpassed! But when I think of the modern human rights-syndrome-in-action there is, thankfully, not a fourth farm still in existence because it would then have had to be called *Deurmekaar* (Discombobulated).

Discombobulated is the right word in a world where human rights-based political correctnesses even began to rob the citizens of a sense of humour. In Britain, by October 2010, following the passage of a new Equality Act, the *Daily Mail* complained that "the office joke is dead." The British law empowered workers "to sue over jokes and banter they find offensive - even if the comments are aimed at someone else and they weren't there at the time the comments were made." Moreover, "firms could be sued if - *without their knowledge* - a member of staff makes an unwise or politically incorrect joke to a colleague, which neither of them finds offensive, but is relayed to another employee who does claim to be upset." Evidently, the only criterion was whether a complainant was upset, which was in line with Canadian decisions that someone could seek redress when he merely *felt* discriminated against, even in the absence of proof of actual discrimination.

In fact, just today, as I'm writing, the Canadian *National Post* is moved to grace its front page with an article headlined "The Death of Humour" because in Canada, it says, being offended has been taken "to a whole new level." "When the urge to complain is enabled and encouraged, and every humourless butt-inski has a global audience, the danger is that Canada becomes a nation of prudes, unable to laugh at itself, and scared to laugh at anyone else."

Actually, not so much a nation of prudes, as a nation of fearful citizens afraid to open their mouths to voice an opinion or state a belief. *Christians especially had to be careful.* Because, if any one incurred the brunt of the country's human rights regimes, they were Christians who had strong convictions about matters of public and private morality, or about what their children were taught in the schools. Traditional Catholics could no longer invoke the natural law, let alone Scripture, in their opposition to active homosexualism, even when it encroached upon their own institutions. Here is not the place to list a lengthening litany of woes suffered on these accounts, not even the compulsory sex education curricula foisted on the schools in the province of Ontario in early 2015, and lauded as a model for all the other Canadian provinces. The British Bishop of Winchester is reported to have said that "the Human Rights Act is protecting the rights of minority groups while encouraging judges and politicians to discriminate against Christians." He gave the example of Christian owners of bed-and-breakfast establishments who suffered because they turned away homosexuals who wished to share a bedroom under their roof, and of church-run adoption agencies, especially Catholic agencies, forced by the government to close their doors after they refused to place children with same-sex couples. (After the British Prime Minister Tony Blair had done just that, one wondered how he managed to gain membership of the Catholic Church.) The Bishop of Winchester added that "there are increasingly professions where it could be difficult for people who are devoted believers to work in certain of the public services, indeed in Parliament."

So much for parochial human rights-related tribulations. Internationally it was the same story with the arrival of the so-called 'second generation' of United Nations-inspired "economic, social and cultural rights" with their undeniable and highly political impetus and character. And it was with *this* project that the struggle for human rights (and the concomitant loss of individual freedoms) became a modern Tower of Babel. Here was such a far cry from the very first extensions of John Locke's tenets, when a certain Christian Wolff (according to Van der Vyver, to whom I'm indebted for several of the following quotations) "postulated the natural right of every person to comply with those duties that contribute toward the perfection of his own personality"; such a far cry from Sir William Blackstone's singling out as a basic right of the human person, "the right to individual security, personal freedom and private ownership"; and such a far cry from the German philosopher Johann Gottlieb Fichte's reduction of "the most fundamental freedom of the individual to the right of every person to act according to reason." "It is one's moral duty," Fichte argued, "to comply with the command of reason, and one has the basic right to carry out that duty." *How very strange in this day and age the old-fashioned idea that ones basic right is the right to do ones moral duty!* As distinct from asserting ones interests!

The new generation of formal economic, social and cultural rights had not fallen out of the sky. They were said to have had their origin in the Mexican constitution of 1917. Only too often the most impressive lists of human rights have been found in the constitutions of the most corrupt, lawless or tyrannical societies. In the case of Mexico, the constitutional list of economic and social rights was subdivided into no fewer than 31 principles, along with 14 separate provisions. So much for human rights in a country that has since fallen into a drug-ridden state of anarchy. And as for the accompanying mayhem, no right to life there (at least not in practice!) The 1924 constitution of the Soviet Union even guaranteed the right to work and the right to leisure. Eventually these extended notions were to permeate the *Universal Declaration of Human Rights* of 1948 and the *International Covenant on Economic, Social and Cultural Rights* of 1966. Those instruments of the United Nations were the bailiwick of the Economic and Social Council, at one session of which, in New York, the Canadian delegation would be led by this writer, of all people. Those two young erstwhile school friends in the city of Durban were truly destined to end up in the most unexpected places...

The new generation of human rights not only served as a vehicle for collective (indeed groupist) notions. And not only as a vehicle for entitlements to positive benefits in the form of money, goods and services. They also served as a means of greatly expanding the reach and the power of the organs of the state, since the state would now be saddled with the responsibility—yea, the duty—to provide those benefits. Understandably all manner of groups became politically active *demandeurs* on the public purse. The entire process would be bolstered by the arrival of a potent multi-culturalist political ethos. All in the name of human rights. Who should have been surprised then that freedoms, individual freedoms, would soon have to take a back seat? In Canada, as in other places, even freedom of speech and of conscience had to yield to the demands of a veritable human rights-based entitlements industry. The entitlements were not only material, but also psychic, as was well illustrated in the domain of active homosexualism, where even the age-old institution of marriage was formally appropriated in the name of equality and self-esteem. On this score Americans were not far behind.

By 2008, one sign of a mounting concern in the United States was American law professor Peter Spiro's *Beyond Citizenship: American Identity.* He noted how few foreigners (albeit permanent residents) even bothered to apply for American citizenship. Rights and benefits and green cards were far more important than the civic duties of what ought to have been an undifferentiated (non-groupist) polity. Even more pointed was a report produced in Britain by Lord Goldsmith (titled *Citizenship: Our Common Bond*) which showed an awareness of how the British Human Rights Act of 1988 contributed to the situation that "there are few citizens' rights; most rights are human rights." In effect, group memberships were more advantageous than the status of the (individual) citizen. Sheldon S. Wolin would have understood! The meaning of the truly political (as seeking the general good of the *individuals* making up the nation) had been fundamentally transformed.

But even Towers of Babel must reach their limits, so that one had to wonder whether the high priests of the church of human rights realized what was happening when they started to demand yet a *third* generation of rights, also called "solidarity rights." In fact, according to one K. Vasak, in demand was not just the benefits of solidarity but "the Right to Solidarity" itself. This third generation of rights included "the right to peace, the right to development of disadvantaged sections of a political community or, in the international context, of developing countries, the right to nature conservation... the right to share in the common heritage of mankind," and so on. More than ever before, the emphasis was *"no longer on the individual but beneficiaries of these rights are collectively perceived, either in the sense of humanity as a whole, a particular political community, or a distinct section of the population within the body politic"* (read 'groups'). (Emphasis added.) I could not but be reminded of how, in the Law of the Sea negotiations, that same principle was behind the new, and strange, doctrine of participants' right, not to disagree, but a "right to agree." Nothing was as solidaristic as a consensus (a "feeling togetherness").

And yet the clincher was the accompanying demand that the new generation of rights would also have to be universal ("on the global or regional scale"). Echoes here of Prime Minister Trudeau's insistence that, to be effective, transformative schemes had to be "global in scope, and universal in application." In other words, all or nothing. The same globalistic and universalizing urgings of a Canadian Trudeau were to repeat themselves decades later, as we have seen, in the utterances of a Barack Obama. In Berlin, Obama was speaking mainly to Europeans who had already effectively abandoned national boundaries—not to mention sovereignties—with their voluntary subjection to a European Convention on Human Rights. A year later Lord Hoffman (a former South African who became Britain's second most senior Law Lord) attacked the European Court of Human Rights for its intrusive rulings, he said, that had gone against domestic decisions and whose rulings were like "teaching grandmothers to suck eggs." By 2009 the European Court was already facing a backlog of 100,000 cases.

In 2010 a commentator noted that Obama's 2008 election campaign had "unfolded on an entirely different plane from ordinary politics. It signaled the emergence on a worldwide scale of the 'Religion of Humanity' for which Obama became the symbol… He was no longer running for president of the United States. He was being selected for the much grander 'office' of leader of a new world community," and seeing himself as "the plausible representative of the teeming masses of the Third World." Here we would do well to remember that the religion of humanity was first inspired by the French social philosopher Auguste Comte, who believed that faith in the transcendent was no longer possible in a positivist age. He therefore wanted to "replace God with humanity... The aim of this religion without God was to build a global community that assured the betterment of man's lot." One aspect of Obama's invocations in Berlin was how it aligned with Comte's belief that "those who continued to view the world in terms of nations and their conflicts" were "retrogrades."

*Replacing God with Man himself is, of course, the very essence of the new form of secular humanism.* And if this was aligned with a universalist philosophy, how potent indeed was the symbolism of Canada's euphoric Expo '67, called *Man and his World.* If, however, one considered how just about all human rights complaints relied on the complainant's membership of one group or another, how then—might one ask—could *group-based* interests be *universalized* because, on the universal scale the only real common denominator could only be and had to be the human person, the individual. And if that was the case, the doctrine of human rights and freedoms would be right back where it started centuries ago, namely, with the interests of the same individual! This was why an early commentator in the *Wisconsin Law Review* warned that "to the extent human rights increasingly embrace the whole range of social aspirations, their usefulness as an ordering concept may be distorted" and that "the present broad and indiscriminate use of the term 'human rights' may obscure what are in fact very different types of social ends, and that various human rights may have very little in common but their label." Consider that these words were written in 1969, long before the apotheosis of groupism and multiculturalism, and matters really got out of hand.

Nevertheless, even the aforementioned commentator had it wrong. He simply assumed and accepted that human rights entitlements were utilitarian devices. He was miles away from the proposition that rights and freedoms—at least insofar as they pertain to natural persons (and not corporations)—are surely rooted in the nature and character of the person. Humans—made in the image of God—are possessed of inherent dignity and worth and it is for *that* reason that their rights and freedoms are human. And least of all for the reason that they belong to a particular group, or even worse, derive their very identities from their membership of one group or another.

---

"Oh, Professor Montoya, I have no concern for such matters. Rights are a thing of man. God is a God of love. You do not love your neighbor by giving your neighbor a right. You give the poor man or the black man a right and you feel you have done your duty to him. You may even feel that he now owes you a debt of gratitude. But if you had loved him to begin with, the question of right would never have arisen."
Stephen L. Carter, *The Emperor of Ocean Park*

---

In the land of apartheid a philosopher by the name of H.G. Stoker gave much thought to the source of the natural rights and freedoms of persons. He called it the 'ontic right'—a term denoting the most basic right of the human person—to fulfil his special and personal (God-given) calling in life; and he opposed all laws and social institutions that would obstruct the realization of this 'ontic right.'

Christians in particular have, or should have, no difficulty with such a proposition. And here is where I have problems with Columbia

University professor Samuel Moyn's otherwise meritorious *Last Utopia: Human Rights in History*. Moyn argues, persuasively, that to leave the creation and protection of human rights to constitutions and to judges and courts and tribunals fails to take account of the historical facts. He claims that human rights "can only be secured by an effective state." According to a reviewer, Moyn holds that "human rights might in some sense exist prior to the state, but without the state they counted for nothing."

Yet the problem we are facing is that today's oppressive human rights regimes in the "modern and effective state" are the handiwork not only of judges, courts, and tribunals, but the product of constitutions and charters and laws passed by politicians and governments! *Timeo Danaos et dona ferentes* (Beware the Greeks when they bear gifts)! And as we know, almost invariably, group-based assertions of human rights are *political* actions, typically the result of political power struggles; of a politics of equal opportunity; of a spurious 'equality' where there is never any real equality except in the eyes of God; and of a highly political and politicized multiculturalism.

Moyn also argues that the belief that rights are fundamental in political ethics is "a late twentieth-century fancy." Yes, they would be fanciful if they were nothing but an element or product of political ethics. But then he lets the cat out of the bag when he recognizes (as noted by a reviewer of his book) that older political rights theorists were influenced by a belief that rights were "*dictates of natural law, which had to be obeyed because they emanated from God.*" (Emphasis added.)

Which is no news to any believing Christian who may also happen to respect the natural law—the handiwork of the Creator—as well as the inherent dignity of the human person created in the image of God. If we think of the primary tenets of the divine law, with the injunction to love neighbour as self, how can a human right also be no other than a right to meet ones responsibilities and carry out ones duties? We can ask the same question about freedom, because what are our freedoms for?

But could one have a polity beholden to a humanist religion that did not also have its dedicated temples? Evidently not.

A harbinger and interpreter of the 20th century New Age cult, Fritjof Capra wrote *The Turning Point: Science, Society, and the Rising Culture.* There was another turning point, in the early 1930s: the subject, in 2008, of a summer-long exhibition at the National Gallery in Ottawa, an event titled *The 1930s: The Making of the New Man.* That was the time, in Voegelin's Germany, when science and technology were harnessed in the service of eugenics. There too, as in Capra's case, was an encounter involving science, society, and culture.

On the eastern side of Ottawa's prestigious Sussex Drive stands the Catholic Cathedral of Notre Dame. Right across from it, on the western side, and also facing Parliament in the other direction, is Canada's mock Gothic glass cathedral of arts and culture, the National Gallery, for which Canadians had to thank a transformationist prime minister. On the eastern side the faithful are invited to a certain transformation of mind and spirit, even a trans-substantiation. A different form of transformation is offered on the western side, courtesy of a newly appointed director, who said: "What I'm interested in doing is finding what we can do with this collection to make a visit to the National Gallery a transforming experience."

Moreover, as against those who, on the eastern side, are beholden to the Traditional, the new director is devoted to the Contemporary. Thus, in front of the Gallery looms a giant black spider on spindly legs, the handiwork of Franco-American sculptor Louise Bourgeois. Art for the people. While across the road there is veneration of a woman who was pregnant with the Son of God, the female spider is pregnant too, her pouch heavy with eggs, and ready to spin her web. Even more symbolic, and perhaps conclusive, is the presence inside, at the very heart of the Gallery, of a large historic reassembled Christian chapel that had been moved lock, stock and barrel from its original site. In its new location, *utterly captive,* its sterility is palpable.

Close to both edifices is a glitzy and newly constructed Islamic Global Centre for Pluralism financed by the Aga Khan, and inaugurated by him in the presence of the Canadian prime minister of the day. It seeks to convey that antagonism toward Islam is based on a misunderstanding rooted in a lack of knowledge. Now there will be an opportunity for visitors to shed their ignorance and acquire the necessary *gnosis*. The building is described as "an essay in glass." The main facades are clad in white Neoparies, "a crystallized glass material that has a soft, pure colour and smooth, marble-like texture."

Canadians liked their secular crystal temples. For a long time Americans had at least one of their own, but at least it was Christian: Robert Schuller's postmodernist Crystal Cathedral, described by Veith as "something like a religious theme park, featuring babbling brooks and luxuriant plant life and multimedia sensory overload." The crowning glory of Canada's Expo 67 was a glass-clad geodesic globe. In 2015 Canadians learned that the National Arts Centre in Ottawa "will build a glittering entrance that will embrace Confederation Square to celebrate Canada's 150th anniversary."

The year before a remarkable glass-sheathed Museum for Human Rights had risen above the Canadian Prairies in the city of Winnipeg; in this case not a mock Gothic cathedral but (as the architect proudly pointed out) a stylized Babylonian *ziggurat*. It had been described as a monument to Canada's transformative Charter of Rights and Freedoms, and intended to have world-wide appeal, not unlike the glass-panelled pyramid outside the Louvre in Paris, home of the original human rights-driven revolt. The pursuit and celebration of human rights had become *the* pivotal and indeed dominant cultural transformationist force in the life and the psyche of the Canadian polity and was inextricably linked with both the multiculturalist and the groupist elements in a saga that had unfolded over the course of almost five decades.

Symbols play a vital role in the sensibility and imagination, and no stronger symbol could have been conceived than the new Museum for Human Rights. But it was not just the symbolism of the architectural

293

design that was so compelling. It was the scope and the reach of the project, whose official status was reflected by the patronage of no less than the Governor General of Canada, supported by a National Advisory Council of thirty leading citizens of the land. They included a retired Justice of the Supreme Court; two former prime ministers; the ubiquitous Maurice F. Strong; and one of the sons of Pierre Elliott Trudeau; the son himself an aspiring future prime minister.

Long before the project got off the ground, Canadians had been told that the government-funded operating budget would cover the cost of *pilgrimages*, including guided tours and educational sessions for young people. Those young people, according to plan, would be transported to Winnipeg from near and far at a rate of 20,000 a year.[15] As an "international education centre" the museum would also feature "an observatory with current (i.e., real-time) information on human rights issues and situations from activists situated around the world." Visitors would be able to learn about international rights groups and immediately register "to be advocates of these groups if they choose." Using dioramas, collections, audio-visual testimony, photography and dramatic re-enactments, "the Museum will feature never-before told stories" of an open-ended list of victims. Thus the stories would cover "the experiences of *groups* as diverse as Aboriginal peoples, women, French Canadians, Jews, Ukrainians, African Americans and Canadians, Acadians, the disabled, labour, the Chinese, Japanese, Doukhobors, Sikhs and many others." (Emphasis added.)

A year or two later assurances were given that the original list of qualifying groups would be greatly extended. And a somewhat different categorization came from the president and chief executive officer of the museum when he wrote "Be assured, the content of the museum will be inclusive… Yes, indigenous rights and the Holocaust will be examined. So will many other issues: mass atrocities, gender issues, the rights of persons with disabilities, sexual orientation, children's rights, poverty, racism,

---

15    On June 15th, 2015, in a full-page advertisement in national newspapers, the Museum proudly announced that "tens of thousands of visitors and students [had] experienced a life-changing journey of education and discovery."

language rights, age, migration/immigration and others. The CMHR will explore past successes like the adoption of the Universal Declaration of Human Rights, and current human rights abuses like the situation in Darfur." A veritable self-validating venue for any distressed and anguished Gnostic! Whether Canada's principal champion of abortion rights, Dr Henry Morgentaler (whom Prime Minister Trudeau had praised as "that great humanist," and whose work earned him the prestigious Order of Canada), would also be honoured, was not yet known, but there would be no memorial for the largest group of them all, the non-human humans; the more than 60 million *untermenschen* whose lives had been wantonly, forcibly, and legally terminated in North America alone.

According to the official web site "this museum is envisioned to be the largest human rights centre in the world - a national and international destination... a beacon for the world (and) Canada's greatest legacy." Visitors would be encouraged to wear a stylized star (with a strong resemblance to the Star of David) and exhorted to be a "Human Rights Star."

> "We can change the world.
> One 'star' at a time.
> The Canadian Museum for Human Rights.
> Human Rights stars in the making."

With its Babylonian inspiration, what more eloquent symbol could have been conceived of a self-propelled self-transcendent humanism-in-action? And what more eloquent a symbolism could have been conveyed than by one Michael Kirby, Clerk of the Privy Council under Prime Minister Trudeau, who stood by when Her Majesty the Queen signed the Canadian Charter into law on April 17, 1982, two years after he (Kirby) delivered a formal lecture at a local university calling for *Rebuilding the Proud Tower?* The task, he said, would have to be approached "with boldness and originality."

What an irony, though, that human rights and a failure to respect the inherent dignity of the human person, made in the image of God, should have so marked both the beginning and the end of this narrative.

The irony being that both the denial *and* the pursuit of human rights should have fallen into the hands of an oppressive regime, admittedly the former a 'hard' (South African) totalitarianism, and the latter the 'soft' (Canadian) variety, but any different in kind? The former in the name of a fundamental inequality; the latter in the name of an equally fundamental but spurious equality. Noteworthy too was that in the case of the former it was very much the oppression of a great majority (of black people) by a distinct minority (of white people). In the case of the latter, in the process of asserting their rights, small minorities were able to force fundamental legal and other changes that were then applicable to and imposed upon the rest of the Canadian polity, like it or not. This happened, for example, when the members of a notorious swingers' club in Montreal were able to secure a Supreme Court decision to the effect that henceforth wider community standards of decency could no longer be invoked in dealing with even the most egregious forms of immorality.

Yet there was one other outstanding difference between the two totalitarianisms. The former was the handiwork of professing Christians, while in the latter case Christians would be at the receiving end—and face the penalties—because they were no longer free to profess and live out their deep convictions, and not even in a defensive manner. *Secular humanism had become a church, the church of the oppressive state.* Judging from the signs the same thing was happening in the United States.

My thoughts went back to that architectural icon of Afrikanerdom in South Africa, the Voortrekker Monument—in that case built entirely out of granite—whose religious significance was highlighted by a sarcophagus on which a beam of sunlight fell on the 16th of December, each year: the Day of the Covenant. Canadians no longer had a Covenant, but they had their Charter. They had dropped their Covenant when they changed the name of the country from the Dominion of Canada, because it had been intended by the founding fathers to honour Canada's Christian foundations, the name having been taken from Psalm 72: "He shall have dominion also from sea to sea, and from the river unto the ends of the earth."

In 1995 Pope John Paul II told a correspondent that in the currents of history (including the history of ideas) "it is the 'turning point' that is the most important, as when a train enters a switch where an inch decides its future direction." Turning points vary, but the major and definitive turning point in the history of Gnosticism, toward the end of the 12th century, said Voegelin, involved the person and work of an Italian monk by the name of Joachim of Fiore. He was the one to whom New Agers constantly referred in their annunciation and celebration of the Age of Aquarius, "a Third Age of the Spirit." In Joachim's eschatology, said Voegelin, was created *"the aggregate of symbols which govern the self-interpretation of modern political society to this day."* (Emphasis added.) Among other things, Fiore predicted that the Church hierarchy would cease to exist and that Christians would unite with infidels in an "Order of the Just."

Could one fairly argue that the arrival of the political Gnostics of the 20th century, with their singular interest in harnessing the means and the method, became the next major turning point in the Gnostic story? When Jacques Ellul wrote so compellingly about the new domination of *La Technologie* in the life of western man, did he have any idea what that might comprise? Had he also foreseen that the crudeness of eugenics would be so overtaken by a wave of biogenetically engineered transformations, potentially of just about every life form? If that too was not an epochal turning point in the history of *gnosis*, what would be? Anyway, as Voegelin observed, "the third age of Joachim... will transform men into members of the new realm without sacramental mediation of grace." There would be no need either for the Son of God or for the healing presence of the Holy Spirit. Instead, the self-managing immanentist harnessing of self-referentialism and self-idolatry would become yet another "leading power of the culture." This was the real New Atheism, not a notional atheism, but an active and activist atheism.

Voegelin recounted how, in the days of Rome, when Christianity first came on to the scene, its major effect was the disablement of the Roman gods in a self-divinizing society, and especially in the light of Saint Augustine's two cities. Thanks to Christianity society was de-divinized.

*Cobblestones*

In the new age of Joachim, a slow but relentless immanentization would take root, which would eventually blossom into a full-scale radical re-divinization of a self-preoccupied polity. Even Gaia—the physical world itself—would become an object of worship, looked upon reverently from outer space. All that was needed was to concentrate on the means and the methods to bring about the requisite transformations of both 'man and his world.'

This story began with human rights and seems to end on the same note. Yet we shall have to dig a little deeper even than the parameters of a humanist mindset, and the focus of the next and final chapter.

# CHAPTER SIXTEEN
# NIHILISM

"A nihilist is a man who judges the world as it is that it ought not to be, and of the world as it ought to be that it does not exist."

Friedrich Nietzsche, *The Will to Power*

"Our nada who art in nada, nada be thy name thy kingdom nada thy will be nada in nada as it is in nada. Give us this nada our daily nada and nada us our nada as we nada our nadas and nada us not into nada but deliver us from nada; pues nada. Hail nothing full of nothing, nothing is with thee."

Ernest Hemingway, *A Clean, Well-Lighted Place*

"Fate stitches together elements that seem unrelated on the surface. It's only when the truth emerges you see how the bones are joined and everything connects."

Sue Grafton, *U is for Undertow*

At a certain level, and seen from a certain distance—in both space and time—seemingly disparate things can and often do come together. Patterns emerge. There can even be order in chaos. And since human nature does not change, there too patterns of conduct and belief can and do repeat themselves.

In his foreword to Thornton Wilder's *The Bridge of San Luis Rey*, Russell Banks may have had something similar in mind when he said that "one merely has to consider the central question raised by the novel, which, according to Wilder himself, was simply: 'Is there a direction and meaning in lives beyond the individual's own will'... It is the question that defines us as human beings." Thornton Wilder was not only a Christian but a strict Calvinist, so it was not as if he was fatalistic. Neither was Shakespeare fatalistic when he wrote about tides in the affairs of men.

Getting closer to the end of this story one can ask similar questions not only about the change agents who have been working in and upon the Canadian microcosm, but also their soul brothers south of the border. Was there a direction and meaning in the lives of the actors—and in the life of the two countries—that went beyond their own respective circumstances, wills and assorted actions? Was there some underlying impetus beyond their conscious control? Something as pervasive and persistent as Original Sin in the Christian lexicon? Or more simply expressed: Was there more than met the eye? And more important, did the associated experiences have meaning and did they hold lessons for a wider community; wider than North America, encompassing Europe as well? If we pose the question in that context, we are indeed referring to the historical domain of a Christian civilization. What single element, if there is such, could then account for the possible twilight of such a civilization and not just a decline in comparison with the rise of the East? The latter so challengingly evoked by a Samuel Huntington, a Robert Kaplan, and the economic historian Niall Ferguson when he wrote *Civilization: The West and the Rest*? I believe that we can identify such an element as a fundamental and systemic loss of faith.

Thus I believe that the foregoing questions can be mostly answered in the affirmative, and not for the better. Certainly, with respect to the Gnostic movement, over the centuries, said Hans Jonas, it had erupted "in many places, many forms, and many languages." Nor has it ceased to do so, except that its modern extension is no longer confined to existentialist modes of thought and behaviour (which was the modern form identified by Jonas) but has morphed into Eric Voegelin's political mutation.

Of course, existentialism was already a turning back towards and upon self and the world and no longer—at least insofar as it was linked with the Gnostic spirit—merely escapist. At the same time Gnosticism—and notably in its political garb—was closely aligned with, and indeed expressed by, various manifestations of an immanentist view of 'man and his world.'

And yet it has remained to try to understand what precisely lay at the heart of these movements. It was more than just a rebellious spirit. Just as humanism was 'merely' an element of an immanentist ethos, immanentism was also a symptom of something else, something more profound. Of that, in Cornelio Fabro's mind, there was no doubt. In his mind it was nothing other than an expression and expansion of a profound atheism: a denial, a negativity.

But then one had to recognize that immanentism could still lay claim to *positive* attributes. Even Fabro spoke about a "positive" or "constructive" atheism, which—as we've already noted—he called a "new principle of immanence." In his words: "The notion of 'positive' or constructive atheism is peculiar to the modern era; more exactly, it is the quintessential distillation of the principle of immanence", even as he recalled that "atheism is a professedly negative term." Surely, if humanists and immanentists were determined to construct a new and better world and were even prepared to pull God himself into the project, was that not a positive thing? One might even be tempted to cite Satan's temptation of Jesus Christ, where whatever he was offering was nothing but positive! Who would be so rash as to accuse all humanists of a congenital negativity (even though we can see much evidence to the contrary)? And indeed, Fabro observed that "this positive character of the new atheism (whether Marxist, existentialist, neo–positivist or pragmatist, or any other variety) finds expression in the ambitious title of 'humanism'..."

Clearly—as we've reached the end of this story—we can see that quite a few threads have been pulled together. Or, to use a different metaphor, a recognizable tapestry has been taking shape. Or, to use yet another metaphor, have we not, having stripped away the layers of an onion, begun to arrive at its core?

Thus, notwithstanding the positive appearances of immanentism-as-the-new-atheism, none less than Hans Jonas had no difficulty in conflating "Gnosticism, existentialism, and nihilism," and in doing so, had in mind a nihilism which was both ancient and modern. Cornelio Fabro reached the same conclusion. He quoted Jean-Paul Sartre's assertion that "it is necessary to find the foundation of all negation in a nihilation which is exercised *in the very heart of immanence*, in absolute immanence, in the pure subjectivity [where] we must discover the original act by which man is to himself his own nothingness..." Most forcefully, Fabro insisted that the insight that immanence was a quintessential "denial of God, from the very outset... has been our main point throughout, the very heart of our interpretative endeavour; and it cannot be too trenchantly stressed." (And we have to remember that this was a project running to more than 1300 pages.)

Extending his analysis, Fabro saw the modern affliction as an *autogenesis* that "reveals itself terminally as elusive and mortally vanishing into the nothingness that lies at the root of the immanentized human mind, or more exactly the human thinking act when that act is deprived of all transcendent substantiation and foundation." Elsewhere, Fabro alluded to the "Will-to-Power" which becomes a "Will-to-Death" which "itself merges into the nadir of nihilism, the Will-to-Nothingness." As we know all too well, nothing relates to or fits the will-to-power more closely than the political.

Fabro did not make political excursions, but he did link these elements to "the great centipetal whirl of the principle of immanentism" that became "so patently clear in Lenin, whose tactical shrewdness should not obscure his deeper philosophical traditions... Practice, the inevitable and inevitably changing pull of the here-and-now; the concrete situation, *is* ultimate reality for this arch-immanentist." How typical of Barack Obama's mentor Saul Alinsky's belief that "the standards of judgment must be rooted in the whys and wherefores of life as it is lived, the world as it is, not our wished-for fantasy of the world as it should be." For Alinsky, morals did not count, as when he berated "the means-and-ends moralists, constantly obsessed with the ethics of the means..." Even

Hillary Clinton, in her academic thesis on Saul Alinsky "had singled out the single most important contribution to the radical cause - his embrace of political nihilism." How reminiscent too of both the Maoist and the Trudeauesque pursuits—naked pursuits—of *praxis*, strategy and tactics as the only things that really counted. And how reminiscent too of the New Ager Fritjof Capra's invocation of a world that "accepts no fundamental entities whatsoever - no fundamental constants, laws, or equations... No moving objects; there is activity but there are no actors; there are no dancers, there is only the dance." In fact, said Capra, there is "neither matter nor consciousness." And not far removed from Robert Jay Lifton's citation of Sartre's saying that human consciousness is nothing more than "a great emptiness, a wind blowing toward objects."

In yet another domain, the postmodernist world, David Harvey, referring to the deconstructionists, explained how they "produced a condition of nihilism that prepared the ground for the re-emergence of a charismatic politics," a charismatic politics of which there could not have been any better examples than a Canadian Pierre Elliott Trudeau or an American Barack Obama. In other western countries as well one could detect the influence and power, in the new politics, of mere leadership charisma and the victory of style over substance.

We might also touch on the phenomenon of a time- and space-compressed globalism in which postmodernist fiction, says David Harvey, reflects "the flattest possible characters in the flattest possible landscape rendered in the flattest possible diction," a featureless world where Everyman has become not only One-dimensional Man, but No-man. And all that notwithstanding the sanctification of Humanism! More than just overtones of C.S. Lewis's *Abolition of Man* and his "men without chests."

So we may ask again: What is nihilism? In seeking the answer to that question we can detect many echoes of themes and events already touched upon. In its modern form, at least, it is not just a 'belief in nothing.' In the first place, it rejects belief in the form of faith, if faith is defined as "the firm belief in something for which there is no proof." The other element is that it rejects belief in final purpose; especially if one is as beholden to *process* as the leaderships we have already encountered.

According to one commentator, just as there are two kinds of immanentism, there are also two kinds of nihilism: "The first is passive and usually goes by the term existential or 'social' nihilism," but the second is "active and is termed 'political' nihilism." The former certainly, but not exclusively, was manifest in the (now to us familiar) expressions of a "sense of isolation, futility, angst and the hopelessness of existence increasingly prevalent within the modern digital world..." But the "words used to describe political nihilism include: active, revolutionary, destructive and even creative." Call the former *negative* nihilism, but the latter, most aptly, *positive* nihilism. But what a contradiction in terms! Positive, political, nihilists have a program. They are bent on transformation because of their lament that "conditions in the social organization are so bad." Moreover, positive, political, nihilism deals with "authority and social structures rather than simply the introspective, personal emotions of existential nihilism."

Remarkably, Alinsky and his soul brothers embodied, and were prepared to exploit, *both* kinds of nihilism. When Alinsky observed "the despair (that) is there," he immediately launched into the second kind— the active kind—with his Leninist call for organization. There's more to some community organizers than others! Indeed, suddenly I also seem to better understand that there is only a difference in degree between "community organizing" and the way such powerful change agents as Verwoerd, Mao Tse-tung, and Trudeau had kicked off their political careers by getting involved in labour issues; it even marked the origins of the Nazi movement. *Because that was where one looked for despair, coupled with a readiness on the part of the distressed to resort to action.* Perhaps I'm now also beginning to understand why I should have spent several years of my life in Canada assisting the only Christian labour union in North America and its associated Work Research Foundation, given that theirs was not a voice of despair but of Christian hope.

And in all those cases—down to a Barack Obama—they would take direct aim at the nation's "authority and social structures." As an example, one would only have to revert to both Mao and Trudeau's scathing polemics against existing social and religious bodies, and Obama's effort in 2012 to force Catholic institutions involved in healthcare and health insurance to supply their employees with contraceptive and abortifacient benefits. Further undermining the authority of the Church was Obama's ability to garner the political support of all too many Catholics—nominal or otherwise—and therefore a classic wedge issue.

Given what we've seen of rebellious pronouncements, it's been observed that the best "definition of a (political) nihilist came from Ivan Turgenev's 1861 novel *Fathers and Sons.*" Such a nihilist was "a person who does not bow down to any authority, (and) who does not accept any principle on faith, however much that principle may be revered." In Russia, nihilism was identified with rejections of the authority of state, church and family. In the light of what we ourselves have seen, these elements too are not unfamiliar either, as we saw in Trudeau's triumphalist parading of the achievements of the Quiet Revolution in Quebec. And not to mention the mind set of a Saul Alinsky with his admiration for the ultimate and original rebel: Lucifer.

One could also recognize a natural link between nihilism and anarchism. In the anarchist attitude to law (whether the laws of God or natural law or even the laws of nature) Hans Jonas was struck by the prevalence of Gnostic antinomianism and the fact that "antinomistic Gnosis appears crude and naïve in comparison with the conceptual subtlety and historical reflection of its modern counterpart." In the old Gnosticism, Jonas said, "what was being liquidated... was the moral heritage of a millennium of ancient civilization", but added to this, of late, has been the denial of "two thousand years of Occidental Christian metaphysics as background to the idea of a moral law." More recently, and for the first time in history, the rejection of a very old tradition pertaining to the nature, origin and purpose of the institution of marriage—resulting in a fundamental and most *unnatural* redefinition (now so familiar to all of us)—was only the latest example of a Gnostic antinomianism at work. Not for nothing that

Jonas remarked of Nietszche, that for him "the meaning of nihilism is that *'the highest values become devaluated (or 'invalidated').'* (Emphasis added.) Here was yet another price to pay for the rejection of the transcendent. Whereas one of the complaints of the old Gnostics was that thanks to the hidden God "no *nomos* emanates from him, no law for nature and thus none for human action as a part of the natural order", this time the problem was not the dereliction of an absent and doubtful God, but the lawlessness of a rebellious human spirit.

And here, by itself, there was a problem, because for the old as well as the modern Gnostic, freedom was not, said Jonas, a matter of the soul "which is as adequately determined by the moral law as the body is by the physical law, but wholly a matter of the 'spirit.' "As we know," he added, "the world of the modern immanentist Gnostic has been rife with all kinds of "spirituality." (By Christian standards, we would add *false* "spiritualities;" *self-generated* "spiritualities.") The "*pneumatios,* 'spiritual' man, who does not belong to any objective scheme, is above the law, beyond good and evil, and a law unto himself in the power of his 'knowledge.'"

Jonas noticed that for this "spirituality"—which had both a spatial and a temporal dimension—"life is a kind of trajectory projecting itself forward into the future." In the North America of a burgeoning political Gnosticism one of the most potent watchwords was *futurism.* An eschatological futurism. Futurists abounded. Many of the acolytes of a Willis Harman and the Canadian change agent I identified as X were 'futurists.' Strange sentiments emanated from the aforementioned World Futures Conference held in Washington, DC. Futurism was a projecting forward (magically by Harman) of a desired future (not even a predicted future) whose content would then be projected back into the present (in the real Feuerbach style) as a transformative device. *Since the future is unknown, it too is still a nothingness.* But on that basis was future 'history' to be written in the past tense. That the exercise was religious (read 'spiritual') one could not doubt. I remember a conference addressed by a notable futurist, Herman Kahn of the American Hudson Institute. Speaking in Montreal, he stood messiah-like with widespread arms before a spellbound audience, whose expressions rivalled those of any religiously intense gathering, not excluding the audiences of an ascendant Barack Obama.

In fact there was something odd about the Gnostic *present* whereinto the future was projected back, Jonas observed. *The Gnostic present did not have any real duration.* It was but a passing moment, perhaps denoted best by the German *augenblick* (the blink of an eye). Was this because the Gnostic was divorced from reality, living in a dream world of his own making?

I've always wondered about the New Age representation of Janus, the god of doors. There, Janus is depicted as two faces, back to back, looking in opposite directions, but with nothing in between, no body behind the faces. I interpreted that symbol as an illustration of Jonas's diagnosis, namely, that for the Gnostic "no present remains for genuine existence to repose in." In other words, yet another instance of an overarching existential nihilism. And here too was a further clue to the Gnostic angst, because, said Jonas, "I repeat, there is no present to dwell in, only the crisis between past and future." Not only is the Gnostic homeless in space but also in time. No longer, for the Gnostic, is it eternity "that grants a present and gives it a status of its own... it is the loss of eternity which accounts for the loss of a genuine present." There is neither baby nor bath water.

As for the Gnostic's dislocation in space, how ironic that when the political Gnostic has turned back into and upon the world, *he should still be lost in space.* Not rooted in any specific locale, there were the Trudeauesque and Obamaesque dreams of the new one world, a world of universalisms, where all transformative actions would have to be not only "global in scope, but universal in application." Here was the new globalism, where national identities would have to disappear, as well as the boundaries forming the subject, *inter alia*, of Robert J. Lifton's *Boundaries: Psychological Man in Revolution*. On this score Obama's Berlin oration, intent on "tearing down" just about every wall, was a classic example.

We were already living in a world transformed by communication and other technologies into a series of mere 'instants.' In this new world, marked by mere process, there soon arose a new form of lostness and alienation. Strangers communicating and forming vacuous and instant 'friendships' with hundreds and sometimes even thousands of other strangers. Even worse—we now know only too well—this was also a world of interconnected systems and the systems mind, where man himself would be no more than a pliable and manipulable object. On a lesser scale the same universalizing aspiration asserted itself in the domain of the European Community. Little wonder that in such an environment young indigenous Europeans were grasping at the promise of Islam to give them some sense of identity, belonging and purpose.

The same sense of being exposed in amorphous space had already developed in the Canadian psyche, where one contemporary writer after another would extol the usefulness of Canada's blankness and nowhere-eness. Here was the kind of existential nihilism Jonas must have seen when he observed that in the world of the modern Gnostic "extension, or the quantitative, is the one essential attribute left to the world..." An amorphous world without any graspable quality, other than the subjective qualities its inhabitants would themselves try to inscribe on it.

If we hark back to Canada's celebrated *Man and his World* event of 1967, it would seem that Jonas put his finger on a deep truth. He argued that at the root of the repeated outbreaks of Gnosticism in the history of the western world, it has always been a matter of a radically dualistic mood in the Gnostic psyche. This has been the "dualism between man and the world, and concurrently between the world and God." The old Gnostic felt himself separated and alienated from both God and world. Of course, Jonas (as far as I know) never or hardly touched on the importance of the immanentist solution—not in so many words—but if he had, he would have recognized, as a sought solution, man's determination to pull God back into the very fabric of the world, and indeed, to inextricably 'fuse' him with his own Creation, with both 'man and his world.'

So, in the end, the riddle of the political Gnostic has been of a religious character. It had been thus from the beginning, and thus it will continue.

In *Spe Salvi*, his Encyclical *On Christian Hope*, Pope Benedict XVI posed the opposite, Christian view of reality, and the consequences of its denial. "Once the truth of the hereafter had been rejected," he wrote, "it would then be a question of establishing the truth of the here and now. The critique of Heaven is transformed into the critique of the Earth, the critique of theology into the critique of politics. Progress towards the better, towards the definitively good world, no longer comes simply from science but from politics... and thus points out the road towards revolution, towards all-encompassing change."

"In order to have a sense of who we are, we have to have a notion of how we have become, and of where we are going."

Charles Taylor,
*Sources of the Self*

# EPILOGUE

On the ground, at my feet, something's glittering in the afternoon sun. Bending down, I pick it up and hold it in my hand. A small silver penknife, delicately wrought.

Stretched out below me is a wide basin surrounded by heather-clad hills. There's a solitary house in the far distance.

All of a sudden I'm thinking of a man by the name of John Buchan, Lord Tweedsmuir, because I'm looking at the headwaters of a river, the River Tweed, that forms part of the southern border of the land of the Scots.

For me, things have come full circle because this setting symbolizes and brings together my South African, my adopted Scottish, and my Canadian histories.

Because John Buchan was a member of a small team of highly educated and talented young men who were brought to South Africa in the wake of the Treaty of Vereeniging, to help Lord Milner to deal with the aftermath of the ravages of the Anglo-Boer War. There he developed a deep love of the land of my fathers. And that was before Buchan became a Governor-General of Canada, where he was destined to die after he had fallen in his bath in Government House in Ottawa.

And I'm thinking of John Buchan at the end of this my story, when I have to ask myself two questions: What have we learned, and where are we going?

It happens that Buchan had the answer when he wrote: "It is a vicious business to look backward unless the feet are set steadfastly on a forward road… An open and flexible mind, which sets itself to apprehend new conditions, is a prerequisite of man's usefulness."

He continued: "But if (the past) is regarded as the matrix of present and future, whose potency takes many forms but is not diminished, then he will cherish it scrupulously and labour to read its lessons, and shun the heady short-cuts which only end in blank walls."

So we have to ask ourselves whether, and in what way, western societies might confront the challenges posed by the groupist ideologies of multiculturalism and human rights, and might reverse the groupist abuses of the political process.

On the latter score it may well be too late to do much about the disintegrative techniques of political electioneering and governance. Not when one considers the way computer and networking technologies enable politicians to slice and dice the electorates.

We have also seen how—as far as Americans are concerned—multiple voices have warned over the years that "groups are us." Almost as if groupism has become irreversible even in a land supposed to be a cultural melting pot.

In South Africa we have seen how groupism in the form of apartheid came to a sticky end. But it may well endure in the tribalism of African societies.

Societies that have become disillusioned by their multicultural fracturings might be able, albeit slowly, to deal with it by means of an array of legislative and administrative corrective measures, whether through public education, tax policies, immigration policies, or even the way neighbourhoods are designed and settled. *But the problem is that such measures are still statist, and they have not worked.* This was amply illustrated by one of the most incisive analyses of the European debacle I have seen— published in the prestigious international journal *Foreign Affairs* in early 2015. In an article titled "The Failure of Multiculturalism: Community

Versus Society in Europe," the author, Kenan Malik, showed that where governments, notably in France, have tried a policy of assimilation it has failed. He argued that "Europe should separate diversity as a lived experience from multiculturalism as a political process... managed through state policies and institutions." "Real integration, whether of immigrants or of indigenous groups, is rarely brought about by the actions of the state; it is shaped primarily by civil society, by the individual bonds that people form with one another, and by the organizations they establish to further their shared political and social interests."

In the land of apartheid, groupism was an artifact of the state. In Canada, constitutionally entrenched; legislatively and judicially supported; and bolstered by an array of grants and subsidies, multiculturalism became a state-designed straitjacket from which the society will most likely be unable to escape. Especially when the country regarded itself as definitionally multiculturalist, and set itself up as a model for the rest of the world. What a warning *pour les autres!*

An even greater challenge comes in the domain of human rights. Notably in Canada where human rights are not only governed by a virtually unchangeable Charter of Rights and Freedoms; where the judiciary has taken precedence over Parliament; and where a system of extra-legal human rights tribunals have wielded far-reaching powers. All of that besides the fact that the domain of human rights is also yoked and beholden to a groupist philosophy.

The overarching problem is that the human rights syndrome is so firmly anchored in a human-centred and gnostically-inspired immanentism that it becomes a religious problem requiring an extraordinary *volte face* of a religious nature.

There remains, of course, the Gnostic phenomenon, in general; a seemingly permanent affliction, while constantly looming below the horizon are the periodic outbreaks of Gnostic political leaderships. Fortunately they prove to be relatively short-lived.

## Cobblestones

Yet, how can we do otherwise than to continue to live in hope and how can we afford not to try to learn about the lessons that history may offer?

Here I find myself looking at a little silver penknife, and trying not to forget the wise words of a remarkable Scotsman.

The road was anything but smooth, yet much was learned on a journey from the south to the north.

# MILESTONES

1689     Three brothers de Villiers, French Huguenots, arrive at the Cape of Good Hope

1838     The Great Trek and the Battle of Blood River

1899 to
1902     The Anglo-Boer War

1908     Sir Henry de Villiers visits Canada

1910     Formation of the Union of South Africa

1918     Founding of the *Broederbond*

1934     The Kimberley Conference, the birth of ideological apartheid, and the year of my birth

1938     Commemoration of the Great Trek

1944     Schism with the Dutch Reformed Church, and the start of the fight against the *Broederbond*

1945     Fernande Coulson, Igor Gouzenko, and the start of the Cold War

1950     Death of Field Marshal Jan Christiaan Smuts. The launching of *Cité Libre*

1959    Chief Albert Luthuli. A torture trial. First emigration (to Britain)

1963    The dark face of apartheid in an African township

1967    *Man And His World* (the Canadian Expo 67). Second edition of Chairman Mao's *Little Red Book*. Political debut of one Pierre Elliott Trudeau

1970    Second emigration (to Canada)

1981    The Constitutional fight. A day at the Berlin Wall

1982    Canadian Charter of Rights and Freedoms signed into law

1989    The Bloemfontein Congress and the end of apartheid

2014    The Canadian Museum for Human Rights

CPSIA information can be obtained at www.ICGtesting.com
Printed in the USA
LVOW06s0001241015

459558LV00001B/30/P